European Painting and Sculpture
Before 1800

Italian School XV century
Profile Portrait

European Painting and Sculpture before 1800

Ursula Hoff

National Gallery of Victoria

First Published 1961
Revised and Reprinted 1967
Third edition published 1973
Published by The Trustees of The National Gallery of Victoria

ISBN 0 7241 0007 5
Printed and bound in Australia by
Brown Prior Anderson Burwood Victoria
Registered in Australia for transmission by post as a book

Note to First Edition

The present catalogue deals with oil paintings, painted by artists born before 1800, in the possession of the National Gallery of Victoria. Many of the pictures included here were listed in the general catalogue of 1948, and appendices 1950, 1954.

Owing to the publication in recent years of the London National Gallery Catalogues, the first of which was brought out by Mr. Martin Davies in 1945, a new conception of cataloguing has gained ground which demands the inclusion of more detailed research than had been attempted in the 1948 catalogue. As much information as could be obtained from locally held records and from research during a period spent by the compiler abroad has been included here. However much this catalogue may fall short of its prototypes, the compiler is deeply conscious of her indebtedness to the publications of the London National Gallery.

The following plan has been adopted throughout the entries: the biographical notes aim at giving a brief outline of the main dates and facts of each artist's career; reference has sometimes been made to the place of the Melbourne work in the oeuvre of the master; and to works in other media by the same artist held in the collection of prints and drawings.

The title of the painting is followed by a reference to the support (i.e., canvas, board) and size. (A note on the measurements is to be found on page X under *Explanations*). Any inscriptions, signature and dates that may be found on the painting are noted. These are followed by a description of the *Condition* of the work. This note has been drawn up in consultation with the Conservator; it aims at giving a general idea of the state of the surface of the picture to the visitor and to note any permanent important damages or conditions likely to be recurrent (i.e., blistering). These notes are not based on exact scientific examinations of the painting for which both time and facilities are lacking.

Under *Comment* explanations have been given of the subject matter of the picture; and such evidence has been discussed as has a bearing on the dating and authorship of a work.

The *Provenance* aims to record all that is known of the whereabouts and ownership of the pictures prior to their acquisition for Melbourne.

References, related to the Comment and Provenance, indicate the sources used for each statement. All reference material quoted has been consulted unless marked "not seen".

Work on this catalogue has extended over many years, and much of it was carried out in Melbourne with the correspondence files of the National Gallery of Victoria, those of the archives of the State Library of Victoria and the art sections of the State Library and of the Baillieu Library of the University of Melbourne. Owing to the generosity of the Trustees of the National Gallery of Victoria it was possible for the compiler to carry out eight month's research abroad, where the following institutions were of assistance: The British Museum Library and Department of Prints and Drawings; the Courtauld Institute of Art, University of London; l'Institut Royal du Patrimoine Artistique, Brussels; The National Portrait Gallery, London; The Rijksbureau voor Kunsthistorische Documentatie, The Hague; The Victoria and Albert Museum, Library and Department of Sculpture and Prints and Drawings; The Warbug Institute, University of London.

I wish to acknowledge my gratitude to these institutions and to the scholars who so generously gave their time and help. Wherever possible such help has been acknowledged in its place in the catalogue. I have also received much assistance from my collegues at the National Gallery of Victoria and at the Fine Arts Department of the University of Melbourne; to them, and especially to the Gallery's Conservator, Mr. Harley Griffiths, I wish to express my thanks. I owe a special debt of gratitude to two of the Gallery's Trustees, Col. A. H. L. Gibson and Mr. Justice Scholl, for reading the manuscript and making pertinent comments, to Miss Marguerite Kay, London, for checking the references, and to Miss June Stewart, Mr. David Lawrence and Mr. Daniel Thomas for reading the proofs.

Ursula Hoff

1961

Note to Second Edition

The present catalogue is a revised and enlarged edition of the catalogue of 1961. Some of the previous 186 entries have been amended and 20 new entries of acquisitions made between 1961 and April 1967 have been added. To facilitate identification, all works described have been illustrated in small reproductions.

The compiler records her thanks to the Centre national de Recherches "Primitifs Flamands" for permission to quote from Ursula Hoff and Martin Davies, *Les Primitifs Flamands I. Corpus de la Peinture Flamande des Anciens Pays-Bas Meridionaux au Quinzième Siècle, 11, Le Musée de Melbourne,* Brussels, to appear in 1968. Acknowledgement has been made in the text of information kindly made available to me by scholars. I wish to thank Miss Marguerite Kay, London, for again checking references for some of the new entries, and Miss June Stewart and Mr. Franz Philipp for kindly reading the proofs.

Ursula Hoff

1967

Note to Third Edition

This revised and augmented edition of 'European Paintings before
Eighteen Hundred' includes for the first time the Gallery's small collection
of Sculpture from the same period, and records new acquisitions in both
fields made between 1967 (the publishing date of the second edition)
and July 1972. All new entries had to be compiled in Australia but the
compiler has had very generous help from colleagues overseas whose
names are recorded in the relevant places. All literature quoted has been
consulted, except where marked 'not seen'. The compiler wishes
particularly to thank Professor Zeri for the kind interest he has taken in the
collection and the helpful re-attributions he supplied for Nos. 736/2 and
553/4 published in the previous catalogue as Italian School 17th and ditto,
18th century.

I would also like to record my indebtedness to the late Professor emer.
Rudolf Wittkower to whom we owe the documentation of the two sculptures
by Bernini.

Melbourne, 1972
Ursula Hoff

Forward to Third Edition

In 1961 as part of the programme marking the centenary year of the
National Gallery of Victoria, the Trustees issued the first edition of this
book under the title *Catalogue of European Paintings before Eighteen
Hundred* written by Dr. Ursula Hoff, the then Keeper of the Department of
Prints and Drawings, now the Assistant Director of the Gallery. The second
edition called *European Paintings before 1800* was issued in 1967 to
include a number of important paintings which had entered the collection
since 1961. This edition was published to mark the opening of the new
building in 1968.

The present third edition is being published in response to the continued
demand for this book. The inclusion of sculpture widens its coverage
of the Gallery's holdings. The sculpture section has considerably increased
in interest through the addition in 1971 of two bronzes by Gian Lorenzo
Bernini, the greatest sculptor of the Italian Baroque.

Once again acknowledgement is made of the enormous part that has
been played by the two bequests — those of Alfred Felton and Everard
Studley Miller — upon which our Gallery has been so largely built. Despite
ever increasing prices and an ever dwindling supply we have been able
to add further works of quality to our collections. The Miller Bequest is
handled by the Trustees themselves; but both Trustees and staff wish to
record their indebtedness to those who continue to handle the Felton
Bequest with such sympathy and understanding of the needs of the Gallery.

As with the two previous editions this volume is entirely the responsibility of Dr. Hoff, and the Trustees wish to thank her most sincerely for her work. Without her profound scholarship it would have been impossible for such a volume to be produced. At the same time they would also like to thank all those who have assisted Dr. Hoff in the compilation of the material and whose names have been appropriately recorded by her.

N. R. Seddon   Eric Westbrook
President   **Director**

Explanations

Condition: All original canvases may be taken to have been re-lined, unless the contrary is stated.

Measurements: All pictures listed in this catalogue have been remeasured; stretcher or panel measurements have been given, unless otherwise indicated; where the painted surface differs markedly from the measurements of the support, both measurements have been given. Height precedes width.

Terms Used: Qualifying terms have been used after the names of certain artists. "Studio of" refers to a work coming from the immediate circle of assistants of a master; "School of" refers to the wider circle of contemporary followers of a master; "Follower of" designates later followers of a master; "attributed to" refers to a picture showing some elements of the style of a master but admitting an element of doubt; "after" means that the picture is a repetition of a work of a master named and not by the hand of the master himself.

A.R.A.	Associate, Royal Academy (London).
Burl. Mag.	*The Burlington Magazine.*
ca.	About.
C.N.G.	*Catalogues, National Gallery, London.*
D.N.B.	*Dictionary of National Biography.*
E.W.A.	*Encyclopedia of World Art,* 1960.
l. left;	*l.c.* left centre; *l.l.* lower left; *l.r.* lower right.
loc. cit.	Locus citatum.
N.G.	National Gallery.
N.P.G.	National Portrait Gallery.
op. cit.	Opus citatum.
q.v.	"see under."
R.A.	Royal Academy, London. *bildenden Künste.*
Th.B.	U. Thieme, F. Becker, *Allgemeines Künstlerlexikon der*
u.c. upper centre;	*u.l.* upper left; *u.r.* upper right.

List of Attributions Changed from the General Catalogue of 1948 and Appendix I of 1950, II of 1954

Stockbook No.	1948 Catalogue and Appendices	Present Catalogue
662a/4	Balen, Hendrick van	Italian School 17th or 18th century
553/4	Baroccio, Federigo	Italian School 17th or 18th century
552/4	Bassano, Jacopo, attributed to	Bassano, Francesco, School of
1109/4	Beechey, Sir William	Brown, Mather
304/1	Bega Cornelisz Pieters	Dutch School 18th century
550/4	Caravaggio, School of	Reni, Guido, after
962/3	Cotman, John Sell	Cotman, Miles Edmund
4590/3	Dürer, School of	Flemish School, 16th century
557/4	Florentine School, 14th century	Italian School 15th century
217/4	Lely, Sir Peter	Dyck, Anthony van, School of
1827/4	Pisanello, School of	Vivarini, School of
214/4	Ribera, Jusepe de	Giordano, Luca
219/4	Ribera, Jusepe de	Strozzi, Bernardo, School of
2974/4	Russian, School of Stroganov	Byzantine-Russian School
310/1	Ryckaert, David	Dutch School
2124/4	Sienese School, XIV century	Bartolo, Domenico di
184/4	Tiepolo, School of	Italian School, 18th century
3729/3	Tiepolo, School of	Italian School, 18th century
1541/4	Uccello, Paolo, attributed to,	Italian School, 15th century
303c/1 (?)	Unknown	British School, middle 18th century
303d/1 (?)	Unknown	British School, early 18th century
304/1	Unknown	British School, late 18th century

Note: Changes in the qualification of a name (as *after Claude* instead of *Claude)* are not included in this list.

Stockbook No.	1948 Catalogue and Appendices	Present Catalogue
305/1	Unknown	French School (?), 18th century
4694/3	Unknown	British School, Elizabethan
1966/4	Venetian School, 14th century	Paolo Veneziano
306/1	Wilkie, David	British School, 19th century

List of Attributions changed from the Catalogue of 1967:

Stockbook No.	1967 Catalogue	Present Catalogue
553/4	Italian School, 18th century	after Federigo Barocci
2124/4	Domenico di Bartolo	Italian, Florentine, 15th century
965/3	Canaletto	Bernardo Belotto
736/2	Italian, 18th century	Jean Boulanger, after
184/4	Tiepolo, School of	Sebastian Bourdon
3729/3	Italian School, Venetian 18th century	Valerio Castello
306/1	British School, early 19th century	attributed to John Jackson

Jacopo Amiconi (also Giacomo Amigoni)   1675-1752

Italian. Born at Venice; his work shows the influence of Sebastiano Ricci (*q.v.*) and Solimena. Stood in the service of the Elector of Bavaria, for whom he painted ceiling paintings in the castles of Schleissheim and Nymphenburg; altarpieces were in the Frauenkirche in Munich. In 1729 he went to London where he carried out commissions for portraiture and decorative paintings in country houses, such as Powis House, Moor Park, and also for the Covent Garden Theatre in London. In 1736 in Paris; he returned to Venice in 1739; in 1747 he accepted an appointment as court painter to King Ferdinand VI of Spain, and remained in Madrid until his death. One of his two daughters was married to one *Castellani,* and is not to be confused with the Teresa *Castellini,* portrayed in the Melbourne picture.

Reference: Th.B.

Illust. 1   2226/4 **Portrait Group**

canvas, 172.8 x 245.1 cm. Signed *G. Amiconi* on the handle of one of the brushes held by the painter. Undated; painted between 1750 and 1752. Inscriptions: On base of pedestal to left: *P. Metastasio;* on paper held by female figure: *C.B.F.* (Carlo Broschi Farinelli) *Canzonetta,* music and the words:

Ecco quel fiero istante Nice mia Nice addio come vivro ben mio cosi lontan da te lo vivro sempre in pene lo non avro piu bene e tu chi sa se mai ti sovuerrai di me.

In Burney's translation:

> Nisa, the dreadful time is come to bid adieu
> Nor to a distant clime must I thy steps pursue,
> No hope will fate allow to soothe the harsh decree
> Yet who can tell if thou will ever think of me.

On a sheet of music at the feet of the female figure is inscribed: *Teresa Castellini*; on dog's collar: *C.B.F.*

Condition: Cleaned prior to purchase; a good number of re-paints; varnish darkening.

Comment: The figures united in this conversation piece were close friends. They are, from left to right: The Abate Metastasio; Teresa Castellini; Carlo Broschi Farinelli; Jacopo Amiconi; a page and a dog.

Farinelli (1705-1782), famous Italian castrato singer, made his debut at Naples; in 1734 he sang in London; in 1737 he went to Madrid and became a favourite of Philip V of Spain (1700-1746); his favour continued under Ferdinand VI (1746-1759), who bestowed the order of the Calatrava on him in 1750 which, together with the jewel of the order, is to be seen in this portrait.[1] In 1761 Farinelli retired to Bologna where he died. At Naples

Farinelli had become acquainted with the Abate Metastasio (1698-1780), poet, playwright and librettist, with whom he remained in life-long friendship.

Metastasio, since 1729 court poet to Charles VI at Vienna, enquired in his letters (addressed to Farinelli in Madrid) after "the beautiful Castellini" (Sept. 6, 1749);[2] she is again mentioned in the correspondence on May 2, 1750.[3] The canzonetta held by her was written by Metastasio and is probably the one referred to in the correspondence of May 3, 1750, as having been sent to Farinelli.[4] On June 13, 1750, Metastasio noted that Farinelli had set the canzonetta to music.[5] The British Museum Add. Ms. 14207 (Nos. 3-9) preserves the music to which this canzonetta was set by such contemporary composers as D. G. Cafarelli, O. Gravina, A. Monticelli and others.[6] The music on the sheet in our painting differs from all these and is perhaps Farinelli's. According to Burney, the title of the canzonetta was *La Partenza.* Its heroine, disguised under the name Nice, was a Viennese opera dancer for whom Metastasio procured an appointment in Madrid to separate her from a married Viennese nobleman who had fallen in love with her.[7]

Three of the people portrayed in the picture were thus certainly together in Madrid in 1750. Metastasio was in Vienna, and the portrait bust in the picture was, it appears, not painted from life. Farinelli had asked Metastasio to supply him with several portraits of himself which arrived in Madrid in 1749 and 1751.[8]

The figures are shown accompanied by a page in a fanciful Hungarian uniform. Since the dog close to him wears Farinelli's initials on his collar, the boy must be Farinelli's page.[9] Burney, mistaking the Castellini for Faustina, attributed the picture to Amiconi's Venetian period; he was followed in this dating by Vernon Lee and most recent writers.[10] All available sources however point to the work having been executed in Madrid after 1750 and before 1752 (the date of Amiconi's death).

Provenance: The painting was seen by Burney in Farinelli's house in Bologna in 1761;[11] owned by Mrs. Clinton Dawkins in 1885; by Lady Templemore in 1926 (exhibited Magnasco Society, 1926, No. 19, owner the Dowager Lady Templemore); after 1931 in possession of Mr. Ronald Tree, Ditchley, Oxon, from whom it was purchased through T. Agnew and Sons, on the advice of Sir Kenneth Clark and A. J. L. McDonnell for the Felton Bequest in 1949/50.

Exhibition: *Life in XVIII Century England,* Iveagh Bequest, Kenwood, London, 1966, Cat. No. 1.

Other Versions: Another portrait of Farinelli by Amiconi painted c. 1750 and closely related to the one in 2226/4 was in 1969 in the possession of Thos. Agnew & Sons, London. Farinelli here appears alone, in three quarter length, wearing the jewel and order of Calatrava, a sheet of music in his left, his right hand resting on the neck of a pug dog. A landscape with a water pageant forms the background.[12]

References: (1) Mr. Edward Croft-Murray has drawn my attention to the undermentioned sources and allowed me to consult his entry on Amiconi in his *Decorative Painting in England,* 1537-1837, Vol. II (shortly to appear). Charles Burney, *The Present State of Music in France and Italy,* London, 1771, pp. 210-213 (to be quoted as *Burney*). (2) Charles Burney,

Memoirs of the Life and Writings of the Abate Metastasio, Vol. I, 1796, p. 289 (to be quoted as *Memoirs*). (3) *Memoirs,* p. 359; see also Franz Haböck, *Die Gesangkunst der Kastraten,* Vienna, I. Notenband, p. L, who says: "We know that he (Farinelli) sometimes gave instructions to individual artists, thus for example to the singer Teresa Castellini from Milan who had been called to Madrid by Queen Barbara and who seems to have been a favourite of Farinelli's." (4) *Memoirs,* pp. 349, 359. (5) *Memoirs,* p. 365. (6) According to Haböck, *op. cit.,* p. L, this was Metastasio's most popular and most admired creation. (7) *Memoirs,* pp. 347-9. (8) *Memoirs,* pp. 206-7, 210, 259, 261, 276, 390, 391. (9) E. Croft-Murray, *op. cit.;* and old label on the back of the picture describes the page as an Archduke of Austria. (10) Vernon Lee, *Studies of the Eighteenth Century in Italy,* 2nd ed. 1907, p. 271; Sir Newman Flower, *Handel,* 1923, p. 220; A. J. L. McDonnell, *Quarterly Bulletin N.G. Victoria,* 1950, IV, (1), 3, repr.; J. Woodward, *Burl. Mag.* Vol. XCIX, 1957, pp. 21-3; M. Levey, *Painting in Eighteenth Century Venice,* 1959, p. 146, fig. 69. (11) Burney, p. 212. (12) *Burl. Mag.,* Vol. CXII, Dec. 1970, Supplement, pl. XLVIII.

Federico Barocci   1526-1612

Italian. Born at Urbino, as the son of a Milanese sculptor. His first master was Battista Franco; later he was with Girolamo Genga in Pesaro and later still spent some time in Rome. The major influence on his art came from Correggio whose soft light and shade and sweetness of style determined Barocci's manner.

Reference: *Encyclopedia of World Art.*

after Barocci

Illust. 2   553/4 **Portrait of a Young Girl**

canvas, 50 x 34.8 cm. Unsigned, undated.

Condition: Fair; cracked and rubbed.

Comment: acquired, and listed in the 1948 catalogue as by Federico Barocci; it is however a copy; a better version exists at Williams College in Williamstown, Massachusetts.[1]

Provenance: According to Howard Spensley[2] his London dealer, R. E. A. Wilson, had it from Lord Barrymore's sale, 21 June, 1933. The picture is not listed in the sale but may have been sold with one of the Barrymore pictures under the heading "and another". Howard Spensley Bequest, 1939.

References: (1) corr. June 19, 1969, Hoff-Burton F. Frederickson, Curator, the Paul J. Getty Museum, Malibu, California. (2) *Howard Spensley Mss.* Book I, pp. 50/51, Cat. No. 529.

George Barret   1728?-1784

British. Born at Dublin. Self-taught. Went to London, 1762. One of the foundation members of the Royal Academy at which he was a constant exhibitor of landscapes until 1782.

References: *Th.B.;* M. H. Grant, *A Chronological History of Old English Landscape Painters,* Leigh-on-Sea, Vol. III, 1958, p. 193 ff.

Illust. 3　4712/3 **View of Windermere Lake, Early Morning**

canvas, 149 x 240.5 cm. Signed and dated l.l. *G. Barrett 1781.*

Condition: Satisfactory.

Provenance:　Exh. R.A. 1781, No. 40 (owner Sir J. W. Ramsden). George Audley, Esq., late of Birkdale Lodge, Southport, Christie's, 12 May, 1932, lot 11, acquired by Randall Davies for the Felton Bequest. Arrived 1933.

Francesco Bassano II　1549-1592

Italian. The eldest surviving son of Jacopo Bassano, *(q.v.).* His art closely followed that of his father.

Reference:　C.N.G.

School of Francesco Bassano II

Illust. 4　552/4 **The Mocking of Christ**

canvas, 47.6 x 83.2 cm. Unsigned, undated.

Condition: apart from an old mend in the canvas, in good condition.

Comment: Formerly attributed to Jacopo Bassano;[1] the stylistic similarity to Francesco, however, and the rather lower quality make Prof. Arslan's re-attribution convincing. Prof. Arslan notes a prototype in the Pitti Gallery, Florence.[2]

Provenance:　Purchased by Howard Spensley from R. E. A. Wilson, Ryder Street, London;[1] bequeathed by him in 1939.

References:　(1) *Howard Spensley Mss.* Vol. I, p. 86, Cat. No. 528; N.G. Victoria Cat. 1948; B. Berenson, *Caravaggio,* London, 1953, p. 57, pl. 79. (2) E. Arslan, *I Bassano,* 1960, Vol. I, p. 352.

Jacopo Bassano active ca. 1535, d. 1592

Italian. His name was Jacopo dal Ponte, called Bassano after the city of his birth. Probably born between 1510 and 1519. His father, Francesco I Bassano, was also a painter. Jacopo's early work shows the influence of Bonifazio Veronese and Lorenzo Lotto. His presence in Venice is documented for 1535 and again later when he advised his son, Francesco II Bassano, in the execution of paintings for the Doge's Palace. His presence in Bassano is frequently documented. Painted religious paintings into which he introduced the animal studies for which he was already noted by Vasari.

References:　Th.B.; C.N.G.

Illust. 5   554/4   Portrait Of An Old Man

canvas, 94.2 x 73.6 cm. Unsigned, undated; painted between 1570-80.

Condition: Howard Spensley reported that additions to the canvas were removed by R. E. A. Wilson.[1] Presumably cleaned at that time. In good condition.

Comment: Prof. Arslan groups this portrait together with those at the Prague and Boston Museums as late works by the artist, and a fine example of his style.[2] Previously thought to represent Titian.[1]

Provenance: Apparently acquired by R. E. A. Wilson of Ryder Street at Sotheby's before 1935,[1] but it has not been possible to identify the sale; exhibited at Wilson's, July 1935, No. 1 (no owner stated);[1] presumably acquired by Howard Spensley after this date and bequeathed by him in 1939.

References: (1) *Howard Spensley Mss.* Book I, p. 76, Cat. No. 530. (2) T. Arslan, *Annual Bulletin, N.G. Victoria,* 1959, Vol. I, pp. 18-19; and *I Bassano,* 1960, Vol. I, pp. 143-4, 171, pl. XII; Vol. II, fig. 194; other references: B. Berenson, *Italian Pictures of the Renaissance, Venetian School,* 1957, Vol. I, p. 18.

Pompeo Girolamo Batoni   1708-1787

Italian. Born at Lucca; went to Rome in 1727 where he spent most of his life. He was influenced by classical antiquity, Raphael, Annibale Carracci and, among contemporaries, notably by Imperiali. Painter of history and portraits. Famous for his portraits of princes, aristocrats and celebrities, often painted while they were in Rome on the Grand Tour, standing against a background of classical antiquity.

References: *Th.B.; C.N.G.*

Illust. 6   1211/5   Gaetano Sforza-Cesarini, Duke of Segni

canvas, 97.8 x 73.2 cm (stretcher size), signed and dated *P. Batoni Pinxit Romae 1768* (?) on waistcoat, lower centre. Inscribed on paper in his l. hand, sua Eccelenza Duca Sforza Cesarini, Roma.

Condition: excellent.

Comment: The sitter was born 23rd August 1723; appointed 18th August 1750 *Protonotario Apostolico* and *Referendario delle sue Segnature;* in 1756 became vicar of the College of Santa Maria in the Via Lata. 1759 became head of the administrative council of the papal State. On the death of his eldest brother Gaetano resigned his ecclesiastical offices and was made Captain of the Cavalry Guard in 1766 by Clement XIII; in 1769 Ferdinando, Duke of Parma, appointed him gentleman of the Bedchamber and Maggiordomo Maggiore to the Duchess Maria Amalia's household. Resigned this position in 1770 and died 17th March 1776 in Rome.[1]
Until its acquisition, this portrait was accompanied by a pendant representing the Duchess Sforza Cesarini now in the Birmingham City Museum and Art Gallery.[2]

Provenance: The picture remained in the family of the sitter until its acquisition from P. & D. Colnaghi, London, on the recommendation of A. J. L. McDonnell under the terms of the Everard Studley Miller Bequest 1961.

References: (1) P. Litta, *Famiglie Celebri Italiane*, Milan 1819, I, tav. III. (2) H. Preston, *Two Portraits by Pompeo Batoni,* in *Annual Bulletin, N.G. Victoria*, VI, 1964, p. 17 f. fig. 14.

Illust. 7   1325/5 **Sir Samson Gideon And His Tutor Signor Basti**

canvas, 275.6 x 189 cm (stretcher size) signed and dated beneath the tread of the lower step to the left in simulated incised letters, *Pompeo Batoni/Pinxit Romae* (last two letters in monogram)/*An. 1767.* The letter held in the sitter's left hand is inscribed in script *To/Sir Sampson Gideon Bart/Roma.* White lettering added later at the lower left corner *Lord Eardly (sic) and his tutor, Signor Basti/Batoni Pinxit* were removed when the picture was cleaned prior to despatch to Melbourne.[1]

Condition: Cleaned after purchase. In good state of preservation.

Comment: Behind Sir Sampson a bust of Minerva, a reduced section of the Minerva Giustiniani at the Vatican which reflects a lost Greek 5th century original; in the distance the Temple of Vesta, at Tivoli. Sir Sampson shows the miniature of a lady to his tutor. He was in Rome in 1765, married in England in 1766; this suggests that the picture, dated 1767, was completed from drawings.[2] For similar procedures by Batoni see Preston,[2] p. 14. A drawing for the costume of Sir Sampson is in the Courtauld Institute, Witt Collection.

Provenance: Was at Belvedere, the seat of Sir Sampson Gideon, who was created Lord Eardley in 1789. Inherited by Lord Eardley's son-in-law Lord Saye and Sele (1769-1844); listed Dr. Waagen, *Galleries and Cabinets of Art in Great Britain,* London 1857, p. 284; passed to Lord Eardley's second son-in-law, Sir Culling Eardley and was removed with other pictures from Belvedere to Bedwell Park, Herts., in 1860; mentioned in T. Lejeune, *Guide Théorique et Pratique de l'Amateur de Tableau, Etudes sur les Imitateurs et les Copistes,* Paris, 1863-65, III, p. 10. Owned successively by Sir Culling Eardley's daughters, Mrs. Culling Hanbury and the Hon. Mrs. William Henry Fremantle; passed to her son, Sir Francis Edward Fremantle (d. 1943); sold by his son Lieutenant Colonel F. D. E. Fremantle, Christie, Dec. 14, 1945, lot 15; bt. Mr. and Mrs. Basil Ionides, Buxted Park, Kent; sold Sotheby, 3rd July, 1963, lot 34; bt. Leggatt. Acquired on the advice of A. J. L. McDonnell from Legatt's under the terms of the Everard Studley Miller Bequest, 1963.

References: (1) Reproduced in colour with the old inscription in *Country Life Annual,* Christmas, 1949, p. 45, fig. 7, p. 49. (2) Harley Preston, *Two Portraits by Pompeo Batoni* in *Annual Bulletin, N.G. Victoria,* Vol. VI, 1964, pp. 11-15. See also C. Gould, *The English Conversation Piece,* in *Country Life Annual,* 1949, pp. 40-49, fig. 7; *The Ivory Hammer—The Year at Sotheby's,* 219th Season, 1962-1963, London, 1963, pp. XXIII, XXIV, pl. 37. p. 45, fig. 7, p. 49.

Sir William Beechey   1753-1839

British. Born at Burford, Oxfordshire; studied at the Royal Academy Schools in 1772 under Zoffany (*q.v.*) 1793 A.R.A. and portrait painter to the Queen. 1798 R.A.

Reference: *Th.B.*

Illust. 8   301/1 **Portrait Of A Lady**

canvas, 125.7 x 93.3 cm (oval). Unsigned, undated.

Condition: In good condition; old varnish.

Comment: Purchased as "anonymous, portrait of Lady Hamilton";[1] the attribution to Beechey is convincing. The sitter resembles the artist's wife.

Provenance: Offered from an undisclosed source in 1863;[1] purchased in 1865.[2]

References: (1) Minutes of Fine Arts Commission 01 Oct. 1863 Archives, State Library of Victoria. (2) Ibid. 31 Jan., 1865.

Abraham Jans Begeyn   1637-8—1697

Dutch. Born at Leyden; travelled in France and Italy and settled in Amsterdam in 1672. Later active in the Hague, London and Berlin where he stood in the service of the Elector of Brandenburg. His landscapes show the influence of the Italianate work of Asselyn and Berchem; he also painted port scenes in the style of Weenix and plants with insects like Mathaeus van Schriek.

References: Th.B.; C.N.G., W. Bernt, *Die Niederländischen Maler des 17. Jahrhunderts,* 1948, Vol. I, No. 57.

Illust. 9   4503/3 **Landscape With Cattle**

canvas, 97 x 76.7 cm. Unsigned, undated.

Condition: Satisfactory, but for dirty varnish.

Comment: Italian architecture and bridge form the background.

Provenance: Acquired for the Felton Bequest from Lieut. Col. E. J. H. Nicholson of Western Australia in 1931 on the recommendation of Bernard Hall; according to the vendor the picture was in Western Australia before 1900.[1]

References: (1) Archives, State Library of Victoria (Ni Box) 1931.

Bernardo Bellotto   1720-1780

Italian. Nephew and pupil of Antonio Canaletto, whose surname he added to his own. He went to Dresden in 1747, and became famous for his views of Dresden, Pirna and Königstein which he made while in the service of Frederick Augustus. From 1767 he worked in Warsaw for King Stanislas Poniatowski until his death.

Reference: Peter and Linda Murray, *A Dictionary of Art and Artists,* London, 1959.

Illust. 10   964/3 **Ruins of the Forum, Rome**

canvas, 87 x 148.1 cm. Unsigned, undated; painted between 1740-44.

Condition: good; old varnish.

Comment: Foreground, left, the Temple of Castor and Pollux; right, the Fountain of Giuterna. Mid-distance, right, the Columns of Phocas and the Temple of Saturn, behind them the buildings of the Capitol.

Extreme left foreground, a corner of S. Maria Liberatrice (this was taken down in 1901-2, to reveal S. Maria Antiqua). A smaller version is in the possession of H.M. the Queen at Buckingham Palace. The Temple of Castor and Pollux is higher in proportion; the fountain is closer to the lower edge, less being seen of S. Maria Liberatrice, and the handling is more summary with sharper contrasts of light and shade than in H.M. the Queen's painting[1] which, like 965/3 was formerly attributed to Canaletto.[3a]

A drawing of the subject, by or after Canaletto is in the British Museum,[2] another version was formerly at Paxton House.[3] An upright version of the same subject, signed and dated 1742 is at Windsor Castle.[4]
Michael Levey accepts the upright version only as by Canaletto, giving the oblong versions, including 964/3, to Canaletto's nephew and pupil, Bernardo Bellotto (1720-80).[5]

Provenance: Said to have come from the Duchess of Marlborough (in no Marlborough sale nor Blenheim Catalogue); Earl of Bessborough, sold Christie's 14 March 1891, lot 149, bt. Agnew; Hope Heirlooms (Lord Francis Pelham Clinton Hope), sold Christie's 20 July 1917, lot 76, as by B. Canaletto, Bt. Pawsey and Paine; with A. H. Buttery, London; acquired by the Felton Bequest on the advice of Robert Ross in 1918.

References: (1) W. G. Constable, *Canaletto,* p. 359, No. 379, Oxford, 1961. (2) Th. Ashby, W. G. Constable, *Burl. Mag.* XLVI, 1925, 208; W. G. Constable, *op. cit.* (3) W. G. Constable, *op. cit.* 3a see 1967 ed. of the present catalogue. (4) C. H. Collins Baker, Cat. *Principal Pictures at Windsor Castle,* 1937, p. 44, pl. 12. (5) Michael Levey, *The Later Italian Pictures in the Collection of Her Majesty the Queen,* London, 1964, No. 418. For a discussion of the series of five Roman views of which 964/3 is one, see *ibid.* No. 368.

Gerrit Berckheyde   1638-1698

Dutch. Born at Haarlem; pupil of his elder brother Job B., with whom he visited Cologne and Heidelberg. Member of the Haarlem guild since 1660. Mainly engaged in architectural views of Dutch towns which he frequently repeated.

References: *Th.B.; C.N.G.*

Illust. 11   1050/3 **The Town Hall, Amsterdam**

canvas, 52.8 x 62.6 cm. Signed and dated *Gerrit Berckheyde 1690,* l.l.

Condition: Satisfactory, old varnish.

Comment: The seventeenth-century Town Hall of Amsterdam, which is now the Royal Palace, designed by Jacob van Campen in 1648 in a style combining Italian classicism on the outside with baroque on the inside, is among the greatest works of Dutch architecture.[1] Dated views of the Town Hall, by Berckheyde, related in type to 1050/3 (but with variations in effects of light and figure groups) in public collections are: 1668 (Antwerp Museum); 1672 (Rijksmuseum, Cat. No. 477); 1673 (Rijksmuseum, Cat. No. 478), (on loan to the Amsterdam Historical Museum); 1680 (Vienna Academy); 1689 (Karlsruhe Museum); 1693 (Rijksmuseum, Cat. No. 481). See also: 1697 (View of the Dam) Dreesman Sale, Amsterdam, March 22, 1960, lot 2.[2]

Provenance: Exhibited R. A. 1879, No. 59 by Major Corbett, Vaynor Park, Berriew, Montgomeryshire; acquired on the advice of Frank Rinder in January, 1920, for the Felton Bequest.[3]

Reference: (1) K. Fremantle, *The Baroque Town Hall of Amsterdam*, 1060. (2) W Stechow, *Dutch Landscape Painting of the Seventeenth Century,* London, 1966, p. 210, (note 22). (3) Rinder corr. 27.1.1920, files N.G. Victoria.

Jean Boulanger   1566-1660

French-Italian. Came early to Italy and into the studio of Guido Reni. In 1638 he became court painter at Modena where he founded a school modelled on that of the Carraccis.

Reference: *Th.B.*

after Boulanger

Illust. 12   736/2 **Bacchus and Satyrs**

canvas, 73.5 x 98 cm. Unsigned, undated.

Condition: Satisfactory.

Comment: Previously attributed to Hendrick van Balen, but does not show his style. A better version, of 736/2 together with a companion piece, both attributed to Jean Boulanger, were on the Florentine art market in 1969.[1] The composition relies closely on groups from Annibale Carracci's *Triumph of Bacchus and Ariadne*;[2] the resting female figure in the r. lower corner, the Bacchus on his carriage and a female, back view to the left of him, the dancing figure playing the cymbals in the centre, all have their counterpart in Annibale Carracci's fresco.

Provenance: Presented by John H. Connell in 1914.

References: (1) corr. Zeri-Hoff 21.X.69. (2) In the Farnese Gallery, Rome, Palazzo Farnese, 1597-1604; H. Voss, *Die Malerei des Barock in Rome,* 1924, p. 168 repr. of Carracci's fresco.

Sebastian Bourdon   1616-1671

French. Born at Montpellier; pupil of Jean (?) Barthélemy, 1623-30 in Paris. Visited Italy from 1634 to 7, and was influenced by Poussin in Rome. He was an original member of the Academie; 1652-4 court painter of Christian of Sweden at Stockholm.

Reference: *C.N.G.*

c

Illust. 13   184/4   **The Adoration of The Magi**

Copper, 45.4 x 35.7. Unsigned, undated.

Condition: Flaked-off paint in many places replaced by re-paints in recent years.

Comment: Previously attributed to the school of Tiepolo (see catalogue N.G.V. 1948; Cat. *European Painting before 1800,* N.G.V. 1962 and 1967).

Professor Federico Zeri discovered the similarity of 181/4 to *A Sacrifice of Iphigenia* in the Musée des Beaux Arts at Orléans there described as a work of Bourdon.[1]

Provenance: Acquired by Barnard Hall for the Felton Bequest in 1934 from the collection of Rev. Patrick Gorry, County Kildare, Ireland.

References: (1) corr. Zeri-Hoff, 30.3.1970; The Orléans picture is reproduced in the *Gazette des Beaux Arts,* Feb. 1970, supp. p. 9, No. 46.

British Elizabethan Period

Illust. 14   4694/3   **Portrait of a Lady in Rich Attire**

panel, 42.2 x 29.5 cm. Inscribed *1570* u.l. *Ae 19* u.r.

Condition: Not in good condition, retouches in face and background.

Comment: According to an old label on the back formerly attributed to F. Zuccaro.

Provenance: Acquired by Bernard Hall from the Fine Arts Society, Melbourne, for the Felton Bequest in 1932.

British Elizabethan Period

Illust. 15   3017/4   **Robert Dudley, Early of Leicester**

panel, 45.3 x 33.5 cm. Unsigned, undated; painted between 1565-70.

Condition: Good; cleaned prior to purchase.

Comment: Robert Dudley, Earl of Leicester, 1532?—88 was Queen Elizabeth's favourite. The portrait here belongs to the early period, reflecting the type seen in the half length in the Wallace Collection, attributed to Steven van der Muelen (active 1543—to after 1563) and is closest to one in a private collection, also possibly by the same painter.[1]

3017/4 has been traditionally ascribed to Federigo Zuccaro (1540/3-1609 Italian School), who was in England from May to October, 1575.[2] Many portraits of the Elizabethan period have been ascribed to Zuccaro but such ascriptions have been disputed by recent authorities.[3] Prof. Ellis Waterhouse points out that "all that he is recorded with any certainty to have painted in England are full-length portraits of Queen Elizabeth and the Earl of Leicester. All that survives is a pair of drawings for these in the British Museum".

Provenance: Exhibited by Mrs. Whatman at the Tudor Exh., The New Gallery, London, 1890, No. 257 (as *Zuccaro*); Sale Vinters, in Maidstone, 4 April 1951, Lofts Warner, lot 608. Acquired on the advice of A. J. L. McDonnell from P. & D. Colnaghi, London, in 1952/3 for the Felton Bequest.

References: 1. Roy Strong, *Tudor and Jacobean Portraits* National Portrait Gallery, London 1969, Vol. 1, p. 195, Vol. II, figs. 378, 379. 2. On purchase this portrait was ascribed to Zuccaro. For Zuccaro's stay in England see Roy C. Strong, *Journal of the Warburg and Courtauld Institutes,* Vol. XXII, 1959, pp. 359/60. 3. L. Cust, *Apollo,* Vol. 1, 1925, p. 254; Vol. IV, 1926, p. 6; F. Kelly, *Apollo,* Vol. XIII, 1931, p. 223; Ellis Waterhouse, *Burl. Mag.* 1936, Vol. LXIX, p. 134; and *Painting in Britain, 1530-1790,* 1953, p. 20.

British, early 18th century

Illust. 16   2925/4 **Acting Lieutenant Thomas Wallis**

canvas, 76.5 x 63.5 cm. Unsigned, undated; painted before 1782.

Condition: in moderate condition; circular priming cracks; mounted on a panel by Harley Griffiths in 1953.

Comment: A label on the back of the canvas gives the name of the sitter and continues "Acting Lieutenant of His Majesty's Ship Superb, killed in action with the French Fleet in the East Indies, 12th April, 1782, aged nineteen years". He wears the midshipman's uniform, in use between 1748 and 1787.[1] The painter is probably not English, since the hair is painted in a style quite different from the English tradition.[2] *Albany Wallis*, portrayed by Sir Joshua Reynolds in 1783, was a relative of the sitter.[3]

Provenance: Brought to Tasmania about 1870 by the descendants of the sitter; the Wallis family retain a letter referring to the portrait having been shown to Sir Charles L. Eastlake, Director of the London N.G. in 1862.[4] Acquired by Daryl Lindsay, Director, in 1952 from S. Lipscombe in Sydney.

References: (1) Correspondence, N.G. Victoria files, 13 March 1952, M. S. Robinson, National Maritime Museum, Greenwich, to Director. (2) Correspondence, N.G. Victoria files, 18 June 1953, C. K. Adams, National Portrait Gallery, London, to Director. Mr. Adams had shown the photograph to Mr. C. H. Collins Baker, whose opinion is quoted here. (3) Exh. R.A. 1783, No. 23; Ellis Waterhouse, *Reynolds*, 1941, pl. 241 (4) Information supplied by S. Lipscombe who obtained the picture from the descendants of the sitter.

British, early 18th century

Illust. 17   303d/1(?) **A Gentleman With Long, Dark Wig**

canvas, 75.6 x 62.4 cm. Unsigned, undated.

Condition: in fair condition; broad craquelure.

Comment: The long, dark wig and the costume belong to the first decades of the 18th century in Britain.

Provenance: Unknown.

11

British, early 18th century

Illust. 18   311/1 **Portait of A Lady**

canvas, 64.3 x 52 cm (oval).

Condition: paint losses and rubbing; old varnish.

Comment: The costume is similar to that worn in portraits by Kneller about 1680; listed in 1948 catalogue under "Unknown".

Provenance: Presented by R. T. Litton, 1886.[1]

Reference: (1) State Library Archives, correspondence, 1886, No. 318.

British, middle 18th century

Illust. 19   303c/1(?) **A Gentleman With Grey Wig**

canvas, 73.7 x 67.5 cm. Unsigned, undated.

Condition: old varnish; paint lifting on l.c.

Comment: The short grey wig and the costume are those of the 1760s in Britain.

Provenance: Presented by G. R. Nash, Melbourne, in 1870.[1]

References: (1) Art Gallery letters, 1867-70, No. 84, State Library of Victoria Archives. (Described as portrait of Richard Nash by Sir Joshua Reynolds). See also Museum of Art Letter Book 1867-70 ibid.

British, late 18th century

Illust. 20   304/1 **A Gentleman in Three-quarter Profile, Facing left with Grey Hair and Black Coat**

canvas, 76.5 x 63.8 cm. Unsigned, undated.

Condition: fair.

Comment: The portrait has some affinity with the manner of Romney.

Provenance: Purchased in 1873 from the dealer James William Hines, Melbourne, 27 June, 1873.[1]

References: (1) National Gallery Ledger, fol. 15, State Library of Victoria Archives; Illustrated Catalogue of the National Gallery, 1918, p. 112, No. 18. (This number also on the frame.)

British, 18th century

Illust. 21   1246/A/B/5 **Two Conversation Pieces** of the Drake-Brockman family of Beachborough: A. Temple Pond with temple in right foreground; B. Temple Pond with temple in the distance on left.

canvas, A. 52.7 x 65 cm. B. 52.7 x 65 cm. Unsigned, undated, in contemporary carved and gilt frames. On label on back: "View of Temple Pond, Miss M. Brockman" in a fairly recent hand.

Condition: excellent; relined after purchase.

Comment: Both pictures are of the 'Temple Pond' of Beachborough House, near Folkestone, Kent, as shown on the six-inch Ordnance Survey Map at TR 166384. Beachborough House, dating from c. 1565, remodelled c. 1810 (the date of the sundial in the pediment), a boys' preparatory school in 1920, burnt down in 1954, had been a seat of the Brockman family since the time of Henry Brockman who died in 1573. The red Tudor roofs and chimneys of the house appear in B on the far right; beyond are the English Channel and the cliffs of France. The pond resembles such waterworks as those at Studley Royal in Yorkshire, which was laid out between 1716-1740 by its owner, John Aislabie, who was acquainted with the architect John Vanbrugh (1664-1726) and who perhaps had the advice of the architect John James (d. 1746) who published a translation of Dèzallier d'Argenville's *Theory and Practice of Gardening* (1712). An engraving of the *Banqueting House from the Round Temple* at Studley Royal (drawn and engraved by A. Walker about 1750) shows the formal cut edges of the pond and a round temple close to the water similar to those in the paintings here.[2]

Though the people in the picture are undoubtedly members of the Drake-Brockman families, none of them can be identified with certainty. Their costumes date from about 1740. At this time Beachborough was owned by William Brockman, who died in 1741, aged 83; he was succeeded by James Brockman, who died, unmarried in 1767, aged 71, leaving Beachborough to the Rev. Ralph Drake, who assumed the name of Brockman. The old man sitting in the Temple in A. could possibly be William Brockman. The man prominently in the foreground in B. in a brown coat could be James Brockman who would have been 44 years of age in 1740. The figure is not unlike a portrait of James Brockman, in the possession of Charles St. Leger Brockman.[2a] The clergyman in B, cannot be the Rev. Ralph Drake-Brockman, since this gentleman was only an 18-year-old student in 1740.[3] Some of the women in the picture could possibly be relatives from Cheriton Manor nearby, which was owned by William Brockman's younger brother Henry (d. 1752) who left three daughters, the youngest of whom, Caroline, later married Ralph Drake-Brockman, but such identifications are only guesswork.

While in the Drake-Brockman family the pictures were thought to be by Hogarth. This attribution cannot be maintained. Professor W. G. Constable has suggested that the landscape and architecture are by George Lambert (1710-1765) with the figures added by Hogarth (1697-1764).[4] Basil Taylor believes the pictures to be by Samuel Scott (c. 1710-1772).[5] John Kerslake and Professor Ellis Waterhouse are in favour of Peter Andreas Rysbrack (1690-1748).[6] Infra-red photographs do not suggest that the figures were by another hand. John Kerslake refers for comparison to Rysbrack's *Richmond Ferry* of c. 1740[7] which seems closer to 1246/A/B than the paintings by Samuel Scott.

Provenance: 1246/A/B are said to have remained in the Drake-Brockman family until 1961 when they were offered by a descendant, Mrs. W. Arkle, for sale at Leggatts. Acquired on the advice of A. J. L. McDonnell under the terms of the Everard Studley Miller Bequest in 1963.

References: (1) I am indebted to Mr. Cecil Farthing and Mr. Nicholas Cooper of the National Monuments Record, London, for information on Beachborough House and grounds. (2) Geoffrey Beard, in *Country Life,* Aug. 10, 1961, p. 286, fig. 7. I am indebted to Professor Joseph Burke for drawing my attention to this article and to the correct quotation of Antoine Joseph Dézallier d'Argenville, *La Théorie et la Pratique du Jardinage,* Paris. J. Mariette 1709. First published under the initials L.S.A.J.D.A., later under the name of Alexandre Le Blond. (2a) *The Records of the Brockman and Drake-Brockman Family* compiled by Brig. Gen. D. H. Drake Brockman, C.M.G. (privately printed) 1936, repr. opp. p. 28; this book was kindly brought to my attention by Mrs. Henrietta Drake-Brockman, M.B.E. (3) For details concerning the Brockman and Drake-Brockman families see *Burke's Landed Gentry.* See also Burford Butcher, *The Brockman Papers,* in *Archaeologia Cantiana,* Vol. XLIII, 1931, pp. 281f. It is stated there that a collection of family deeds belonging to the Brockman family of Beachborough, Newington, Kent, were presented to the British Museum. These deeds include account books and journals dating from 1644-1825 relating to the affairs of the estate. It has not been possible for the compiler to consult these records. (4) *Corr.* W. G. Constable, H. Leggatt, 20. VII, 62. (5) *Corr.* B. Taylor-A. J. L. McDonnell 12. IX, 62. (6) *Corr.* Kerslake-Hoff 30. IV, 64. See also Harley Preston, *Annual Bulletin N.G. Victoria,* Vol. V, 1963, 23, note 2, repr. (7) Reproduced in M. H. Grant, *A Chronological History of the Old English Landscape Painters,* Leigh-on-Sea, Vol. II, 1958, p. 82f, fig. 74.

Mather Brown   died 1831

British. Presumably born at Boston, U.S.A. Studied in London, under Benjamin West. Exhibited portraits at the Royal Academy since 1782 and at the British Institution since 1806.

Reference: *Th.B.*

after Brown

Illust. 22   1109/4 **George, First Marquess Townshend**

panel, 17.7 x 15 cm. Unsigned, undated.

Condition: Satisfactory.

Comment: Previously attributed to William Beechy and the sitter described as Lord Cornwallis;[1] a copy of Mather Brown's George, 1st Marquess of Townshend, after a variant of Brown's portrait at Raynham Hall, showing the sitter in what may be a kind of court uniform.[2]

Provenance: Presented by Mrs. E. Swinburne, 1941.

References: (1) *Catalogue,* N.G. Victoria, 1948. (2) Mrf. C. K. Adams, on seeing a photograph of the picture, immediately recognized its resemblance to the portrait by Brown.

Jan Brueghel   1568-1625

Flemish. Known as Jan Brueghel The Elder or Velvet Brueghel.
Born at Brussels, the second son of Pieter B. the Elder (Peasant Brueghel).
Went to Italy about 1589, 1593-95 in Rome, where he met his patron,
Cardinal Federigo Borromeo. 1597 master in the guild of S. Luke at
Antwerp. Travelled to Prague in 1604, to Nuremberg in 1616. Court
painter to Albert and Isabella, Regents of the Netherlands; a friend of
Rubens with whom he collaborated in later years. Famous for his mannerist
compositions with meticulously detailed representation of foliage flowers,
birds, innumerable figures and deep landscape vistas.

Reference: H. Gerson, E. H. Ter Kuile, *Art and Architecture in Belgium, 1600-1800,* 1960.

Studio of Brueghel

Illust. 23   94/5 **Calvary**

copper, 55.9 x 35.6 cm. Bears inscription *J. Brueghel* left corner in
unevenly spaced capitals, in brown.

Condition: Cleaned prior to purchase; in good condition.

Comment: While in the Lowther Castle collection the picture was
attributed to Jan Brueghel. It repeats however, in exact detail, the figure
composition of the *Calvary* in Munich which not only bears the authentic
signature of the artist but also the date 1598.[1] The Munich Calvary varies
from 94/5 in its more muted tones, in the large shadow areas and its
thin, open brushwork.[2] The brilliantly black costumes of 94/5 are
violet-grey in Munich; the glossy reds of 94/5 appear more subdued and
delicate in the Munich picture. These black and red costumes are
so strongly emphasised in 94/5 as to disrupt the tonal and colouristic
harmony characteristic of Jan Brueghel's authentic oevre. Jan
Brueghel's authentic pictures do not contain strongly marked facial
expressions in their figures. In 94/5 the faces of the holy women are
distorted in grief; the same faces in the Munich picture are idealised
and subdued in expression. The group of the three crosses and some
bystanders as well as several other single figures have been taken from
The Great Calvary drawing, attributed to Dürer or his school (Uffizi,
Florence).[3] Several copies of this are known, the earliest listed being a
painting by Jan de Cock, Museum, Berne, c. 1520; another was made by
Brueghel himself several years after the painting here, dated 1604, also
Uffizi, Florence.[4] The monk-like figure, holding up the tablets of the law
to the bad thief and the (modified) group of the soldiers fighting over
Christ's garments are derived from the *Crucifixion* by Pieter Brueghel
the younger which is thought by Glück to be possibly based on an
invention of Peter Brueghel the Elder.[5] The Melbourne replica is one
of the best of several replicas of the painting at Munich.[6]

Provenance: Mentioned by Waagen as in the possession of the Earl of Lonsdale, Lowther Castle in 1854.[7] Acquired by the Felton Bequest in 1958/9 on the advice of A. J. L. McDonnell from the Eugene Slatter Galleries.

References: (1) T. Brochhagen, in: *Alte Pinakothek, München, Katalog I, Deutsche und Niederländische Malerei zwischen Renaissance und Barock,* Munich, 1961, 12 f, No. 823; Copper, 14⅛ in. x 21 13/16 in. (36.2cm. x 55.4cm.); signed l.l. *BRUEGHEL 1598;* (2) The compiler compared photographs of 94/5 with the Munich *Calvary* on an overseas visit in 1959. (3) F. Winkler, *Die Zeichnungen Albrecht Dürers,* Berlin, 1937, II, No. 317; E. Panofsky, *Albrecht Dürer,* Princeton, 1948, II, 64, No. 523. (4) Winkler, *op. cit.* 42; Brochhagen, *op. cit.* 12; (5) G. Glück, *Brueghel's Gemälde,* Vienna, 1951, Cat. No. 84. (6) Dr. H. Gerson brought to my notice the following replicas of *Calvary,* documented in the Rijksbureau voor Kunsthistorische Dokumentatie in The Hague: 1. from sale Giuseppe Bossi, Vienna, 10 May 1886, No. 22, copper, 35cm. x 35cm. (the latter measurement obviously incorrect, since the painting is oblong in shape). 2. from the collection of Count Prezdzieski, Warsaw, exh. Brussels, 1935, No. 188, copper 46cm. x 40cm. 3. a further version in Collection Karl Landegger, New York, gouache on parchment, laid on wood 14¾ in. x 22 3/16 in. (37.5cm. x 56.25cm.) published by Eric Larsen in *'Artis' Zeitschrift für alte und neue Kunst,* Konstanz, April 1961, p. 14 ff, figs. 2, 4, 5, 6. 4. Collection Karl Landegger, New York, silverpoint on paper, a part of the right foreground half of the figure-group including the fighting soldiers. (7) Waagen, *Treasures of Art in Great Britain,* 1854, Vol. III, p. 264. Other references: D. L. A. Farr, *Burl. Mag.* Vol. C. 1958, p. 221; *The Connoisseur* Vol. CXLI, 1958, p. 253, col. repr. 252. *Annual Bulletin, N.G. Victoria,* 1959, Vol. I, p. 2. *Apollo,* May 1958, p. 151 f.

Byzantine, Post-Byzantine Period

Byzantine art is the art of the Eastern Empire whose capital, Constantinople, was founded by Constantine the Great in 330 A.D. The monuments of the Byzantine style date from the sixth century to 1453, the year of the Fall of Constantinople to the Turks. Post-Byzantine art continued in the Balkans, Asia Minor, Crete and Russia until the 19th century.

Illust. 24   1979/4 **Christ As The Lord Of All**
panel, hollowed, on gesso over linen, 52.7 x 44.8 cm.; painted surface 17¾ in. x 14½ in. Unsigned, undated; painted 16th-17th centuries.

Condition: Talbot Rice remarks that the panel has undergone "severe treatment". Heavily varnished.

Comment: Above the head of Christ the letters *IC XC* (Jesos Christos); on the halo *oun* (he that is); the open gospel reads "Come unto Me, ye chosen of my father" (Matthew chap. 25, v. 34). The fragmentary inscription on the lower margin reads [K] *AITON TEKNON AYT*[Y] (offering of . . . servant of God and of his children).
Talbot Rice dated this ikon 14th or 15th century, rejecting Muratov's date of about 1100.[1] The rounding off of the shoulders and hair, with its loss of human form and the agitations in the folds, however, suggest a post-Byzantine date.[2]

Provenance: Exhibited as in the Charles Seltman collection, Courtauld Institute, London 1933, No. 4; R.A. *Greek Art*, 1946, No. 337; acquired from Mr. Seltman on the advice of A. J. L. McDonnell and Sir Kenneth Clark for the Felton Bequest in 1948/9.

References: (1) D. Talbot Rice, *Courtauld Institute Exh. Ms. Cat.* Jan. 1933, No. 4, pl. II. (2) Dr. K. Weitzmann, John Beckwith, and the authorities of the Byzantine Museum, Athens, have given me the date of this picture. Other references: Paul Muratov, *Ms. Catalogue, Charles Seltman Collection*, 1939, No. 2 (not seen); Jacqueline Chittenden and Charles Seltman, *Greek Art*, 1947, No. 337, pl. 86; D. Talbot Rice, *Burl. Mag.*, Vol. LXXXVIII, 1946, p. 86, pl. A; *Quarterly Bulletin N.G. Victoria*, 1949, III, (4), 4 repr.

Illust. 25   1981/4 **SS. Basil Chrysostom and Gregory With a Kneeling Donor**

panel, 43.4 x 35 cm. Unsigned, undated; painted early 10th century.

Condition: In good condition; panel surrounded by red ¼ in. margin.

Comment: Muratov's attribution to Emmanuel Tzanes[1] was rejected by Talbot Rice.[2] The costume of the donor and the realism of the treatment of folds, the European influence in the pattern suggest the early 18th century.[3]

Provenance: Exhibited as in the collection of Charles Seltman, R.A. *Greek Art*, 1946, No. 367; acquired from Mr. Seltman on the advice of A. J. L. McDonnell and Sir Kenneth Clark for the Felton Bequest 1948/49.

References: (1) *Catalogue, Greek Art*, R.A., 1946, No. 367; Jacqueline Chittenden and Charles Seltman, *Greek Art*, 1947, pl. 99. (2) D. Talbot Rice, *Burl. Mag.*, Vol. LXXXVIII, 1946, p. 89. (3) D. Talbot Rice, *The Icons of Cyprus*, 1937, p. 46, (note 5); verbal information from Dr. K. Weitzmann. See also: P. Muratov, *Ms. Catalogue, Charles Seltman Collection*, 1939, No. 9 (not seen); *Quarterly Bulletin N.G. Victoria*, 1949, III, (4), 5, repr.

Illust. 26   3277/4 **Triptych**

panel, 25 x 19.2 cm. (centre), wings 21 x 9.5 cm. Unsigned, undated.

Condition: Old varnish partly removed by Harley Griffiths in 1954.

Comment: The three wings represent from left to right: *left wing:* S. Gregory the Theologian, S. John Chrysostom, S. Basil; *centre panel: The Dormition* of the Virgin (Koimesis); *right wing: centre figure* S. Anthony; *figure on left:* unidentified; lettering illegible; *on left:* S. Peter the Hermit; the equivalent for Annunciation is written above second figure from the left. The name of John Kontarinis appears on the back of the panel.

Provenance: Unknown.

Byzantine-Italian (Victor of Crete, active 2nd half 17th century)

Italo-Byzantine; worked in Crete and probably also in Venice. Signed works by Victor are a *Nativity* in the Russian Museum, Leningrad (coll. Lichacev); a *Nativity* and a *Death of the Virgin* in the Benaki Museum, Athens, and several ikons in the St. Catherine's Monastery, Mount Sinai.

Reference: *Th.B.* (Ph. Schweinfurth, *Victor von Kreta*), Vol. XXXIV, 1940, p. 330.

Illust. 27   1980/4 **Nativity**

panel, 56.5 x 41 cm. Signed *XEIP BIKTOPOC,* undated; painted about 1650.

Condition: Panel cracked along centre, certain repairs; in good condition.

Comment: Dated by Seltman 1550.[1] Accepted by Talbot Rice,[2] Schweinfurth[3] and K. Weitzmann[4] as the work of the master described above, and dated 1650 or 1660.

Provenance.   Exhibited as with the Seltman collection, Courtauld Institute, London, 1933, No. 20; R.A. *Greek Art*, 1946, No. 347; acquired from Mr Seltman on the advice of A. J. L. McDonnell and Sir Kenneth Clark for the Felton Bequest in 1948/9.

References: (1) Charles Seltman, *The Studio*, Vol. CXXXI-II, 1946, p. 114 repr. (2) D. Talbot Rice, *Ms. Cat. Exh. Courtauld Institute*, 1933, No. 20, pl. XVIII; *Burl. Mag.*, Vol. LXII, 1933, p. 88, pl. A; *Burl. Mag.*, Vol. LXXXVIII, 1946, p. 89. (3) See above. (4) Verbal information. Other references: P. Muratov, *Ms. Catalogue Charles Seltman Collection*, 1939, No. 6 (not seen); *Quarterly Bulletin, N.G. Victoria*, 1949, III, (4), 5, repr.

Byzantine-Russian

Illust. 28   2974/4 **Nativity**

panel, 19.7 x 15.8 cm. (whole panel); 4⅜ in. x 3¾ in. (inside margins).

Unsigned, undated.

Condition: Good.

Comment: Inscribed on upper margin in Russian characters. The short high lights, sloping evenly from right to left, are characteristic of this school. Previously referred to as Stroganoff School.

Provenance: Purchased by Miss E. Spowers in Paris who bequeathed it to Mr. and Mrs. Daryl Lindsay; it was presented by them in 1954 through the National Gallery Society. See also *Quarterly Bulletin, N.G. Victoria,* 1954, VIII, (1), 1.

Edward Calvert   1799-1883

British. Born at Appledore, Devonshire. Joined the navy as a young man. First exhibited at the R.A. in 1825. In 1826 met Samuel Palmer and became a member of the Blake circle. Under Blake's influence he produced a number of small-scale, minutely detailed and imaginative engravings, drawings and watercolours. In 1844 he went to Greece and in the last years of his life produced the generalized oil paintings of arcadian subjects of which the works listed below are characteristic examples.

Reference: *Th.B.*

Illust. 29   1199/3 **Souvenir of Claude**

paper, 25.5 x 36.9. Unsigned, undated; late period.

Condition: Satisfactory.

Comment: This picture bears a distant resemblance to a painting by Claude (LV 172), Nelson Gallery of Art, Kansas City, Missouri, formerly in the collection of Sir Thomas Baring (1799-1873).[1]

Provenance: Acquired for the Felton Bequest on the advice of Frank Rinder in 1921.

References   (1) G. F. Waagen, Treasures of Art in Great Britain 1854, II, 177, No. 5; M. Roethlisberger, Claude Lorrain, New Haven, 1961, I, No. 172, II, fig. 279.

Illust. 30   1198/3   **The Soul Crossing The Styx**

paper laid on canvas, 27.5 x 38 cm. Unsigned, undated; late period.

Condition: Satisfactory.

Provenance: Acquired for the Felton Bequest on the advice of Frank Rinder in 1921.

(Giovanni) Antonio Canaletto   1697-1768

Italian. Born at Venice; studied scene painting under his father; went to Rome in 1719-20. Here he may have studied under the Dutch painter of *vedute* (views) Gasper van Wittel. He is recorded in the guild lists at Venice from 1720 to 1767. For his topographically accurate views of Venice he used the camera obscura with the help of which he made his preparatory drawings. Enjoyed from before 1730 the patronage of Joseph Smith, an English merchant, publisher, collector and later British Consul at Venice through whom an important part of Canaletto's output came into English collections. The Roman subjects painted between 1740 and 1744 may have been made during a second visit to Rome but are more likely based on earlier drawings. In 1745 Canaletto went to London; returned permanently to Venice in 1755.

References: *Th.B.; C.N.G.; E.W.A.*

Studio of Canaletto

Illust. 31   965/3 **Grand Canal and Rialto Bridge From The East**

canvas, 61 x 92.2. Unsigned, undated; painted before 1742.

Condition: Good; old varnish.

Comment: The picture was catalogued in 1943 as by Canaletto and in 1948 as *School of.* Robert Ross[1] had described it as a school piece; its execution is rather harder than authentic work but it must be assumed to come from Canaletto's studio, rather than to be a late copy.[2] It is

19

closely related to the same view engraved in Visentini: *Prospectus Magni Canalis Venetiarum . . . pictis ab Antonio Canale, in Aedibus Josephi Smith, Angli, delineate atque incidente Antonio Visentini 1742, ed. 11, 8, Pons Rivoalti* at *Orientem;* and is also very similar to *Rialto Bridge from the East* in the National Gallery in Rome; (in our No. 965/3 the view is taken from a slightly lower position and there are variations in the boats).

On the right appears the pointed campanile of San Bartolommeo, which was rebuilt onion-shaped in 1754.

Provenance: H. A. Buttery. Acquired by the Felton Bequest on the advice of Mr. Robert Ross, 1918.

References: (1) Felton correspondence, Robert Ross, 1918. (2) Mr. Michael Levey has made this and the following information available to me.

Pieter Candid   c. 1540-1628

Flemish-Italian. Bruges. Original name de Wit or de Witte. Painter of portraits and religious paintings. Karel van Mander, who knew him personally, states that his parents took him to Florence; documented as tapestry worker for the house of Medici 1559-60. Probably apprenticed to Vasari; his connection with the latter is documented for 1569. In 1572 he assisted Vasari with the decoration of the Sala Regia in the Vatican in Rome; before 1574 with the paintings in the cupola of the cathedral in Florence. 1578 in Volterra where he made the altarpiece *Glorification of the Virgin* for the first side altar to the right. In that cathedral; two years later again in Volterra when the *Nativity* and a *Deposition* for the Badia di Sto Giusto outside Volterra are assumed to have been painted. 1585 again documented in Florence where he worked for the Grand Duke Francesco I; 1586 appointed court painter to Archduke William V of Bavaria and continued his service with the Elector Maximilian I (1598-1651).

References: Th.B.; K. Steinbart. *Pieter Candid in Italien* in *Jahrbuch der preussischen Kunstsammlungen*, Vol. LVIII, 1937, 63-80.

Illust. 32   1664/5 **The Lamentation Over The Dead Christ**

panel, 87.6 x 101.9 cm. Unsigned, undated; painted probably 1585-86. Inscribed I.I. on paper nailed to the top piece of the cross now lying on the ground: first four lines illegible, perhaps indicating Hebrew and Greek lettering; last two lines: *jesus nazareniss Rex iudeorum.* Below left the arms of the family of Lisci da Volterra; the bottom shell is barely (if at all) visible in the painting; according to Rietstap the shells and the band should be *azure* and the ground *or;*[1] here the shells are greyish, the ground blue.

Condition: Satisfactory.

Comment: Previously attributed to Daniel Ricciarelli, called Daniele da Volterra, probably on account of its Volterrean origin. The attribution to Peter Candid, suggested among other things by the 'northern' landscape motifs,[2] is confirmed by Michael Levey.[3] Three features stand out in this picture: 1. several motifs may be compared with Vasari's *Lamentation* of 1548 in Ravenna:[4] Christ is shown with his head hanging forward, upraised arms and hands clasped in prayer occur in both compositions; the characterhead of the old woman lamenting in Vasari's picture is close to that on the right in the picture here. 2. the figure of Christ half upright, head in profile and forward, the bearded apostle in 1664/5 are in the tradition of the Pietà from Luco (Palazzo Pitti) of 1524 by Andrea del Sarto.[5] 3. the colour scheme consisting of red, dark-green, blue and yellow and grey-white, with a marked absence of 'changeant' colours[6] is described by Steinbart as characteristic of a work of Candid's late Florentine period, the *Madonna with Saints* in S. Niccolo del Ceppo in Florence, signed and dated 1585. Candid's connection with Vasari is documented (see biography). Despite certain similarity of motifs, the picture here is markedly less mannerist in composition than Vasari's *Lamentation* and also more loosely arranged than Candid's *Lamentation* executed for the Badia di S. Giusto of 1578.[7] As Steinbart has shown, the work certainly carried out after Candid's return to Florence in 1585-6 shows a marked turning away from Vasari's style and even more than the S. Giusto *Lamentation,* a turning towards the style of Andrea del Sarto. It would seem therefore that 1664/5 is perhaps attributable to Candid's last two years in Florence, i.e., 1585-6. For the low near view, the half-cut-off ladder and cross one may refer to Dürer's *Lamentation* in the Small Woodcut Passion B. 43.

Provenance: Lisci da Volterra (no recorded information available); Ragois de Bretonvilliers (it has not been possible to verify this source); Phillippe, Duc d'Orléans, engraved in J. Couché, *Galerie du Palais Royal,* 1786, Vol. I, pl. X (by P.—C. Baquoy (1759-1829) after A. Borel (1743—after 1810) as Daniel de Volterre, Exh. *Lyceum, The Orléans Italian Pictures,* 1798, 144 as Daniel de Volterre, bt. Earl of Suffolk; G. F. Waagen, *Works of Art and Artists in England,* London 1838, Vol. I, p. 336 (Daniele da Volterra, list of Orléans pictures, bt. Lord Suffolk). The same, *Treasures of Art in Great Britain,* London, 1854, Vol. III; p. 170; Daniele da Volterra, Earl of Suffolk, exh. *British Institution,* 1852, 107 Daniele da Volterra, Earl Suffolk; *R.A. Old Masters,* 1878, 203, Daniele da Volterra, Earl Suffolk; acquired for the Felton Bequest 1966, on the advice of M. Woodall, from W. R. Jeudwine, London.

References: (1) J. B. Rietstap, *Planches de L'Amorial Général,* Ed. V. Rolland, Paris, 1912, Plates, Vol. IV, pl. LXXV. (2) Such motifs occur in Candid's S. Giusto *Lamentation;* Steinbart compares them to the background in Dürer's *Lamentation* of the Great Woodcut Passion; Kurt Steinbart, *Pieter Candid in Italien* in *Jahrbuch der preussischen Kunstsammlungen,* Vol. LVIII, 1937, 71. (3) Felton letter No. 13 M. Woodall, 25 III 66. (4) Hermann Voss, *Die Malerei der Spät Renaissance,* Berlin, 1920, Vol. I, illus. 94. (5) John Shearman, *Andrea del Sarto,* Oxford 1965, Vol. 1, pl. 126, Vol. II, No. 68. (6) Steinbart, *op. cit.* p. 68 describes the garment of the shepherd in the S. Giusto Nativity which he dates c. 1580, as blue-yellow 'changeant'. (7) Steinbart, *op. cit.* pp. 70 ff, fig. 7.

Carlo Innocenzo Carloni   1686-1775

Italian. Born Scaria, Lombardy, in 1686, the son of Giovanni Battista Carloni, sculptor, architect and stucco worker, member of a family famous for stucco work. About 1698 his father took Carlo to Germany to teach him the language and to train him as a sculptor. But a little later he was apprenticed to Giulio Quaglia from Laino with whom he is thought to have visited Udine and Venice; in the latter place he became acquainted with the art of Sebastiano Ricci and Pellegrini. He also worked for Quaglia at the church of Lublana of which Andrea Pozzo was the architect. Between 1706 and 1710 Carlo was in Rome under Francesco Trevisani (*q.v.*). He worked in Switzerland, South Germany, the Rhineland, Austria and other European countries, carrying out wall decorations. Between 1715 and 1725 he returned to Italy and Como where he painted the ceiling, the sketch for which is listed below.
He carried out a large number of decorations in Lombardy in the last years of his life and has been called the major painter of the Rococo in Lombardy.

Reference: A. B. Brini, K. Garas, *Carlo Innocenzo Carloni,* Milan, 1967.

Illust. 33   E1A. 1970. **Hercules Led By Knowledge To Immortality**

canvas, 86.4 x 61.3 cm. Unsigned, undated; painted 1726.

Condition: excellent.

Comment: Hercules, with a lion's skin over his head and a club in his right hand, kneels at the lower centre left, accompanied by Fame blowing her trumpet and Wisdom, holding a flaming torch. She points towards Jupiter who raises the crown he will bestow on Hercules; to the right of Jupiter sits Juno accompanied by her peacock. Below the Olympian pair appears Father Time with his scythe and (seen from the back) Mars, dressed in Roman armour. Opposite the left are Venus and Cupid with Mercury above them. In the lower part of the painting a winged, helmeted Victory (?) pursues the vices who are falling off the cornice. In the upper part figures appear beyond the cornice as on a balcony. "Glorifications" such as this one were popular subjects for ceiling paintings of the 17th and 18th centuries.

Our sketch resembles in every detail the final version of this subject on the ceiling of the Palazzo Gallio in Como painted by Carloni in 1726.[1]

Professor Garas thinks that the sketch is in all probability identical with the *bozetto* of this title mentioned in the artist's estate.[2]

Provenance: Possibly in the artist's estate at his death;[3] later history unknown; acquired from the Hazlitt Gallery, London on the advice of Dr. M. Woodall under the terms of the Felton Bequest, in June 1970.

22

References: (1) Amalia Barigozzi Brini and Klara Garas, *Carlo Innocenzo Carloni*, Milan, 1967, pp. 47, 51, 122, fig. 30. (2) Letter from M. Woodall to U. Hoff, reporting a conversation held with Professor Garas in Budapest. (3) See Fausto Lechi 'Un elenco di abbozzi delle opere di Carlo Carloni', *Arte Lombardo* 1965, vol. X, p. 121 seq.; perhaps identical with panel of same subject listed on p. 130.

Annibale Carracci   1560-1609

Italian. Born Bologna, pupil of his cousin Ludovico (1555-1619). May have travelled in Tuscany c. 1583-4, was in Parma with his brother Agostino and almost certainly visited Venice c. 1585-6. He participated with Ludovico and Agostino in the founding of the leading Academy of Bologna and shared with them in the decoration of the Fava (1584) and Magnani (1588-91) palaces in Bologna. In 1595 he went to Rome and carried out the decoration of the Farnese palace. His ceiling decoration of the Farnese Gallery ranks with Raphael's decorations of the stanze and Michelangelo's Sistine Ceiling as one of the great schemes of decoration in western art. A Drawing of a male nude study for a figure in the Farnese ceiling from the Ellesmere Collection is now in the Print Room.

References: Peter and Linda Murray, *Dictionary of Art and Artists,* London, 1959.

Illust. 34   E20. 1971 **The Holy Family**

canvas, 69.9 x 61 cm. Unsigned, undated, painted about 1589.[1]

Condition: painted on top of a used canvas; old pentimenti above the head of the Virgin and on the Child's breast and elsewhere. Slight paint losses and abrasions in numerous places. Restored and re-varnished by Mr. Delius, London, prior to purchase.
Comment: The composition resembles that of Titian's *Madonna with the Infant Christ, the child John the Baptist and St. Anthony Abbot* in the Uffizi. Annibale Carracci visited Venice in his early period and also shows himself influenced by the handling and tonality of Veronese but the tilt of the Child's head and the sharp features of Joseph are presented with the naturalism of the Bolognese school.[2] The hands and feet are drawn with the distinction typical of Annibale. The picture was earlier known as by Annibale; Scharf attributed it to Agostino but possibly only knew the engraving (see below). Professor Pepper is publishing E20.1971 as by Annibale.[3]

Engravings: Engraved by Ferrantes Rosatti in 1649.

Provenance: Early history unknown; first recorded in 1759 as owned by the Dukes of Marlborough, Blenheim Palace (as 'Carracci');[4] Waagen has Annibale Carracci;[5] sold Christies, London, 7-10 August, 1886, lot 640 (as 'Agostino') bt. R. G. Vivian, (label on back); later history unknown; exhibited at Hazlitt's, London, in November 1971 from where it was acquired under the terms of the Felton Bequest, on the advice of Dr. M. Woodall and Mr. Michael Levey of the London National Gallery.

References: (1) The date has been suggested by Professor Stephen Pepper of the John Hopkins University at Baltimore Maryland, who is publishing the picture in *Arte Illustrata* as by Annibale Carracci. (2) Benedict Nicolson, in *Burl. Mag.* Vol. CXIII, 1971, p. 683. (3) See note 1. (4) *The new Oxford Guide: or Companion through the University . . . to which is added a Tour of Blenheim, Ditchley and Stow . . .* Oxford, 1759, page 84, No. 15, (as hanging in the 5th Apartment and listed as *"A Holy Family by Caracci"*). *The English Connoisseur,* Vol. 1, London, 1766, p. 19, No. 15 as hanging in the 5th Apartment and listed as *"A Holy Family by Caracci"*. (5) G. F. Waagen, *Art Treasures in Great Britain,* Vol. III, 1854, p. 127. Listed as hanging in The Little Parlour, and described as . . . *Annibale Carracci — The Virgin and Child appearing to a Worshipping Saint. A small picture, finished like a miniature; a happy imitation of Correggio.* G. Scharf, *Catalogue Rasonné, or, A List of the Pictures in Blenheim Palace,* London, 1861, p. 49. Listed as hanging in the smaller Drawing Room, and described as *Agostino Carraci — Madonna and Child with St. Joseph. A composition of three figures, life-size, half-length. There is an expression of weakness in the figure of the infant Saviour as he leans back on the shoulder of the Virgin. The head of Joseph is turned in profile to the right, and with closed eyes as if blind. Painted on canvas. Agostino Carracci himself made an etching from this composition. See Bartsch. Vol. XXX, page 155, No. 4.*

Valerio Castello   1625-1659

Italian. Gorn Genoa, possibly self-taught, inspired by works of Perino del Vaga *(q.v.)* and his father Bernardo C. After visits to Milan and Parma he settled in Genoa. Here he was able to study the work of van Dyck and Rubens, which accounts for the unusual warmth of his colour schemes.

Reference: *Th.B.*

attributed to Castello

Illust. 35   3729/3 **Susannah and the Elders**

canvas, 81.5 x 58.6 cm. Unsigned, undated.

Condition: restored by F. W. Colley, St. Kilda, 1928. Satisfactory.

Comment: Attribution by the previous owner to Salvator Rosa; Bernard Hall rejected attribution; 1948 *Catalogue N.G.V.* as Tiepolo, School of; 1961 and 1967 *Catalogue European Paintings before Eighteen Hundred;* as Italian School, Venetian, 18th century. Professor Federico Zeri suggested the present attribution[1] and quoted another version of 3729/3 in the collection of Dr. Angelo Costa, Genoa.[2] A further version exists in the Gerrer collection (no. 3) at St. Gregory's College, Shawme, Oklahoma and is there called "Venetian".[3]

Provenance: Offered by Miss S. J. Wadmore, Melbourne; acquired for the Felton Bequest by Bernard Hall in 1928.

References: (1) corr. Zeri-Hoff 23, VIII, 1969. (2) Photo in Gallery archives. (3) I am indebted to Mr. Burton Frederickson, Curator, Paul J. Getty Museum, Malibu, California for this information corr. Frederickson-Hoff, 19, VI, 1969.

Bernado Cavallino   1616-1656

Italian. Born at Naples, where he apparently spent his whole life;
pupil of G. B. Caracciolo (c. 1570-1636) and Andrea Vaccaro (1598-1670)
through whom he became acquainted with the realist chiaroscuro of
Caravaggio. Also studied under M. Stanzioni (1585-1656) by whom he
was introduced into the more luxurious and decorative world of the
high baroque. He further absorbed features from the work of Artemesia
Gentileschi, Ribera, van Dyck, Rubens and Agnollo Falcone. The most
distinguished painter of the Neapolitan school of the 17th century. He
died it is believed during an outbreak of the plague.

References: *National Gallery Catalogues, Acquisitions, 1953-62,* London, 1963; Francis
Haskell, *Patrons and Painters,* London 1963, p. 208; F. Cummings, R. Wittkower, *Art in Italy,*
1600-1700, Detroit Institute of Art, New York 1965, p. 145.

Illust. 36   1829/5 **The Virgin Annunciate**

canvas, 85.1 x 69.2 cm. Unsigned, undated, painted about 1640.

Condition: cleaned by Herbert Lank, London, 1968.

Comment: The gesture of the Virgin crossing her arms in front of her
often occurs in scenes of the Annunciation; it is assumed that a
painting of the angel once formed the counterpart of 1829/5; both may
have been commissioned for a church "dell Annunziata".

Provenance: Private collection, France; Hazlitt Gallery, London, 1968; acquired under
the terms of the Felton Bequest on the advice of Dr. M. Woodall, with the assistance of Mr.
Denis Mahon and Professor Waterhouse and Miss Ann Percy.

References: (general) J. Daniels in *Art and Artists,* Vol. III, No. 3, 1968, 44-46, repr.;
E. Lucie-Smith, in *Arts Review with Auction Gallery Guide,* 8 June 1968, Vol. XX, No. 11,
p. 327; B.N. in *Burl. Mag.,* Vol. CX, 1968, p. 366, fig. 60. Miss Ann Percy is preparing a
catalogue raisonné of Cavallino's work.

Claude Gellée, Le Lorrain   1600-1682

French. Born at Champagne, Vosges in the French part of Lorraine.
About 1613 in Rome where he stood in the service of the landscape
painter Agostino Tassi. In 1623 in Naples where he worked with the Flemish
artist Godeffro Wals. But for a stay of about two years in Nancy, from
1625-27, he lived all his life in Rome. Having attracted the attention of
imitators and forgers, he formed a pictorial record of 195 of his principal
paintings in an album of drawings known as the *Liber Veritatis*
(British Museum, Department of Prints and Drawings) which form the
basis of the identification of Claude's work. His art has its beginnings
in the tradition of Elsheimer, Brill and Tassi, in the 1640s the influence
of Domenichino and the Carracci makes its appearance.

D

Reference: *C.N.G.;* M. Kitson, *Claude Lorrain* in: *Encyclopedia of World Art,* London 1964, Vol. IX, 339-344.

Illust. 37   1796/5 **River Landscape with Tiburtine Temple at Tivoli**

canvas, 37 x 52 cm.

Condition: cleaned prior to purchase; satisfactory.

Comment: The 17th century appearance of the Temple at Tivoli as recorded in a drawing by Bartolomeus Broenberg made about 1620-29, shows it standing on the edge of a precipice; it was built in the 1st century B.C. in circular form, on a raised podium with a continuous portico of fluted corinthian columns. Claude has altered the proportions of the temple, making it narrower and higher and giving it an imaginary setting, though he retains the edge of the precipice. [1]

Roethlisberger has pointed out that the setting ultimately derives from such works by Elsheimer as the Prague copper with the same temple, but that 1796/5 has a new delicacy and liveliness of form. Similar treatment is found in Claude's *Pastoral Landscape* of c. 1636. [2]

Provenance: First traceable at the sale of the third Earl of Brownlow, Christie's, May 4, 1923, lot 161, bt. Lady Cust, sold by her at Christie's, Dec. 4, 1964, lot 79, bt. Agnew's. Acquired from Agnew's under the terms of the Felton Bequest, on the advice of Dr. M. Woodall, 1967.

References: (1) *Gods and Heroes, Baroque Images of Antiquity,* Cat. exhibition Wildenstein, New York 1969, No. 2, (2) M. Roethlisberger, *Additions to Claude,* in *Burl. Mag.,* Vol. CX, 1968, p. 119, fig. 5.

After Claude

Illust. 38   1719/4 **Landscape with Piping Shepherd and a Flight to Egypt**

canvas, 103.5 x 135.2 cm. Unsigned, undated.

Condition: Cleaned prior to purchase; signs of over-cleaning in the thin passages of foliage; the foliage of the willow trees in the middle distance appears to have been rubbed off.

Comment: 1719/4 was catalogued as by Claude in the 1948 catalogue. it is however an almost exact replica of the painting by Claude in Dresden which is authenticated by the signature and date (1647). [1] The Dresden picture moreover is obviously the one recorded by Claude in his book of references: the Liber Veritatis, No. 110 (British Museum Department of Prints and Drawings). 1719/4 differs from L.V. 110 and the Dresden picture in the following details: the girl fetching water from a well has no fluttering scarf; there are only two goats on the promontory between the bush above, the girl at the well and the rock on the r., not *four* as in Dresden and in L.V. 110; these and other minor differences prove that our picture 1719/4 is not the one recorded by Claude in his book as being from his own hand. 1719/4 moreover does not show the characteristics of Claude's brushwork.

Even if allowance is made for paint loss through rubbing, the foliage does not show Claude's hand and the tonal effects of the painting lack the vividness and airiness of Claude's style. 1719/4 is one of the better of several existing copies of the Dresden picture and was listed as such by Smith,[2] Waagen[3] and Mrs. Mark Pattison.[4] This opinion was sustained by Marcel Roethlisberger in 1961.[5]

Provenance: According to John Purling[6] the picture came from the collection of the Prince de Carignan; it can however not be found in any of the Carignan Sale Catalogues; listed John Purling sale, White, 16 Feb. 1801, lot 102; bt. Thomas Hope; Doggett's Repository of Mr. Hope's pictures, 16 Market Street, 1822, No. 43 (not seen); listed by Westmacott, 1824[7] as in Thomas Hope collection; by Waagen 1854, (loc. clt., note 3), as in Henry Thomas Hope collection; on the death of the latter's widow inherited by Lord Francis Pelham Clinton Hope; bt. 1910 by Fairfax Murray by private treaty; in Scottish private collection until beginning of 1946 when it was acquired from Matthiesen's by the Felton Bequest on the advice of Sir Kenneth Clark. Arrived 1947.

References: (1) K. Woermann, *Katalog d. Königl. Gemäldegalerie zu Dresden,* 1896, p. 242, No. 730. (2) J. Smith, *Catalogue Raisonné,* Vol. VIII, 1837, p. 249/50. (3) G. F. Waagen, *Treasurers of Art in Great Britain,* Vol. II, 1854, p. 114. (4) Mrs. Mark Pattison, *Claude Lorrain, Sa Vie et ses Oeuvres,* 1884, p. 216, No. 110. (5) M. Roethlisberger, *Claude Lorrain,* New Haven, 1961, I, p. 274 f. (6) J. Purling sale, White, 16 Feb. 1801, not in front of catalogue. (7) C. M. Westmacott, *British Galleries of Painting and Sculpture,* 1824, p. 227.

Cola dall'Amatrice, real name; Nicola di Filotesio
ca. 1480/90-ca. 1550

Italian. Son of a certain Filotesio of Amatrice in the Abruzzi. Probably went as a young man to Ascoli, where he could see the works of Crivelli and his school; his early style is close to Crivelli and to Pietro Alamanno. 1525 in Rome; after that the influence of Michelangelo and Raphael dominates his work. He also was engaged in architecture. 1537 in Norcia, 1542 in Perugia, later again in Ascoli.

References: Th.B.; R. Van Marle, *The Italian Schools of Painting,* Vol. XV, 1934, p. 105; G. Fabiani, *Cola dall'Amatrice, Ascoli,* 1952.

Illust. 39   3078/4 **The Finding of the True Cross**

wood, 88.9 x 196.6 cm. Unsigned, undated; painted 1516-33.

Condition: in good condition.

Comment: Federico Zeri has shown that this painting formed part of the vast altarpiece commissioned from Cola 1516 for the high altar of S. Francesco at Ascoli Piceno.[1] It was dismembered at the end of the 18th century, but the central part, the procession to Calvary and other panels are still in the gallery at Ascoli. Zeri supposes that *The Finding of the*

True Cross was the central part of the upper tier, and that it was one of the earliest parts to be completed, in 1516 or soon after. The altarpiece was not finally completed until 1533.

The subject of the picture is based on the *Legenda Aurea.*[1] After Christ's death the Cross on which he had been cricified lay buried at Golgatha for 200 years. Queen Helena, the mother of Constantine the Great, went to Jerusalem and with the help of a Jew, called Judas, unearthed three crosses. Judas placed the crosses over a youth who had died that day and the third crooo rovived him and waɜ thuɜ recognized as the true cross. In Cola's picture, the cross lies over the lap of Queen Helena; the youth next to her on the right has been brought back to life; the man in a turban on the far right who assists in holding up the cross, is presumably Judas.

Provenance: Referred to as at Rossie Priory, Inchture, Perthshire, by Berenson in 1936;[2] sold Christie's, 21 June, 1946, lot 16, as the property of Lord Kinnaird, Rossie Priory, bt. Colnaghi; acquired from Messrs. Colnaghi on the advice of A. J. L. McDonnell for the Felton Bequest in 1953/54.

References: (1) Jacobus de Voragine, *Die Legenda Aurea,* German transl. by Richard Benz, Heidelberg, 1925, pp. 349-358. (2) *Paragone,* No. 41, 1953, p. 42, pl. 27. (3) B. Berenson, *Pitture Italiane del Rinascimento,* 1936, p. 131.

John Constable   1776-1837

British. Born East Bergholt, Suffolk, the son of a prosperous mill owner.

Largely self-taught. In his youth went on sketching expeditions with the amateur painter in East Bergholt, John Dunthorne (1770-1844), became acquainted with the artist J. T. Smith (1766-1833) and met Sir George Beaumont (1753-1827) with whom he formed a lifelong friendship. In 1799 admitted to the Academy Schools on the recommendation of Sir Joseph Farington (1747-1821). Though he studied the landscape painters of tradition in the collection of Sir George Beaumont and elsewhere, he announced in 1802 to John Dunthorne his determination to depict the truth at first hand: "There is room enough for a natural painter." Visited the Lake District in 1806 (see No. 2031/3). Until his marriage to Maria Bicknell in 1816, Suffolk remained his main painting ground. Since 1817 resided in London, painting frequently at Hampstead Heath (see Nos. 549/4, 455/4, 81/5, 467/2) and, since 1824, at Brighton. 1824 exhibited *The Haywaln, A Lock on to the Stour and Hampstead Heath* at Paris, when he was awarded the gold medal by King Charles X and obtained the praise of Géricault *(q.v.)* and Delacroix *(q.v.).* Elected R.A. in 1829. His Diploma picture was *The Lock* (see No. 2900/4).

Reference: John Basket, *Constable's Oil Sketches,* London 1966.

Illust. 40   1940/4 **Naworth Castle, Cumberland**

panel, 24.9 x 34 cm. Unsigned, undated; painted probably 1806.

Condition: Old varnish; in good condition.

Comment: The picture may have been painted on Constable's only journey to Cumberland and the Lake District 1806. [1]

Provenance: The picture was exhibited in 1937 at the Tate Gallery, Centenary Exhibition, John Constable, 1937, p. 45, No. 135, as owned by F. J. Nettlefold, who presented it in 1948.

Reference: (1) C. R. Grundy, A Catalogue of the Pictures and Drawings in the Collection of Frederick John Nettlefold, 1933, Vol. I, p. 106.

Illust. 41   2031/3 **Keswick Lake**

canvas, 26.5 x 44.7 cm. Unsigned, undated; painted in 1807.

Condition: excellent.

Comment: A view of Derwent Water and Skiddaw from the foot of Cat Bells. [1] Constable was invited to a tour of Westmoreland and Cumberland in September-October, 1806. He made many watercolour sketches on this trip and some oils which were exhibited in the R.A. of 1807. Holmes stresses the fresh realism and the truthfulness of the colours in the oils which began to supersede the convention of Girtin still visible in the watercolours made during the same tour. [2] Leslie relates that "the solitude of the mountains oppressed Constable's spirit", but Graham Reynolds points out that between 1807 and 1809 Constable exhibited six or more Lake District scenes at the Royal Academy and at the British Institution. [8]

Provenance: Possibly the picture exhibited by Constable at the R.A. in 1807, No. 98 (in the 1937 edition of Leslie's *Memoirs* Shirley identified No. 98 with the picture in the collection of Michael Sadler), [3] Holmes in 1902 identified No. 98 with our No. 2031/3 [4] so does the editor of the 1951 edition of Leslie's *Memoirs*. [5] It was possibly shown again at the British Institution in 1809, No. 282; [6] owned by C. J. Holmes in 1902. [7] Acquired for the Felton Bequest by Frank Rinder from D. Croal Thomson in 1926.

References: (1) Described thus by C. J. Holmes, *Constable and his Influence on Landscape Painting*, 1902, p. 241. (2) C. R. Leslie, *Memoirs of the Life of John Constable*, ed. A. Shirley 1937, p. 25; A. Shirley, *The Rainbow*, 1949, pp. 69-70; Holmes *op. cit.*, pp. 70, 71. (3) Leslie, *loc. cit.*, see note (2). (4) Holmes *op. cit.*, p. 241. (5) P. 19, n. 3, pl. 5. (6) Leslie, *op. cit.*, p. 30; (Windermere Lake quoted on the same page, is not in Melbourne, as stated there). (7) Holmes, *op. cit.*, p. 241. (Exh. R.A. 1807, 1809, owner Ch. Holmes, handwritten label on back). (8) Graham Reynolds, *Catalogue of the Constable Collection*, Victoria and Albert Museum, 1960, pp. 62-63.

Illust. 42   78/5 **"The Quarters" Behind Alresford Hall**

canvas, 33.7 x 51.7 cm. Unsigned, undated; painted in 1816.

Condition: excellent; cleaned by H. A. Buttery prior to being sent to Australia.

Comment: Referred to in Constable's letter 21 August, 1816: "I am going to paint two small landscapes for the General,[1] Views, one in the park of the house and a beautiful wood and piece of water and another scene in a wood with a beautiful little fishing house where the young lady (who is the heroine of all these scenes) goes occasionally to angle."[2] The fishing house here mentioned, now known as *The Quarters,* seems to have been built by a certain Richard Woods who had worked for Colonel Rebow at Wivenhoe Park in 1765 and 1776-81. An estimate for it survives at the Essex Record Office at Chelmsford headed: "An estimate for building the Chinese Temple for Colonel Rebow." Colonel Isaac Martin Rebow of Wivenhoe Park had married the heiress of Thomas Martin of Alresford Hall. This explains why he employed an architect both at Wivenhoe and at Alresford Hall. The building was used in the 18th century for picnic outings; visitors from the Hall would come down to eat the fish which had been caught from the verandah.[3]

A drawing by Constable for 78/5 is in the Art Gallery at Truro.[4]

Provenance: 78/5 and 81/5 were two of a collection of nine paintings owned by Mr. Benjamin Brookman of Adelaide, who went to London in 1890; on his death in 1932 the pictures went to his daughter, Miss Florence Brookman, who bequeathed them in 1940 to her sister Mrs. Ethel Brookman Kirkpatrick. During the London blitz of 1941 the pictures were given into safe keeping at Victoria House, London. In 1959 they were divided between the Galleries of Adelaide and Melbourne.[5]

References: (1) General Slater Rebow, then the owner of Wivenhoe Park and Alresford Hall. The painting, *Wivenhoe Park,* was exhibited at the R.A. 1817, No. 85; C. J. Holmes, *Constable,* London 1902, 243; (2) C. R. Leslie, *Memoirs of the Life of John Constable,* ed. A. Shirley, 1937, p. 93. (3) M. Girouard, *Country Life,* Vol. CXXIV, Nov. 1958, pp. 1040-1. (4) Information received from Mr. Graham Reynolds and the Curator of the Art Gallery, Truro; photograph on N.G. Victoria files. (5) Correspondence Sir William Leggatt—Director, N.G. Victoria files, 1958. Fr. Davis, *The Illustrated London News,* CCXXXII, Vol. I, Jan.-March, 1958, p. 468 repr. *Bulletin of the N.G. South Australia,* Vol. 21, No. 2, 1959. See also *Annual Bulletin, N.G. Victoria,* 1959, Vol. I, 1.

Illust. 43   81/5 **Sunset**

panel, 11.3 x 16.3 cm (sight measurement 4 in. x 5⅞ in.). Unsigned, undated; painted in the 1820s.

Condition: excellent.

Comment: Like most of the other cloud studies this must have been painted from Hampstead Heath. Handling and colouring are similar to the large *Branch Hill Pond* (No. 339-1888) and *Branch Hill Pond, Hampstead* (No. 125-1888) both in the Victoria and Albert Museum, dated by Baskett 'not later than 1822.'[1] Two other studies of similar dimensions, *Dawn* and *A Summer Sunset* with the same provenance as 81/5 are in the National Gallery of South Australia.

Provenance: This sketch as well as the two others in the National Gallery of South Australia have the same type of exhibition label on the back. The label of 81/5 has been largely destroyed; the label of *A Summer Sunset* reads "purchased by us from the collection of Hugh Constable, 1899". The date 1899 is still visible on the label of *Dawn.* All three sketches were in the possession of Mrs. Ethel Kirkpatrick (see under 78/5) and No. 81/5 was presented by her in 1959.

Reference: (1) John Baskett, *Constable's Oil Sketches,* London 1966, Nos. 18, 19.

Illust. 44   455/4 **Clouds**

Paper, 37 x 49 cm. Unsigned, inscription and date 1822 on the back.

Condition: excellent.

Comment: Inscribed on the back in Constable's own writing: "5th September 1822, 10 o'clock. Morning looking South-East very brisk wind at West, very bright and fresh grey clouds running very fast over a yellow bed about half-way in the sky. Very appropriate for the coast at Osmington".

It does not look from Leslie's account[1] as if Constable had been in Weymouth or Osmington in September 1822. Holmes under "1822, places visited" says "Norfolk?"[2] On 7 October, 1822, Constable wrote from Hampstead to Archdeacon Fisher: "I have made about fifty careful studies of *skies,* tolerable large to be careful".[3]

John Baskett records that Constable was at Hampstead from July to October 1822.[4] Despite the reference to Osmington, 455/4 must have been painted at Hampstead. A similar study, made on the same day (Victoria and Albert Museum No. 590-1888, 11⅜ in. x 19 in.) is inscribed: *Sepr. 5. 1822. looking S.E. noon. Wind very brisk. & effect bright and fresh. Clouds. moving very fast. with occasional very bright openings to the blue.*[5]

Badt[6] has connected Constable's interest in the exact study of clouds with the re-edition of Luke Howard's *The Climate of London,* Vol. 1, 1818, in which his classification of clouds into Cirrus, Status, Cumulus, etc., invented in 1802-3 was reprinted. We also know from a letter to George Constable of 1836 that Constable was familiar with Thomas Forster's *Researches about Atmospheric Phenomena* published 1812, 1815, 1823. Forster repeated the classification arrived at by Luke Howard. Bradt draws attention to the interest in cloud phenomena in the work of some of the romantic artists on the continent, like Gustav Carus, Caspar David Friedrich and others who had been inspired, directly or indirectly, by Goethe's interest in the researches of Luke Howard.[7]

Provenance: Together with nineteen others in the possession of Constable's friend Charles Robert Leslie in 1843;[8] in 1828 possibly in the Paterson gallery in an exhibition of cloud studies;[9] in the collection of Sir Michael Sadler; acquired for the Felton Bequest by Sir Sydney Cockerell from Messrs. Spink and Son in 1938.

References: (1) C. R. Leslie, *Memoirs of the life of John Constable,* ed. A. Shirley, 1937, pp. 131-2. (2) C. J. Holmes, *Constable and his influence on Landscape Painting,* 1902, p. 245. (3) Leslie, *op. cit.* p. 131. (4) John Baskett, *Constable's Oil Sketches,* London 1966, pp. 15, 66-68; (5) *Ibid.* p. 66, No. 24. (6) K. Badt, *John Constable's Clouds,* 1950, Chaps. V, VI. (7) *Ibid.* Chaps. II, III, IV. (8) Leslie, *op. cit.* p. 132. (9) Leslie, *ibid.* See also: Graham Reynolds, *Catalogue of the Constable Collection,* Victoria and Albert Museum, London, 1960, pp. 149-50.

Illust. 45 549/4 **Hampstead Heath**

canvas, 41.3 x 63.8 cm. Unsigned, undated; painted in the 1820s.

Condition: good, but the sky shows signs of rubbing.

Comment: The building on the left would seem to be the 'Saltbox' seen in the London National Gallery's *Hampstead Heath* No. 1236. The technique of the palette knife work resembles that of No. 122-1888 in the Victoria and Albert Museum, dated 'end of Octr 1819', which also has similar sky effects over the distant horizon.[1]

A similar painting (? the same) is illustrated by Charles Holmes, *Constable,* 1902, and listed on p. 246 as Messrs. Obach & Co., Hampstead Heath, 1823, 17½ in. x 25 in.

Provenance: Lt. Com. Horatio M. McKay, Langdown Firs, Hythe, Southampton, England. Acquired for the Felton Bequest from John Mitchell, 30 Bury Street, London, in 1939, by Sir Sydney Cockerell.

Reference: (1) Graham Reynolds, *Catalogue of the Constable Collection,* Victoria and Albert Museum, 1960, p. 118, No. 171, pl. 136.

Illust. 46 467/2 **West End Fields, Hampstead, Noon**

canvas, 33.2 x 52.4. Unsigned, undated, painted before 1830.

Condition: cleaned in 1952[1] by Harley Griffiths; in excellent condition.

Comment: A view over West End Fields, towards Windsor; in the distance the windmill at Kilburn.

Other Versions: A large version is in the National Gallery of Scotland.[2] A free sketch was in the Cecil G. Lawson, H. L. Fison collections.[3]

Engravings: The Edinburgh version was engraved in mezzotint by David Lucas in 1830 under the title *Noon,* forming part of *Landscapes Characteristic of English Scenery* published by Constable in 1830.[4] An example is in the Print Room Collection, N.G. Victoria, No. 906/4.

Provenance: Exhibited by Captain C. G. Constable, R.A., 1872, No. 27 (as *Noon, West End Fields);* by Sir Cuthbert Quilter, R.A., 1895, No. 11, 1906, No. 48; sold by Sir Cuthbert Quilter[5] at Christie's, 9 July, 1909, lot 50; bought Anson. Acquired for the Felton Bequest on the advice of Frank Gibson, 1909.

References: (1) A. Shore, *Quarterly Bulletin, N.G. Victoria,* 1953, Vol. VII, (1) 2.
(2) *Catalogue of Paintings and Sculpture,* National Gallery of Scotland, 1957, p. 51.
(3) Christie's, 6 November, 1959, lot 21; re-sold at Sotheby's, June 17, 1970, lot 36.
(4) Shirley, *The Published Mezzotints of David Lucas after John Constable,* R.A., 1930,
p. 175, No. 16, pl. XVI. (5) W. Roberts, *The Connoisseur,* Vol. XXIV, 1909, p. 167, 171 repr.

Illust. 47   2900/4 **Study of a Boat Passing a Lock**

canvas, 103 5 x 129 9 cm Unsigned, undated; painted in 1825.

Condition: cleaned before purchase. In excellent condition.

Comment: The subject is the lock at Flatford on the Stour in Suffolk; the
view is taken upstream; Dedham church is in the distance; willow trees
appear on the right; to the left a horse stands in the fields. A sail boat is
waiting at the lock gate which is operated by a boy. The crossbeam on the
two posts at the entrance to the lock, to be seen in the drawings No. 1 and
2 below, has been omitted; the posts have been curtailed in height;
according to Beckett pentimenti at the right hand post suggest that this at
least was originally higher than it is now.[1]

2900/4 is usually referred to as the study for Constable's Diploma picture
of 1826, but it is not sketchy; the foreground is highly finished, the
background delicately and smoothly painted as if it had been preparatory
for finishing.[2] W. G. Constable has advanced a theory that the freely
handled versions of more elaborated paintings of the same size are not
necessarily preliminaries but have a claim to be regarded as independent
works made to suit the painter's own taste.[3]

The versions of the Lock preceding the Diploma picture are divided into
an upright and an oblong group. A full account of the various versions may
be found in W. G. Constable's article.[3] Here the oblong versions given by
Constable which are immediately related to No. 2900/4 will be listed.
1. pencil drawing of *Flatford Lock,* British Museum, W. G. Constable, fig.
121. Mr. Beckett noted that this is on Whatman paper 1824.[1] A cross-beam
connects the two posts of the lock.

2. pen and sepia drawing, *A Lock,* Fitzwilliam Museum, Cambridge, W. G.
Constable fig. 122; this is closer in composition to 2900/4 than the previous
drawing. There are posts and cross piece at the entrance to the lock. A boy
at the lock gate and a horse with a rider on the right have been introduced.
According to W. G. Constable it is probable but not certain that this sketch
is derived from the British Museum drawing.

3. pen and sepia drawing, *A Lock,* Fitzwilliam Museum, Cambridge. W. G.
Constable fig. 123. The posts and crossbeam at the lock entrance are
omitted suggesting a later development of the composition. This drawing is
mounted on a piece of paper which carries a note by Lucas "a sketch by
the late John Constable for the Lock. Diploma picture presented to the

Royal Academy given to me by Mr. Constable. D. Lucas." Here the barge is in the lock as in the upright version in the Simon Morrison collection (W. G. Constable fig. 115).

4. An oil sketch in the collection of Viscount Mackintosh of Halifax (W. G. Constable fig. 124) fairly closely corresponds to 2900/4. W. G. Constable refers to "three or four other paintings of the same type" and suspends judgment on the authorship.

5. Oil painting, *The Lock,* signed and dated 1826, accepted by the Council of the Royal Academy in 1829 as Constable's Diploma picture and now at Burlington House (W. G. Constable fig. 119). This painting is close in major details to 2900/4; a dog has been introduced on the right. The handling is much less free.

Further versions, probably replicas and imitations of the paintings by other hands are listed by W. G. Constable.[3]

Provenance: Private owner, Exeter; exhibited Arthur Tooth & Sons, *Recent Acquisitions* V, Nov.-Dec. 1950, No. 4; acquired from here for the Felton Bequest on the advice of A. J. L. McDonnell 1950/51.[4]

Exhibitions: It was exhibited at the London National Gallery in 1951 for two months.

References: (1) R. B. Beckett, *Constable's Lock,* in *Burl. Mag.,* Vol. XCIV, 1952, pp. 252-6. (2) J. G. Böhler, *Constable and Rubens,* Thesis, Munich, 1955 (copy in Library of the Victoria and Albert Museum), p. 80. (3) For a new theory on the relation between highly finished and free versions in Constable's oeuvre and very full information on the pictures quoted in this entry see W. G. Constable, *The Lock as a Theme in the Work of Constable in Essays and Studies in Honour of Sir Daryl Lindsay,* Oxford University Press 1964, pp. 128-144, pls. 110-130. (4) *Quarterly Bulletin N.G. Victoria,* 1951, V, (4), 1-4.

Jean-Baptiste-Cammille Corot   1796-1875

French. Born at Paris. From 1822 to 1825 he received instruction from the classicist landscape painter, A. E. Michallon (who died in 1822) and Jean Victor Bertin. In 1825 he went to Rome, Naples and Venice. In Rome he received encouragement from Carouel d'Aligny, a classical landscape painter whom Corot later referred to as his real teacher. After his return he settled in Paris. He made two further journeys to Italy: in 1834 and 1843, and also visited Switzerland often, Holland in 1854 and England in 1862, but the greater part of his time was spent in the Forest of Fontainebleau. The pictures listed below belong for the most part to the small, freely painted nature studies in which Corot anticipated the Impressionists and which he continued to paint alongside his larger, idealistic landscapes which he exhibited at the Salon. These small landscapes with their just rendering of tone and light exerted a powerful influence on the painters of the Barbizon School.

References: *E.W.A.;* Fritz Novotny, *Painting and Sculpture in Europe (1780-1880);* 1960.

Illust. 48   1510/3 **View of The Quay of the Schiavoni**

canvas, 32 x 46.3 cm. Signed *COROT* lower right, undated; painted
1834.

Condition: described as 'damaged and restored' by Robaut;[1] restored by
W. A. Holder in 1925.[2] Cleaned by Harley Griffiths in about 1945. Apart from
some priming cracks and small paint-losses, in good condition.

Comment: Corot made a journey to Italy in 1834, staying in Venice from
August to early September, when he made 'six or eight little oils'.[3] Robaut
calls our No. 1510/3 'probably nature study for another view of the same
quay dated 1845'.[4] A sketch of the same place, closely related to No.
1510/3 made perhaps during the artist's previous stay in Venice in 1828,
but doubted by Robaut[5] was in Lord Berners's collection, London, in 1932.[6]

Robaut quotes several other paintings by Corot of the same quay.
A later elaboration of the subject, signed and dated 1845 is in the David
Rockefeller Collection; this painting, listed by Robaut as No. 322, 0, 46 x
0.80 was made for Corot's friend M. Robert of Nantes and was still in the
Robert collection in 1905; purchased by Rockefeller from Wildenstein in
New York in 1957.

Provenance: In the possession of Mr. Duz in 1898;[7] according to a note on a photograph
in the Witt Library, Courtauld Institute, London, the painting was owned in 1921 by
Knoedlers; in 1922 it was in an exhibition at Paul Rosenberg's *French Nineteenth Century
Art* in Paris;[8] according to Felton correspondence 1925 it was bought by Lefevre and
Alexander Reid of Glasgow from France;[9] acquired in 1925 by Frank Rinder for the Felton
Bequest. In the same year it was exhibited at the Tate Gallery from 6 February-26 March.

Exhibitions: Arts Council of Great Britain and Edinburgh Festival Society, 1965, Cat.
No. 29.

References: (1) A. Robaut, *L'Oeuvre de Corot*, Vol. II, 1905, No. 321 (repr. in line).
(2) Rinder, Felton correspondence 8 Jan., 2 April, 2 July, 1925. (3) Robaut, *loc. cit.*
(4) Robaut, *op. cit.*, No. 322. (5) Robaut, *op. cit.*, No. 194. (6) *Exh. Catalogue, R.A. French
Art*, 1932, p. 145, No. 294. (7) Robaut, *op. cit.*, No. 321. (8) Roger Fry, *Burl. Mag.*, Vol. XL,
1922, p. 272, pl. I. (9) See note 2; further references: *The Connoisseur*, Vol. LXXI, 1925,
pp. 117, 118, repr.; *Special Studio Number, Venice Past and Present*, 1925, p. 81, repr.;
Roger Fry, *Characteristics of French Art*, 1932, p. 95, pl. XXII B; 1951, p. 62, pl. 22;
K. Roberts, *Corot*, London, 1965, No. 15.

Illust. 49   338/2 **The Bent Tree (Morning)**

canvas, 44.3 x 58.5 cm. Signed *Corot,* lower right; painted about
1855-60.[1]

Condition: excellent; strip lined by Harley Griffiths.

Comment: A larger version much lower in tone with yellow sunset sky,
called *The Leaning Tree Trunk,* with several women but without the cow, is
in the National Gallery, London;[1] there are marked differences in the
delineation of detail between the two paintings.

Provenance: In the Alexander Young collection since 1888;[2] acquired for the Felton Bequest by Sir George Clausen in 1907 from Messrs. Agnews,[3] on the recommendation of Bernard Hall.

References: (1) A. Robaut, *L'Oeuvre de Corot,* 1905, No. 1121 (N.G. London), No. 1122 (N.G. Victoria); Martin Davies, *National Gallery Catalogues, French School,* 2nd ed., 1957, p. 52, No. 2625. (2) Reproduced in *The Magazine of Art,* Vol. XI, 1888, p. 185; also D. C. Thomson, *The Barbizon School,* 1891, p. 45. (3) Felton Correspondence, 15 Jan., 1907.

Illust. 50   1316/3 **Landscape,** Sketch

wood, 20.8 x 37.2 cm. Signed *Corot,* lower left, undated; painted probably about 1855-60.

Condition: excellent.

Comment: The brushwork resembles that of the *Bent Tree.*

Provenance: Hilda Williams, Melbourne, whose father had acquired it in Europe; acquired for the Felton Bequest by the Trustees in 1924.[1]

Reference: (1) Correspondence State Library of Victoria, 24/273.

Illust. 51   271/2 **Sketch at Scheveningen**

canvas, 18.1 x 30.1 cm. *Scheveningen* scratched into the paint lower left; unsigned, undated, painted in 1854.

Comment: An unrecorded painting. Corot visited Holland in 1854.

Provenance: An inscription on the back of the picture shows that it was formerly in the possession of Vollon, the artist. Acquired for the Felton Bequest by Sir George Clausen from Messrs. Obach, London, in 1906.

Illust. 52   1057/3 **The Model, Nude Study**

canvas, 59.8 x 43 cm. Unsigned, undated; probably painted about 1820-30.

Condition: cleaned lightly by Harley Griffiths in 1945; in excellent condition. Not re-lined.

Comment: Mr. Rinder wrote "such figures by Corot are exceedingly rare", and reported that the picture had been seen by the Director of the London National Gallery in 1919.[1] It is not listed by Robaut, *L'Oeuvre de Corot,* 1905.

Provenance: Placed in the hands of a dealer by Edmund Davies and acquired by Frank Rinder for the Felton Bequest 1919-20.

References: (1) Felton correspondence Rinder, 23 Dec., 1919, and 11 March, 1920.

36

Francis Cotes   ca. 1725-1770

British. Pupil of Knapton; exhibited at the Society of Artists from 1760 onwards. Highly praised for his portraits in pastel. One of the founders of the Royal Academy. It appears that the draperies in his portraits were often painted by Toms, who also worked for Reynolds. Romney succeeded to his house and studio in Cavendish Square.

References: Th.B.; C.N.G.; Whitley, *Artists and their Friends in England, 1700-1799,* Vol. I, 1928.

Illust. 53   1250/3 **Portrait of a Flower Painter**

canvas, 76.2 x 63.9 cm. Unsigned, undated.

Condition: satisfactory.

Comment: Marianne Zweig has suggested that this is a portrait of Mary Moser, d. 1819, flower painter.[1] A comparison with Zoffany's profile portrait of Mary Moser in his *Life School at the Royal Academy*[2] remains inconclusive. The lady portrayed was obviously a flower painter, as is shown by the unfinished canvas on the chair and the palette and brush. She is depicted in the attitude of a classical muse. The picture is undoubtedly by Francis Cotes.

Provenance: Purchased through Messrs. Christie, from Mr. Thursby-Pelham, Cadogan Gardens, London, for the Felton Bequest by Frank Rinder in 1922.

References: (1) M. Zweig, *The Connoisseur Year Book,* 1956, p. 104, 110, repr. 1. (2) At Buckingham Palace No. 99; another portrait of Mary Moser is to be found in Singleton's *The President and Members of the Royal Academy,* 1802, at the R.A.; here the features are so generalized as to make comparison difficult. The coiffure has changed. A picture by Huysman often called *Mary Moser with Her Brother (or Father)* probably represents George Michael Moser and his wife, Mary Moser's parents.

Miles Edmund Cotman   1810-1858

British. Born at Norwich. Son and pupil of John Sell Cotman, followed his father as assistant teacher at King's College, London. Painted in oil and watercolours; best known as a painter of seapieces and river landscapes.

Reference: Th.B.

Illust. 54   962/3 **Hay Barges**

canvas, 89.5 x 148.7 cm. Inscribed *J. S. Cotman* and dated 1834 (?) on name shield of boat.

Condition: at the time of acquisition it was noted that the picture had repairs in the sky.[1] There is, however, evidence of many old paint losses and re-paints in all parts of the picture. Paint flaking badly. Seriously deteriorating.

Comments: Formerly attributed to John Sell Cotman[2] but considered to be a Miles Edmund Cotman by Sir Charles Holmes and Mr. Francis W. Hawcroft.[3] The date is nearly illegible but more likely to be 34 than 23 as was stated in the Heseltine catalogue.

A print, published by Simpkin and Marshall, Stationers Court, London, is very close to this picture. It is called Boats off Yarmouth, and is said to be taken "from an original drawing by J. S. Cotman". This drawing may also have been by Miles Edmund.[3]

Provenance: Old labels and inscriptions on the back refer to H. M. Thompson and Heseltine; sale Sir Henry Meysey Thompson (later Lord Knaresborough) Christie's, 16 March 1901, lot 17, bt. Hoseda; sale J. P. Heseltine, Christie's, 7 June, 1918, lot 115, bt. Mrs. Clifton, Carfax Gallery, acquired by Robert Ross from Miss M. Knox, London, for the Felton Bequest, 1918/19.

References: (1) Ross-Knox, Felton corr. 5 June, 1918, N.G. Victoria files. (2) Cat. N.G. Victoria 1948 and previous lit. (3) Correspondence P. Hoff, F. W. Hawcroft, Deputy Curator, Norwich Castle Museum, 1959, N.G. Victoria files.

Lucas Cranach the Elder   1472-1553

German. Born at Kronach (upper Franconia), from whence he derives his name. The main master of Protestant painting. In 1505 became court painter to the Elector of Saxony, Frederick the Wise, and continued in this position under the two following Electors. His sons, Hans and Lucas, worked in his studio. Cranach signed with the device of the flying snake or dragon, derived from his coat of arms.

References: Th.B.; C.N.G.

Illust. 55   4700/3 Philip Melanchthon

wood, 18.7 x 13 cm. Signed with Serpent, dated 1532.

Condition: slightly rubbed and perhaps retouched in signature.

Comment: Philip Melanchthon (1497-1560) was a German theologian. After studying at Heidelberg and Tübingen universities he was called to Wittenberg University as Professor of Greek. Here he made the acquaintance of Luther whom he assisted in his translation of the Bible and became one of the foremost leaders of the Reformation in Germany. He had met Albrecht Dürer probably as early as 1518 and again in 1525 and 1526[1] when Dürer engraved his portrait (B. 105). 4700/3 is one of a large number of replicas, which are dated 1532, 33 or 37. None of the existing portraits can with certainty be described as the original.[2]

Provenance: According to a letter received on purchase from Prof. Witte, Director, Schnütgen Museum, Cologne, 1 Nov. 1932, the portrait came from the Merkens collection. It was acquired on the advice of Randall Davies for the Felton Bequest in 1932.

References: (1) M. Thausing, Dürer, Leipzig 1884, Vol. II, p. 266. (2) M. J. Friedländer, J. Rosenberg, Die Gemälde des Lukas Cranach, Berlin, 1932 No. 252; Prof. R. Oertel informed me that many more replicas than the ones listed here are in existence; two of them are in the Bavarian State collections.

John Crome (Old Crome)   1768-1821

British. Born at Norwich. Apprenticed 1783-90 to Francis Whistler, coach and sign painter. Saw and copied works by Gainsborough in the collection of Thomas Harvey. Became the founder of the Norwich School. His work shows the influence of the landscapes of Richard Wilson as well as that of the Dutch landscape painters of the 17th century.

References: *Th.B.; C.N.G.*

Illust. 56   454/4 **Woodland Path**

panel, 51 x 42.3 cm. Unsigned, undated; painted 1821.

Condition: in good condition.

Comment: Another version closely related to 454/4 is in the Norman L. Goldberg collection, St. Petersburg, Fla., U.S.A.;[1] a photograph of a version in the Viscount Trapian Collection, East Lothian is in the Witt Library. The Cliffords[2] describe 454/4 as a copy of the Goldberg version but know the former only from a photograph.

Provenance: George Salting (1835-1909); passed to Wallis, then to Mr. Williams, sold 1908, bt. Agnew; sold to the Rt. Hon. A. J. Balfour in whose collection the painting was in 1920;[1] acquired by the Felton Bequest from Messrs. Spink & Sons on the advice of Sir Sydney Cockerell in 1937/38.

References: (1) Correspondence Hoff-Goldberg, 1958 N.G. Victoria files. See also: C. H. Collins Baker, *Crome,* 1921, pp. 82, 103, 172, as 'Forest with Pool'; Norman L. Goldberg, *The Connoisseur,* Vol. CXLVI, 1960, p. 216, fig. 9; M. H. Grant, *A. Chronological History of Old English Landscape Painters,* Leigh-on-Sea, vol. V, 1959, p. 404, fig. 432. (2) Derek and Timothy Clifford, *John Crome,* 1968, No. 100.

Aelbert Cuyp   1620-1691

Dutch. Born at Dordrecht. Pupil of his father Jacob Gerritsz C. (1594-1651/2). His early landscapes, to which belongs the one listed here, are in the nearly monochromatic manner of Jan van Goyen. In the 1640s his style changes under the influence of the Italianate painter Jan Both.

References: *Th.B.; C.N.G.*

Illust. 57   4664/3 **Landscape with Cattle**

panel, 65 x 90.3 cm. Signed *A. Cuyp* lower right; undated; painted

Condition: in good condition.

Comment: As Dr. Gerson informs me,[1] the date of the picture is given by the view of Leyden in the distance, in which the 'Marekerk' cannot be seen. Since this church was built in 1639-49, the picture must be from before this time. The earliest known date on one of Cuyp's paintings is 1639. Copies: There is a copy (? by I. v. Strij, 1752-1815) in the collection I. Strengman, Heilo.[2]

Provenance: If the copyist was v. Strij, 4664/3 must have still been in Holland during his life time. The picture was put up for sale as part of the Huntingfield estate, Heveningham Hall, Yoxford, Suffolk, by Christie's 25 June, 1915, lot 76 (bt. by Pell).[3] It has been pointed out that Joshua Charles, 4th Baron Huntingfield was of Dutch descent. The Baron Huntingeld, 1790, was the second son of Sir Joshua Vanneck, baronet 14 Dec. 1751; Sir Joshua descended from Cornelius Vanneck, paymaster of the land forces of the United Provinces (Burke's *Peerage,* 1956) but there is no evidence as to the length of time the picture had been in the Huntingfield family. It is known that Sir Joshua Vanneck bought paintings at auctions. Purchased from an undisclosed private owner on the advice of Randall Davies in 1932 by the Felton Bequest.

References: (1) Correspondence, 1959 N.G. Victoria files. (2) As before. (3) As "Herdsman with Animals".

Jans Frans van Dael   1764-1840

Flemish-French. Born at Antwerp where he was a pupil of the Academy. 1786 went to Paris to settle. Specialized in flower paintings, but also carried out decorative paintings at the palaces of Chantilly, Saint Cloud and Bellevue. Won the favour of Napoleon I and the Empress Josephine. He carries on the Flemish tradition of the meticulously detailed flowerpiece of the 17th century.

Reference: *Th.B.*

Illust. 58   215/4 **Flowerpiece**

canvas, 107.5 x 82.3 cm. Signed and dated *Van Dael* 1811 on table edge, lower right.

Condition: in good condition.

Comment: Two other versions of this composition are known: 1. Le Louvre, Inv. No. 1196, canvas, 1.00m. x 0.76m. signed and dated 1810, bought by Louis XVIII of France in 1819;[1] 2. Sale Hôtel Drouot, Paris, 9. III. 1951, No. 33, signed and dated 1814.[2]

Provenance: Mentioned as in the Rothan collection, Paris, in 1873 and 1888.[3] Sale M. G. Rothan, Georges Petit, Paris, 29-31 May, 1890, lot 27; Mme. X, Paris 15-16 Nov. 1920, lot 4; Mme Hartmann, Paris, 1934; acquired from Knoedlers, London, by Barnard Hall in 1934 for the Felton Bequest.

References: (1) L. Demonts, *Musée National du Louvre. Catalogues des Peintures exposées dans les galeries III Ecole Flamande, Hollandaise, Allemande et Anglaise,* Paris, 1922. (2) I am indebted to Mr. J. Foucart, Musée du Louvre, for information on these two versions. (3) P. Mantz, *Gazette des Beaux Arts,* 1873, p. 433; Champlin and Perkins, *Cyclopedia of Painters and Paintings,* 1888, p. 363.

Jacques-Louis David 1748-1825

French. Born at Paris. On the advice of Boucher studied under J. M. Vien and continued at the Academy. Won the Rome Prize in 1774. The visit to Rome in 1775 induced him to abandon the baroque elements in his early style and to evolve the classicist manner fully developed in his *The Oath of the Horatii* of 1784 (Louvre). In 1804 he became court painter to Napoleon I; after the fall of the emperor in 1815 he left France and settled in Brussels where he carried out a number of notable portraits; the picture listed below shows the influence of David's manner of this late period

References: *Th.B.;* Fritz Novotny, *Painting and Sculpture in Europe (1780-1880),* 1960.

School of David

Illust. 59   408/4 **Head of a Man**

canvas, 51.4 x 43.1 cm. Unsigned, undated.

Condition: reasonable; some re-paints near lower edge; not re-lined.

Comment: An old label on the back describes the picture as 'presumably a portrait of the Greindl Family'. The suggestion that the picture may have been cut down cannot be maintained, since the painted surface does not go to the end of the canvas.

Provenance: A. Besnard; Renée Fribourg;[1] exhibited Brussels, Cinq Siècles d'Art, 1935 (? No. 14), (owner André J. Seligman);[2] acquired on the advice of Sir Sydney Cockerell from André J. Seligman, Paris, 1937, for the Felton Bequest.

References: (1) Felton correspondence Cockerell 2/37. (2) Label on back.

Richard Barrett Davis 1782-1854

British. Born at Watford, Herts. His father, Richard Davis, was huntsman to the Royal Harriers under George III, who placed young Richard Barrett under Sir Frances Bourgeois, R.A. (Farington's Diary, 20 Jan., 1804); later studied at the Royal Academy Schools and partly under Sir William Beechey. 1828, appointed animal painter to William IV. Frequent exhibitor at the British Institution and the Society of British Artists. Painter of sporting pictures, landscapes, and animal genre.

Reference: W. Shaw Sparrow, *A Book of Sporting Painters,* London, 1931, pp. 153-156.

Illust. 60   2885/4 **Equestrian Group**

canvas, 70.7 x 91.5 cm. Signed and dated, *R. B. Davis, August 1845* lower right.

Condition: excellent.

41

E

Provenance: Owned by C. D. Roch, Esq., acquired for the Felton Bequest, 1951/2 from P. & D. Colnaghi, London, on the advice of A. J. L. McDonnell.

Reference: Daryl Lindsay, *Quarterly Bulletin, N.G. Victoria,* 1952, VI, (2), 5.

Ferdinand-Victor-Eugène Delacroix 1798-1863

French. Born at Charenton-Saint Maurice. 1815, pupil of P. N. Guérin (1774-1833); copied paintings by Rubens and Veronese and became an ardent admirer of Géricault *(q.v.)* whom he met in Guérin's studio. Learnt watercolour paintings from Charles Fielding (1793-1837), brother of Copley Fielding, who was in Paris 1823/4. Delacroix's *Massacre of Chios,* 1821-4, the colour of which he altered after seeing Constable's pictures exhibited in Paris in 1824 *(q.v.)* was attacked by the followers of David *(q.v.)* for its brilliant colour and free handling. 1825 in London where he became acquainted with the work of Turner, Gainsborough, Wilkie and Lawrence. In 1832 went to Morocco, after which scenes of African life, Algerian women, Arabs hunting and lions and tigers provided Delacroix with new subject matter as well as with new problems of colour. The greatest French exponent of Romanticism.

Reference: *C.N.G.,* Fritz Novotny, *Painting and Sculpture in Europe (1780-1880),* 1960.

Illust. 61   489/2 **The Confession of the Giaour**

canvas, 23.8 x 32.2 cm. Signed upper left *Eug. Delacroix.* Undated, painted between 1825 and 1838.

Condition: good.

Comment: The picture illustrates an episode from Byron's poem *The Giaour,* first published in 1813, and translated into French by Pichot, 1822-5. Delacroix illustrated a number of episodes from this poem. [1]

The Giaour, a Turk converted to Christianity, had killed the Moslem Hassan; he spent years of self-imposed seclusion in a monastery to expiate his deed; before his death he confessed to a monk.

The picture is listed by Robaut under 1838, the year in which a lithograph of it by Mouilleron appeared in *La France Littéraire.* [2]

Robaut and Moreau only knew this lithograph, not the original painting. [3] Hamilton writes that a large painting of this subject was given by Delacroix to George Sand and subsequently stolen from her grand-daughter. [4] Hamilton, who only knew our picture from the reproduction in the Thiébault sale catalogue, [5] suspected quite rightly that it is not the large work owned by George Sand but a small preliminary version. An engraving by an anonymous artist illustrating the same scene in Pichot's third volume, and another by George Cruickshank which appeared in George Clinton's *Memoirs of the Life and Writings of Lord Byron,* 1825, appear to have stimulated Delacroix's conception of the scene.[6]

Provenance: The picture figured in the sale Guasco, Petit, Paris, 11 June, 1900, lot 24, under the title *Colomb, Monastère de St. Juste.* It occurs in the Thiébault-Sisson sale, Hôtel Drouot, Paris, 23 Nov., 1907, lot 32, and according to records in the Gallery archives was owned by F. Tempelaire (whose father was a friend of Fantin Latour's) in Paris in 1910; it was acquired for the Felton Bequest in 1910 on the advice of Frank Gibson.

References: (1) W. Bach, *The Journal of Eugene Delacroix,* 1937, pp. 87, 88. (2) A. Robaut, *L'Oeuvre complète d'Eugène Delacroix,* Paris, 1885, No. 000. (3) A. Moreau, *Eugène Delacroix et son oeuvre,* Paris, 1873, p. 113. (4) G. H. Hamilton, *Gazette des Beaux Arts,* Vol. XXXVI, 1949, pp. 267-8 and note 13. (5) See under provenance. (6) Hamilton, *loc. cit.,* and figs. 8, 9. See also: *Quarterly Bulletin N.G. Victoria,* 1953, VII (3), 3.

Johann Jakob Dorner   1741-1813

German. Born at Ehrenstetten in Breisgau. Pupil of Frans J. Rösch in Freiburg i. Br. and Joseph Bauer in Augsburg. 1761 in Munich. Was given a scholarship with the express condition to copy paintings of Netherlands artists, particularly Dou and Mieris. 1765 appointed court painter at the Bavarian court, and had to furnish a small painting in the Dutch manner every three months. 1766-69 travelled in the Netherlands and to Antwerp and Paris. Rose to high positions at the Bavarian court.

Reference: *Th.B.*

Illust. 62   347/4 **The Hard Landlady**

copper, 36.6 x 47 cm. Unsigned, undated.

Condition: satisfactory.

Provenance: Frank Godden collection; sold at Joel's, Melbourne, 4 Sept., 1936, and purchased for the Felton Bequest.

François Hubert Drouais   1727-1775

French. Born at Paris. Pupil of his father Hubert; later studied under Nonotte, Carle Vanloo, Natoire and Boucher. Since 1756 "peintre ordinaire au Roy" (Louis XV). Exhibited at the Salon. Since 1758 member of the Academy. Fashionable portrait painter, noted particularly for his portraits of children.

Reference: *Th.B.*

Illust. 63   1359/5 **Madame Sophie De France**

oil on canvas, 72.7 x 59.8 cm. Signed and dated *Drouais le fils 1763*
Condition: cleaned prior to purchase; despite small areas of retouching
in excellent state of preservation.[1] Slightly trimmed at lower edge.
Comment: The identification of the sitter is traditional.
Sophie-Philippe-Elizabeth Justine, b. 27 July 1734 at Versailles
was the eighth child of Louis XV, King of France (1715-1774) and
Queen Marie Leczinska. When four years of age she was sent with
some of her sisters to the Abbey of Fontrevault, Bourbon Lodge,
to be educated. On her return to Versailles in 1750 she was described by
the Marquise de Pompadour: "Madame Sophie is almost as tall as
myself, very good, plump, a fine throat, well built, fine skin and eyes and
in profile as like the King as one drop of water to another".[2]
According to her sister Louise (the venerable Mother Thérèse de Saint
Augustine) her chief virtue was simplicity and her chief study
concealment of her real worth.[3] She died, unmarried, at Versailles
on March 3, 1782.

Other Versions: An unsigned replica, with more summary treatment of
lace and a landscape background, described as "attribué à Drouais"
was advertised by Palais Gallière, Paris 14 March, 1969;[4] the
reproduction suggests that our picture has been trimmed at the lower
edge; probably the same as acquired by the Mustées nationaux de
Versailles et de Trianons in 1970.[5]

Provenance: Professor Bernard Smith kindly brought to my notice the following
documents in the Archives Nationales, Paris; 0[1] 1910 and 1921[B]; fol. 44 Affaires Générales
p. 83 letter from 'Drouais le fils' dated 24 June 1763 stating that he had finished portraits of
Mesdames; p. 100 a memorandum addressed to Monsieur Le Marquis de Marigny (Director
of the King's Buildings) dated 28 July 1767 in which on p. 101 appear the following entries:
"Le portrait de Madame Sophie, avec des mains sur toile de vingt. 1000[H] un second
portrait d'après nature de Mme. Sophie, demême que les precedens. 1000[H]".
No. 1359/5 is clearly one of the portraits listed here; its subsequent history is unknown,
until 1913. Eugène Kraemer sale, Galerie Georges Petit, April 28-29, 1913, lot 11, repr.;
between 1913-1931 (?), owned Hodgkins; exhibited New York, Union League Club, *18th
Century Portraits* April 9-15, 1931, No. 14 (owner Wildenstein & Co.); Los Angeles Museum,
Five Centuries of European Painting, Nov. 25-Dec. 31, 1933, No. 30 (owner, Wildenstein &
Co.); New York World Fair, Pavillon de la France, *Five Centuries of History mirrored in Five
Centuries of French Art,* 1939, No. 191, Cat. p. 69, pl. XXXV (owner Wildenstein & Co.); Sao
Paulo, Museu de Arte, *O retrato na Franca,* Jan. 1952, Cat. p. 445 repr. (owner Wildenstein
& Co.); New Orleans, Isaac Delgao Museum of Art. *Masterpieces of French Painting through
Five Centuries,* Oct. 17, 1953-Jan. 10, 1954, Cat. p. 32 (owner anon.). Acquired from Messrs.
Wildenstein, London, in 1963 on the advice of A. J. L. McDonnell under the terms of the
Everard Studley Miller Bequest.

References: (1) Report Dudley Drown, London, 23. IV, 63, corr. N.G. Victoria. (2) Casimir
Stryinski, *The Daughters of Louis XV,* London 1915, p. 62 (Correspondence de Mme. de
Pompadour, Poulet Massis, Paris 1878, pp. 71-73, 19th October 1750). (3) *ibid.* p. 173 (from
Vie de la Vénérable Mère Térèse de Saint Augustine, II, 165). See also *Art News,* Nov. 25,
1933, p. 12 repr.; Harley Preston, *Annual Bulletin, N.G. Victoria* Vol. V, 1963, p. 25, fig. 21.
(4) *Art and Auction,* Vol. 13, No. 276, Feb. 28th 1969, cover illus. (5) *Gazette des Beaux
Arts,* Chronique d'Art, No. 59, Feb. 1970.

44

Françoise Duparc   1705-1778

French. Born at Marseilles. Daughter and pupil of Antoine Duparc;
trained under J. B. van Loo in Aix-en-Provence; after 1745 in Paris,
came under the influence of J. B. S. Chardin. After the death of her
sister went to London where she exhibited at the Free Society of Artists
in 1763 and at the Society of Artists in 1766. She later returned
to Paris and at the end of her life went back to Marseilles.

Illust. 61   661/1 **Portrait of an Old Lady**

canvas, 42.2 x 32 cm. Unsigned, undated.

Condition: cleaned and re-lined by Mr. Pryse-Hughes in 1937.

Provenance: Henry Tonks Sale, Christie's, 29 July, 1937, lot 43, as by Hogarth; bt.
Adams; acquired from R. E. A. Wilson by Howard Spensley in Oct. 1937 and bequeathed
in 1939.

Reference: Howard Spensley Mss., Vol. I, p. 120; Cat. No. 527.

Dutch   17th Century

Illust. 65   4563/3 **Interior with Soldiers**

wood, 55.6 x 45 cm. Unsigned, undated; painted in the 1620s.

Condition: cleaned in 1954 by Harley Griffiths. In good condition.

Provenance: Purchased from the Castlefield collection, owner Lucy Smith at Joel's,
Melbourne, 20 Aug., 1931, by the Felton Bequest. An old piece of newspaper on the back
refers to London, and carries the date 1850.

Dutch   18th Century

Illust. 66   304/1 **Death and the Fortune Teller**

panel, 37.3 x 33.7 cm. Signed *C.B.* on table; undated.

Condition: Cleaned and restored by Mr. David Lawrence, 1972.

Comment: A skeleton prepares to stab the fortune teller who sits to the
right, right head on hand, asleep. Crucifix, cards, money bag, a painting
of another skeleton and two inscriptions reinforce the message. The
picture was in the 1948 catalogue attributed to Cornelis Pietersz Bega
(1620-1664) but the monogram is not his and the work does not show
his style.

Provenance: From a label on the frame the picture appears to have been in Norwich, in
England. Purchased 1874, from James William Hines, art dealer, Melbourne.

Dutch or Flemish

Illust. 67   301 / 1 **Reading a Letter**

canvas, 41.8 x 60 cm. Unsigned, undated.

Condition: numerous paint losses and re-paints.

Comment: Listed in the 1948 Catalogue as attributed to David Ryckaert, 1612-1661, but is obviously of a later period, and the motifs seem derived from Teniers the Younger.

Provenance: Presented by Dr. Thomas Black, as by Teniers,¹ Melbourne, 1885.
Reference: (1) corr. great-grand daughter, II, VII, 71.

Sir Anthony van Dyck   1599-1641

Flemish. Born at Antwerp. Pupil of Hendrik van Balen. In 1618 master of the Guild of St. Luke; in the same year he became the chief assistant of Rubens, in whose house he lived until 1620. After a stay of four months in London in the service of James I he went to Italy in 1621 where he remained, but for a short visit to Antwerp, until 1625. He went to Venice, Rome, Palermo and Florence, and made visits to Genoa where, in his portraits of members of the noble Genoese families, he laid the foundations for his future style. 1625-6 back in Antwerp. Returned to London in 1632 where he remained, but for two visits to Antwerp, until his death. He was the court painter of Charles I and his portraits have been emulated by all great English portrait painters from Dobson to Lawrence. The two portraits listed belong to his second English period. A drawing and the Landau-Finaly collection of his *Iconography* are in the Print Room.

Reference: *Th.B.*

Illust. 68   457 / 4 **Philip Herbert, Earl of Pembroke**

canvas, 105.4 x 83.8 cm. Unsigned, undated; painted between 1635-38.

Condition: in very good order and condition; the hand, a little high in tone, may have been overcleaned. Cleaned prior to purchase.

Comment: Philip Herbert, Earl of Montgomery (since 1605), and 4th Earl of Pembroke (since 1630), was the favourite of James I and of Charles I. In 1626 was appointed Lord Chamberlain to the Royal household, a post from which he was removed in 1641. Adhered to parliamentary party during the civil war and retained his seat at Wilton until his death.¹ Famous for his patronage of van Dyck, whose paintings still fill the Double Cube Room at Wilton, designed by Inigo Jones as part of the garden front of Wilton which Jones and Philip Webb rebuilt between 1647 and 1652.²

The Earl appears with the wand of office of Lord Chamberlain and the Order of the Garter hanging on a blue ribbon; he wears a white and gold jacket and black cloak; cloudy sky, sea (?) and rocky foreground appear on the right, a yellow damask curtain on the left.

Provenance: The picture came from Kyre Park, the seat of the Baldwyn-Childe family.[3] Kyre Park had been inherited by this family from Jonathan Pytts, 1780-1807, who left his estate to the descendants of his aunt, Mrs. Childe.[4] The picture is said to have been exhibited in the Worcestershire exhibition in 1882 but is not listed in the catalogue and there is no label on the back. On the death of Mrs. Balwyn-Childe in 1930 the property passed to Charles Edward Childe-Freeman, the entire estate was shortly afterwards sold to Mr. George H. Heath.[5] The picture is mentioned as In the possession of P. & D. Colnaghi in 1931.[6] In 1934 it was sold to Garabed Bishirgan; exhibited at the Orangerie, Paris, in 1936;[7] acquired from Colnaghi for the Felton Bequest on the advice of Sir Sydney Cockerell and W. G. Constable in 1937.[8]

References: (1) D.N.B. (2) John Summerson, Architecture in Britain, 1530-1830, 1953, p. 89 seq. (3) Provenance recorded in The Times, 25 Oct., 1937. (4) Cat. Worcestershire Exh., p. 148, No. 49 under Jonathan Pytts. (5) Burke, Landed Gentry, 1952. (6) G. Glück, van Dyck, 1931, p. 564 refers to it. P. Wescher, Pantheon, Vol. XIX, 1937, p. 22 repr. (7) Rubens et son Temps, Paris, Musée de l'Orangerie, 1936, p. 58, No. 17 (misprint for No. 32), (owner P. & D. Colnaghi), date given as 1637-38. (8) Felton letter 37/1032, 39. See also Quarterly Bulletin, N.G. Victoria, 1946, I (4), 4.

Illust. 69   1246/3 Rachel De Ruvigny, Countess of Southampton

canvas, mounted on panel, 223.2 x 131.8 cm. (sight measurements). Inscribed with title in a later hand; unsigned, undated; probably painted in 1640.

Condition: cleaned by Harley Griffiths in 1959. The old varnish had been mixed with yellow-green colouring matter; the cleaning revealed the strong contrasts between white and pale blue lights and dark blue shadows in the garment, also to be found in the cleaned version at Althorp. The cleaning revealed an alteration in the position of the necklace on the left side.

Comment: The sitter, known as "la belle et Vertueuse Huguenotte", was the eldest daughter of Daniel de Massue, seigneur de Ruvigny; married to Thomas Wriothesley, fourth Earl of Southampton (1606-1667) in France in August 1634. She died on Feb. 16, 1640.[1]

This is the first of eight variants, copies and adaptions of which the versions at Althorp and Welbeck have also been published as by van Dyck.[2] Several factors suggest that 1246/3 was the original version:[3] (a) it was the only one to be chosen for engraving,[4] (see below); (b) while the other versions were in possession of the Earl's daughters, 1246/3 was inherited by the Earl's third wife, presumably with the contents of Southampton House;[5] (c) an alteration in the Althorp picture shows convincingly that the painter started this version with the design of 1246/3 in mind; below the right foot, fully depicted

47

at Althorp, the remnants of the scalloped hem of the garment can still be seen which cover the foot in Melbourne; to reveal the foot was therefore an afterthought.[6]

On McArdell's mezzotint the date of 1636 follows the title of the painting. Lionel Cust retained this date;[7] Schaeffer dated the Welbeck version 1632-40;[2] Glück agreed with Collins Baker[8] who analyzed the changes in costume in the 1630s in van Dyck's portraits and placed the Melbourne picture later, between 1638-1640; the free manner of handling also belongs to the artist's late period. The symbols showing the sitter in triumph over death and fortune strengthen the probability that the picture was painted in 1640.[9]

The composition may be compared with Rubens, an *Allegorical Portrait of Emperor Charles V,* derived from a portrait by Parmigianino painted during Charles V's visit to Bologna in 1530, later in the collection at Mantua, where Rubens saw it. Ruben's portrait is illustrated in *Northwick Park* sale catalogue, *Christie,* Oct. 29, 1965, No. 40.

Provenance: Probably painted for her husband, Thomas Wriothesley, 4th Earl of Southampton. The Earl bequeathed the contents of Southampton House to his third wife, Lady Frances Seymour, who later married Conyers Darcy.[10] Lord Darcy sold the painting to Anthony Grey, Earl of Kent in 1683;[11] from Anthony Grey, Earl of Kent, it pased to his son, Henry Grey, Duke of Kent; then to the Duke's grand-daughter, Lady Jemina Campbell who married, in 1720, Philip Lord Royston, afterwards second Earl of Hardwicke;[12] Lady Jemina became Baroness Lucas and Marchioness de Grey.[13] The picture was inherited by her daughter Amabel, who became Countess de Grey in 1816;[14] Earl de Grey[15] whose elder daughter married the 6th Earl Cowper of Panshanger.[16] In 1905 the picture was inherited by Earl Cowper's nephew, Lord Lucas, and after his death in 1916 it passed to his sister, Lady Lucas who died in 1959. Acquired for the Felton Bequest from Lady Lucas, on the advice of Frank Rinder in 1922.

References: (1) *D.N.B.* (Wriothesley, Thomas); R. W. Goulding, *Wriothesley Portraits, Walpole Society,* Vol. VIII, 1920, pl. XLIII, pp. 39, 76-7 (to be quoted as "Goulding"). (2) See G. Glück, *Van Dyck,* 1931, pl. 455 (Althorp); Schaeffer, *Van Dyck,* 1909, pl. 412 (Welbeck) note p. 517; R. W. Goulding, C. K. Adams, *Catalogue of the Pictures . . . The Duke of Portland, Welbeck Abbey,* 1936, No. 346. (3) See Goulding, *op. cit.,* p. 136, quoting Sir Claude Phillips in *Daily Telegraph,* 27 February, 1909. (4) Glück erroneously assumed that the Althorp version was engraved. (5) Goulding, *loc. cit.* (6) Glück believed the Althorp version to be the first on account of the sceptre "das nach der Haltung der Hand doch ursprünglich sein dürfte"; the position of the hand in the Melbourne picture differs however considerably from that at Althorp. (7) Lionel Cust, *Anthony Van Dyck,* 1900, p. 125 *seq.* (8) Glück, *loc. cit.,* and C. H. Collins Baker, *Burl. Mag.* Vol. XXXIX, 1921, p. 267 seq., pl. 11C. (9) Ursula Hoff, *Annual Bulletin, N.G. Victoria* Vol. II, pp. 1-4. For the symbolism of the crystal globe see Erwin Panofsky, *Problems in Titian; mostly iconographical,* London, New York, 1968, p. 126 *seq.* (10) Goulding, *loc. cit.* (11) *Catalogue of Pictures belonging to Thomas Philip, Earl de Grey, St. James,* 1834, No. 68 note; (I owe the knowledge of this catalogue to Prof. Ellis Waterhouse). (12) See note on McArdell's engraving, J. Chaloner Smith, *British Mezzotint Portraits,* Vol. II, 1879, p. 896, No. 168; Paget-Toynbee. (See note 10.) (13) Exh. British Institution 1815, *Cat. of the Dutch and Flemish Schools,* p. 18, No. 87, owner Lady Lucas. (14) Rev. J. Granger, *A Biographical History of England, 5th edition,* 1824, Vol. III, with annotations giving the pedigree of the picture from 1758 to 1816, by G. Scharf; (by courtesy of the National Portrait Gallery, London). (15) British Institution June, 1852, p. 10, No. 62, owner Earl de Grey. (16) M. L. Boyle, *Biographical Catalogue of the Portraits at Panshanger,* 1885, p. 391, No. 9 (describes her as holding a wand in her r. hand); R.A. 1873, Gallery No. III, p. 12, No. 111; Grosvenor Gallery Cat. Van Dyck Exhibition, 1887, No. 42, owner Earl Cowper.

School of van Dyck

Illust. 70   217/4 **Mary Lucas**

canvas, 119 x 99.2 cm. Unsigned, undated; painted about 1635; inscribed in a later hand l.r.: *Mary Lucas, Sister of John, Lord Lucas, Grandfather of Henry, Duke of Kent.*

Condition: re-lined; the original canvas had been cut before it lining. About 1 in. of the lower edge of the painted canvas is bent around the stretcher; inscription in old but not contemporary handwriting, possibly made at the time of Henry, Duke of Kent.

Comment: Listed in the 1948 catalogue as Sir Peter Lely, Margaret Lucas, later Duchess of Newcastle. Prof. Ellis Waterhouse informed me that the portrait was labelled School of van Dyck, while in the Wrest Park collection. It was listed as such in the old Wrest Park inventories and the sitter was called Mary Lucas.[1] In 1917 at Christie's (see provenance) the painter was given as Sir Peter Lely, the sitter as Mary Lucas. The sitter's name was changed to Margaret Lucas after the Christie sale; she is first referred to as Margaret Lucas in a letter from P. Dunthorne of the Rembrandt Galleries to Bernard Hall in 1934.[2] Since the inscription clearly reads *Mary* and not *Marg.,* the old identification of the sitter as *Mary Lucas* has been reverted to. Mary Lucas was born between 1606-1613 and married in 1625 to Peter Killigrew.[3]

She was the daughter of Thomas Lucas, of St. John's, Colchester, and the elder sister of Margaret, later Duchess of Newcastle. Since Mary died in 1647[4] and is certainly only in her twenties in the portrait she cannot have been portrayed by Sir Peter Lely, who did not come into prominence until 1647.[5] The costume,[6] the tight manner of painting point to a date in the middle thirties, by an artist closely related to van Dyck.

Provenance: The picture was at Wrest Park for a long time, possibly from the time of Henry, Duke of Kent, who married a niece of the sitter. Sold Christie's, 16 Nov., 1917, lot 78 (as Sir Peter Lely), bt. Legatt; prior to 1934 in the possession of P. Dunthorne, according to whom it had been previously in the possession of H. Bendixson. Acquired for the Felton Bequest in 1934 on the advice of Bernard Hall.

References: (1) The Hon. Mrs. Spencer Loch gave me the information from the Wrest Park inventories. (2) Felton Correspondence, Hall, 1934, N.G. Victoria, files. (3) J. L. Vivian, *The Visitations of Cornwall,* 1887, p. 269; *reference* obtained from Miss P. Reynolds, Research Department, State Library of Victoria. (4) Douglas Grant, *Margaret the First,* 1957, p. 98. (5) Ellis Waterhouse, *Painting in Britain, 1530-1790,* 1953, p. 63. (6) C. H. Collins Baker, *Burl. Mag.,* Vol. XXXIX, 1921, p. 267 *seq.* for the dating of costumes in van Dyck's portraits.

After van Dyck

Illust. 71   149/2 **Cornelius van der Geest**

panel, 82.5 x 66.6 cm. Unsigned, undated.

Condition: very yellow old varnish; paint flaking in places.

Comment: Old copy of the original by van Dyck in the National Gallery, London.

Provenance: Bequeathed by Alfred Felton, 1904.

After van Dyck

Illust. 72   301a/1 **The Marriage of St. Catherine**

canvas, 142.5 x 120.4 cm. Unsigned, undated.

Condition: good.

Comment: The original is in the collection of Her Majesty the Queen at Buckingham Palace.

Provenance: Bought at Christie's, prior to 26 Feb. 1867, by Alfred T. Thomson, for the National Gallery of Victoria.[1] Shipped 26 Feb. 1867.

Reference: (1) N.G. Victoria letter No. 95, archives, State Library of Victoria.

William Etty   1787-1849

British. Born at York. 1806 entered the Academy Schools and studied for one year 1807-8 under Thomas Lawrence. Exhibited at the Royal Academy and the British Institution from 1811. In Italy together with Richard Evans 1822-3; stayed for nine months in Venice where he made copies after Titian, Veronese, Tintoretto and others. In Paris he studied Rubens, Poussin, Velasquez, Veronese, etc.; became R.A. in 1828. The *Study of a Nude* listed below was painted during the last nine years of Etty's life, during which he enjoyed his greatest reputation and prosperity. A drawing by Etty is in the Print Room.

Reference: Denis Farr, *William Etty*, 1958.

Illust. 73   556/4 **Nude Woman Asleep**

canvas, 48.5 x 63.3 cm. Unsigned, undated; painted in the 1840s.

Condition: satisfactory.

Comment: An unpublished picture; an old handwritten label on the back says: *Study for the Deluge 1834*; a drawing of a similar figure is in the City Art Gallery, Birmingham.[1] No painting by Etty of the Deluge is known. The dating given above was suggested by Mr. Denis Farr.

Provenance: Exhibited by R. E. A. Wilson, Ryder Street, London, in 1933, No. 6 (as *Study for the Deluge)*, owner Howard Spensley;[2] 132nd Exhibition of the Oxford Arts Club, April, May, 1935 (Cat. not seen); bequeathed by Howard Spensley in 1939.

References: (1) Denis Farr, *William Etty,* 1958, No. 311, pl. 76a; (date possibly 1828-30). [2] Howard Spensley Mss., Book I, p. 26, Cat. No. 533.

Illust. 74   1110/4 **Dorothea Bathing**

panel, 69.2 x 51.4 cm. Signed *W. Etty* lower left.

Condition: broad craquelure; the panel slightly warped.

Provenance: Presented by Mrs. E. Swinburne, 1941.

Jan van Eyck   active 1422, died 1441

Flemish. Traditionally assumed to have been born at Maaseyck. Between 1422-24 painter and "varlet de chambre" to John of Bavaria, Count of Holland, working in the Count's castle at the Hague. On the Count's death in 1425 he was appointed court painter and "varlet de chambre" to Duke Philip the Good of Burgundy. There is evidence that he made long secret journeys on behalf of the Duke and that he was active in Lille from 1426 to 1428 and visited Tournai. From 19 October 1428, until Christmas 1429, on a mission to Portugal. Married in 1429 and in 1430, probably, established himself in Bruges. In 1430-32 worked on the Ghent altarpiece, left unfinished by his brother Hubrecht (d. 1426). Several of Jan's works carry signatures and these appear always on the frame, except in the case of the Wedding Portrait of Giovanni Arnolfini in London where the inscriptions, serving a special documentary purpose, appears on the panel itself. In the "Timothy", London National Gallery, Jan's signature also occurs on the panel.

Reference: L. Baldass, *Jan van Eyck,* 1952.

After van Eyck

Illust. 75   1275/3 **The Madonna and the Child**

panel, 26.3 x 19.4 cm. Inscribed.

COPLETV ANO D	ꓮꓥC	Completed in the year
MCCCCXXXIIJ	IXꓮ	of Our Lord 1433 by
P IOHEM DE EYC	XꓮN	Johannes de Eyck, Bruges
BRVGIS		As I can

51

Condition: except for the heavy craquelure in good condition.
Cleaned and examined by the Institut Royal du Patrimoine Artistique,
Brussels, in 1958.

Comment: The picture was discovered by Waagen at Ince Hall, Liverpool,
in 1850; Waagen wrote in 1854:[1] "I understand from a friend that a
small picture of the Virgin and Child now hangs in this apartment
(Drawing Room) which was formerly in the chaplain's room and was
there recognised by me as a Jan van Eyck".[2] The history of the growth
of the Ince Hall collection makes it appear most likely that the picture
was acquired by Henry Blundell (1723/4-1810) between 1803 and 1810.[3]

It was seen at Ince Hall by Crowe and Cavalcaselle in 1857[4] and
James Weale in 1883.[5] After its exhibition at the Royal Academy in 1884,
at the Guildhall in 1892, and the Burlington Fine Arts Club in 1892-3,
where it was seen by continental experts, certain criticisms appeared.

H. von Tschudi noted that the detail was treated with less precision
than one would find in the best of van Eyck's work; von Tschudi further
commented on the unusual placing of the inscription and the "childish
and uncertain" nature of the letters which contrast with the known
hand-writing and manner of signing by van Eyck. He further doubted
the date 1433 which, for stylistic reasons, seemed to him too early.
Von Tschudi further remarked that Dr. Bode had told him of a
replica with the same inscription occuring in the same positions
in the picture in the collection of the Duke of Verdura in Palermo.[6]

In 1900 the picture was rejected by Karl Voll on account of its
inscription and manner of execution. He regarded the painting as
based on an original by van Eyck. Voll had not seen the Ince Hall
picture in the original and many of his comments were inadequate.[7]

Von Bode in 1901 reserved judgement on the authenticity of the
inscription "since the picture is strongly and crudely overpainted";
he referred to two other versions, the Verdura copy and another which
seemed a Sicilian work of the early XVI century, then in the Museum
of Catania.[8] After having seen the picture again at the Guild-hall, in
1906, Friedländer decided to retain the work in the oeuvre of van Eyck,
but assumed that the inscription was taken from an inscription on the lost
original frame, later copied on to the picture itself.[9] He repeated and
elaborated these views in his later book on *Early Netherlandish Painting,*
1924.[9a] He assumed that the inscription on the Verdura picture was
identical with the Ince Hall inscription, and that the Verdura picture was a
copy of the Ince Hall inscription, and that the Verdura restorer Zink, who
cleaned the picture prior to its sale to Melbourne, discovered that the
inscription was contemporaneous with the painting, but refrained from
comment, perhaps because he then had no longer access to the work
which had been in Melbourne since 1923. Erwin Panofsky, who had seen
the picture at the New York World's Fair in 1939, believed that the face
was partially re-painted.[10] Other experts who had seen the work at this and

related exhibitions in the States between 1939-41, while still adhering to the theory that the inscription was added later, raised doubts as to the reliability of the date, which had been variously read as 1432 or 1433. J. S. Held wrote "it does not add to our confidence that the date is written in Roman numerals contrary to Jan's general practice of using arabic ones, or—exceptionally—a combination of both."[11] Grossmann, who saw the picture during its exhibition in Bruges in 1956,[12] allied himself with Pächt[13] in assessing the date as 1428, partly on epigraphic grounds, partly because the earlier date seemed to them to agree with the style of the work.

It seems clear from the above account that misgivings felt about the Ince Hall Madonna as early as 1892-3 had been allayed by the theory that the inscription, the most obviously un-Eyckian feature, had been added later. Another reason why the picture was retained as an original was that the un-Eyckian characteristics, such as the features of the Madonna, were regarded as due to later over-painting. Other factors were the assumption that there existed an old copy which was in every way identical with the Ince Hall Madonna. An examination carried out by Dr. Paul Coremans and the technicians of the Laboratory of the Institut Royal du Patrimoine Aristique in Brussels in co-operation with Mr. F. I. G. Rawlins of the Laboratory of the London National Gallery and the art historian Mr. Martin Davis, Keeper of the London National Gallery, have somewhat changed these premises. The examinations were carried out with all available physical and microchemical means, including a study of micro-samples. Reports tendered to the Trustees of the N.G. Victoria in 1958 and summarized more fully in *Corpus* No. 12 made the following points:[13a]

1. They re-affirm Zink's observation that painting and inscription are of the same date and by the same hand. No sign was found that remnants of an original inscription underlie a later, re-drawn inscription. Peculiarities of the lettering such as the loss of the K in Eyc, the addition of an A to the IX instead of an H (it should be IXH, not IXA), the use of Anno D instead of the customary Anno DNI, as well as the clumsy lettering prove that the inscriptilon was done by a hand which did not understand what it was writing and had little skill in lettering. Since the inscription, as stated above, is coeval with the painting, the painting cannot be by van Eyck's own hand.

2. No over-painting such as would explain away the weaknesses of the picture was found. The un-Eyckian features of the Madonna, certain errors in the construction of the cupboard and the window frame and shutters further support the conclusion suggested under 1 that the painting is not an original van Eyck.

3. The discovery of an old photograph of the Verdura version showed

that the inscription, though close in wording to the Ince Hall picture, was differently distributed on the panel; it is also possible that the text of the inscription was slightly different but the photograph does not allow an exact reading. In addition to this there are other slight differences between the two pictures.

These factors allow the assumption that both the Ince Hall Madonna and the Verdura picture are copies of a lost original by van Eyck. As Dr. Erwin Panofsky has pointed out, this lost original "must have enjoyed a great reputation throughout the 15th century. This is demonstrated not only by the comparable Verdura Madonna and the Covarrubias picture (possibly by a South German Master operating in Spain) but also by the inherent qualities of the composition and by the very imporatant fact that the uncontested "Duran Madonna" by Rogier van der Weyden in the Prado, datable about 1437 or so, is unthinkable without his having had access to the composition recorded in the Ince Hall Madonna as well as the Verdura picture".[14]

Provenance: Probably acquired between 1803 and 1810 by Henry Weld-Blundell (see note 3).[15] It was identified as a van Tyck by Waagen (see note 1) and was seen (or described as being at) Ince Hall by Crowe and Cavalcaselle in 1857 (see note 4) and by R. A. M. Stevenson in 1883 (The Athenaeum, 6 Oct., 1883, p. 440) and Weale (see note 5). The picture was exhibited at the R.A. Winter Exhibition, 1884, No. 267 (owner Thomas Weld-Blundell); the Guildhall, 1892, No. 48 (owner as before); The Guildhall, 1906, No. 3 (owner as before); in 1922 the Felton Bequest acquired the picture on the advice of Frank Rinder through the agency of Captain Langton Douglas from Mr. C. J. Weld-Blundell; arrived in Melbourne 1923.

Exhibitions: It was exhibited at the London National Gallery, Room XV, from 16 Oct. to 30 Dec., 1922; later at the New York World's Fair in 1939, No. 113, and in the same year at the Golden Gate International Exposition in San Francisco. Owing to the outbreak of World War II it remained in the States and was shown in the Cleveland Museum of Art in 1940 and in the Cincinnati Art Museum in 1941. In 1956 it hung in Room XX in the London National Gallery, prior to being sent to Belgium for the exhibition in Bruges, l'Art Flamand dans les Collections Britanniques, 1956, No. 2.

References: (1) G. F. Waagen, Treasures of Art in Great Britain, 1854, Vol. III, p. 249. (2) Waagen's entry would seem to be the earliest printed reference to 1275/3. (3) In a foreword to the Catalogue of the Pictures at Ince Blundell Hall, Walker Art Gallery, Liverpool, April 3-31, 1960, p. 7, 8, John Jacob (J.J.) quotes an entry in The Farington Diary of 1806 showing that Henry Blundell "granted an annuity of £500 a year to a person aged 52 or 3 for a collection of works of art". Blundell's collection increased from 197 pictures in 1803 to 314 listed in an inventory taken on Charles Blundell's death in 1841; Jacob states that there is no reason to suppose that Charles was responsible for the additions. (4) J. A. Crowe and G. B. Cavalcaselle, Lives of the Early Flemish Painters, 1897, 3rd ed. p. 90-92 (1st ed. 1857). (5) J. Weale, Les Trésors de l'Art chrétien en Angleterre, Revue de l'Art chrétien, 1883, p. 193. (6) Repertorium für Kunstwissenchaft, Vol. XVI, 1893, p. 101, "eigt den Meister nicht in seiner höchsten Vollendung. Die Nebendinge sind etwas flüchtig behandelt, das Muster auf dem Teppich hintr der Madonna wirkt unhuhig; dazu kommt ine nicht besonders gute Erhaltung." Von Tschudi's observations are reflected in the comments of Ludwig Kaemmerer, Hubert and Jan van Eyck, 1898, p. 58. (7) Karl Voll, Die Werke des Jan van Eyck, 1900, pp. 87, 88. (8) W. Bode, *Jahrbuch d. Königl. Preuss. Kunstsammlungen*, Vol. XXII, 1901, p. 122, n.l. (9) M. J. Friedländer, *Repertorium für Kunstwissenschaft*, XXIX, 1906, p. 574, No. 3. (9a) M. J. Friedländer, *Die Altniederländische Malerei*, 1924, Vol. I, p. 53-5, pl. XX, and *Early Nertherlandish Painting, I, The Van Eycks—Petrus Christus*, Leyden/Brussels, 1967. (10) Erwin Panofsky, *Early Netherlandish Painting*, Vol. I, 1953, p. 183; so also Millard Meiss, "Highlands" in the Lowlands, in *Gazette des Beaux Arts*, 57, VIe P., 1961, 278, note 12. (11) *The Art Bulletin*, Vol. XXXVII, 1955, p. 217 (review of Erwin Panofsky, *Early Netherlandish Painting*). Waagen, *op. cit.*, had read the date as 1432; Weale, *op. cit.*, and other writers followed him in this reading; von Tschudi, *op. cit.*, read 1433 but the 1432 date continued to be quoted; Weale in *Burl. Mag.*, Vol. IX, 1906, p. 185, after re-examining the picture at the Guildhall, corrected his earlier dating to 1433. There is indeed a third stroke on the white border which runs along the brocade hanging of the canopy. (12) F. Grossman, *Burl. Mag.*, Vol. XCIX, 1957, p. 3-4. (13) Otto Pächt, *Burl. Mag.*, XCVIII, 1956, p. 274, n. 32. Dr. Pächt feels that the plain border of the garment of the Madonna, the particular nature of the folds are close to such paintings as the Madonna by the Master of Flémalle in Leningrad; he also states in his note in the *Burlington Magazine* (quoted above): "there is a transition from the thorax to the knee section which, together with the serpentine movement of the main current of folds and the lack of precision in the sitting posture", is more closely allied to the early style of the Flémalle master, and therefore suggests an earlier phase of van Eyck's art than that of 1433. (13a) Ursula Hoff and Martin Davies, *The National Gallery of Victoria, Melbourne, (Les Primitifs Flamands, I. Corpus de la Peinture des Anciens Pays-Bas Méridionaux au Quinzième Siècle* 12) Brussels 1971. (14) Letter to the Director, 24 Feb., 1959, N.G. Victoria files; for the Covarrubias picture see Josua Bruyn, *Van Eyck Problemen*, Utrecht 1957, pp. 122 f, fig. 51. (15) It is often stated that the picture had a note on the back saying that the panel was pledged in Italy in 1619 (see for example Baldass, *van Eyck*, 1952, No. 7) but this is due to a misunderstanding. Weale, in 1883 (see note 5) reported that he saw the small red seal which is still on the back. It has not been possible to identify this seal.

John Ferneley   1782-1860

British. Born Thrussington, Leics. Trained by his father, wheelwright to the Duke of Rutland, and during this time did some cart painting.
1803 to London. 1804 to Dover, painting for some officers of the garrison. 1805 studied under Marshall *(q.v.)* in London. 1849 to Ireland, where his chief patrons were Lord Belmore and Lord Lismore. Later settled in Melton Mowbray, where he remained until his death.

Reference: Walter Shaw Sparrow, *A Book of Sporting Painters*, 1931, pp. 157-168.

Illust. 76   2971/4 **Squire George Osbaldeston on Ashton taking the Fence Side by Side with Sir Francis Holyoake-Goodricke on Crossbow**

canvas, 101.5 x 127.5 cm. signed and dated, *J. Ferneley, Melton Mowbray, 1830* lower centre. Inscribed below on right; *Sir F. Holyoake-Goodricke on Crossbow;* below horse on left: *G. Osbaldeston Esq. on Ashton;* in corner lower left. *Two of the figures from the . . . picture in possession of H. Goodricke.*

Condition: fair, cleaned in 1952.

Comment: Squire George Osbaldeston, 1787-1866, was one of the greatest all-round sportsmen of his time, a famous breeder of hounds and well-known steeple-chase rider; master of the Pytchley Quorn, from 1827-1834.[1] 2971/4 is a repetition of a painting by Ferneley of 1824 showing Squire Osbaldeston on Ashton going out with Mr. Holyoake and Sir Harry H. Goodricke on "Dr. Russell", which in 1927 was in the collection of Major Mervyn Thorneycroft.[2] Mr. Holyoake became Sir Francis Holyoake-Goodricke in 1833. The above quoted inscription must therefore have been added after 1832.

Provenance: Purchased on the advice of Daryl Lindsay in 1952 from Gordon Lyton, Esq., Melbourne.

References: (1) Guy Paget, *The Melton Mowbray of John Ferneley,* 1931, p. 21. (2) Paget, *op. cit.,* p. 66 repr.; *Squire Osbaldeston, His Autobiography,* ed. E. D. Cuming, 1927, p. 120 *seq.,* p. 49 repr.; G. T. Burrows, *Gentleman Charles, A History of Fox Hunting,* 1951, p. 32; both sources describe the Thorneycroft picture.

Flemish about 1500

1247/3 Triptych with the Miracles of Christ

panels. Unsigned, undated; painted about 1500.

Condition: excellent; fine priming crackle; "antiquated" varnish, removed by Harley Griffiths in 1957 from centre panel. Reframed by Mr. Draper, London National Gallery in 1922.

Provenance: Nothing is known about the early history of the triptych; Collection F. J. Gsell, Vienna by 1886;[1] F. J. Gsell sale, Vienna (Georg Plach) 14.3, 1872, lot 215 (as Memling);[2] bt. Sedelmeyer; sold for Lady Leyland by W. H. Romaine-Walker (architect) in London to Frank Rinder for the Felton Bequest in 1922. (Rinder corr. 22 Sept., 1921 (as by Mostaert) and 12 Nov., 1922.

Comment: The triptych is fully discussed in the following publication: U. Hoff, M. Davies, *The National Gallery of Victoria, Melbourne (Les Primitifs flamands, I, Corpus de la peinture flamande des anciens Pays-Bas méridionaux au quinzième siècle No. 12)* Brussels 1971, referred to hereunder as *Corpus Melbourne.*

References: (1) G. F. Waagen, *Die vornehmsten Kunstdenkmäler in Wien,* Vienna 1866, p. 316. (2) Th. v. Frimmel, *Lexikon der Wiener Gemäldesammlungen,* G.-L. Munich, 1914, 82 seq.

Illust. 77   Centre Panel: **The Multiplication of the Loaves and Fishes**

panel, total height 113.9 x 83.4 cm.; shoulder height 32 in.; width 32⅞ in.

Comment: The centre panel depicts the *Multiplication of the Loaves and Fishes,* as recorded in all four Gospels, Matthew XIV (15-21); Mark VI (35-44); Luke IX (12-17); John VI (3-13). Details peculiar to

John's account VI, 3 and 9, Mark VI, 43 and Matthew XIV, 21
are shown in the picture. In the distance Christ sits on a mountain
surrounded by seven disciples; a small lad holds a basket with five loaves
and two fishes which Christ blesses; the foreground scene shows the
moment after the multitudes have eaten; the disciples collect the
left-over bread and fish bones in twelve baskets. There is an unusual
emphasis on drinking; two members of the crowd are shown drinking;
water bottles stand on the ground, to the right a woman takes water
from a spring. Subsidiary scenes representing miracles occurring in the
gospels just before and after the miracle of the multiplication are shown
in the background; to the left Christ heals the sick; to the right Christ
dismisses the multitudes; further to the r. the apostles have apparently
entered the boat on the sea of Galilee; further back Christ and Peter
are walking on the water; in the background the town of Capernaum as
in John VI, 17 or Bethsaida as in Luke IX, 10.

Several figures are certainly or possibly derived from other paintings.
The foreground figure to the left is a repetition of S. Mary Magdalene
in a *Lamentation* attributed to Rogier van der Weyden.[1] The two dogs
resemble those in the *Columba altarpiece* by Rogier van der Weyden;[2]
the seventh figure from the front in the left hand row resembles a portrait
drawing of Michelle de France.[3] Figures 4 and 5 from the front in the
right hand row resemble drawings of Philippe and Jean IV, Dukes of
Brabant.[4] Figure 7 in the same row can be connected with the portrait
of Isabella of Portugal.[5]

The possibility of a eucharistic significance of these miracles in this
and the left hand panel (*Marriage at Cana)* is discussed in *Corpus
Melbourne.*

Following Friedländer, the centre panel had been attributed to the Master
of the Legend of S. Catherine, sometimes identified with
Pieter van der Weyden, the son of Rogier van der Weyden. The delineation
of the features closely resembles those in the panels of the *Legend of
S. Catherine* in the collection of Baron van der Elst.[6]

References: (1) M. J. Friedländer, *Altniederländische Malerei,* Vol. II, 1924, pl. XXXIX.
(2) G. Glück, *The Art Quarterly,* Vol. V, Detroit, 1942, p. 56, note 3. (3) *Corpus Melbourne;*
it is there identified by comparison with a drawing in the *Codex Succa,* Brussels (II, 1862,
I, Fol. 11). (4) These are identified by comparison with drawings in the *Codex Succa* and
with two silverpoint drawings, John of Brabant (van Beuningen coll.) and Philip of Brabant
(formerly Mannheimer coll. now destroyed) see E. Panofsky, *Netherlandish Painting,* 1953,
(Vol. II, figs. 380, 382). (5) cf. portrait on panel now reasonably claimed to be Isabella of
Portugal d. 1473, by Rogier van der Weyden, John Rockefeller Jnr. Coll. repr. Panofsky, *op.
cit.,* Vol. II, fig. 363. (6) M. J. Friedländer, *op. cit.,* Vol. IV, 1926, p. 101 seq., pl. XLV; 105
seq., pl. XLVII See also: F. Winkler in Thieme Becker's Dictionary, Vol. XXXV, 1942, p. 468
under Pieter van der Weyden.

F

Illust. 78a   L. wing obverse: **The Marriage of Cana**

panel; total height, 113 cm.; width, 37.2 cm.

Comment: The Marriage at Cana is recorded in the Gospel of
John, II, 1-11. In a hall framed by an arch nine people in rich dress
are seated along an L-shaped table on the right. At the short arm of the
table under a canopy the bride between an older and a young woman.
On the consoles of the arch to the left Samson and the Lion, to the right
six apostles among whom S. Peter is recognizable by his round head,
short curly beard and tonsure. In front of them six stoneware urns, one
of which is being filled with water by a servant; some indecipherable
lettering is around the hem of his garment. In the foreground three figures
in rich dress; in the centre the "ruler of the feast" receives the wine in
his cup; to the right the bridegroom (bearing the initials I. M. on his purse)
who was called when the ruler of the feast tasted the wine.
On the consoles of the arch to the left Samson and the Lion, to the right
Gideon's fleece; in the centre medallion David killing Goliath. Above in
two niches statues of the serpent of the Garden of Eden and Adam
and Eve after the Fall.

Several of the figures appear to be derived from portraits of members
of the house of Burgundy. In the foreground centre Adolph of
Cleves-Ravesteyn;[1] to the left probably Englebert II of Nassau;[2] at the
short end of the table from the back, Philip the Good of Burgundy
(1396-1467);[3] presumably Margaret of York (1446-1503);[4] her husband,
Charles the Bold;[5] probably Mary of Burgundy;[6] her husband,
Maximilian I;[7] their son Philip the Fair.[8]

The three women at the short arm of the table could be expected to be the
three wives of Philip the Good but do not resemble known portraits of
Michelle de France, Bonne d'Artois and Isabella of Portugal.

The attribution of the Marriage at Cana to the Magdalen Master, recorded
in *Catalogue 1961* is not upheld in *Corpus Melbourne.* No alternative
attribution can be suggested.

References: Versions of the following portraits may have served as prototypes or are
cited for comparison: (1) panel coll. Prince de Croy Rumilies, Catalogue of the Toison d'Or
exhibition, Bruges, 1962, No. 29 repr. (2) for a comparable portrait, in reverse, see *Catalogue
of Paintings, Rijksmuseum,* Amsterdam, 1960, 200 f. (3) panel after Rogier van der Weyden,
Dr. A. Janssens de Bisthoven, *Stedelijk Museum voor Schone Kunsten,* Brugge, 1957, No.
13, 110-113; (4) compare H. Adhémar, *Le Louvre,* Brussels 1962, 79, (9); (5) Rogier van der
Weyden's portrait in Berlin shows the roundness of the head; M. J. Friedländer, *Die
Altniederländische Malerei,* Berlin II, 1924, No. 42; for a better comparison see *Corpus
Melbourne.* (6) position of head and hand resemble those on a 15th century stained glass
window in the Victoria and Albert Museum (C.439-1918); cast down eyes occur in Codex
1857 Vienna National Library, fol. 14v (O. Pächt, *The Master of Mary of Burgundy,* London
1948, 48-49). (7) compare stained glass panel, Victoria and Albert Museum, C.439-1918.
(8) panel coll. Mrs. Tudor Wilkinson, c. 1490, M. J. Friedländer, *Die Altniederländische
Malerei,* XII, 1935, No. 31, pl. VIII. See also: Walter S. Gibson, *Some Notes on Pieter Bruegel
the Elder's Peasant Wedding Feast* in The Art Quarterly, Vol. XXVIII, No. 3, 1965, pp.
194-208.

Illust. 78b   Left wing reverse: **Rest on the Flight to Egypt**

Comment: The legend of the Rest on the Flight to Egypt seems to have
its origin in Pseudo-Matthew, Ch. XX, where it is recorded that on the third
day of the journay, the Virgin, sitting down under a palm tree, longed for
its fruit; Jesus, sitting in Mary's lap, bade the tree bend down, which it
did, to her feet and she gathered dates. Parts of the composition are based
on Schongauer's engraving Lehrs 15,[1] dating from the early 1470s.[2] The
palm tree with angels, the trees on the left, and the figure of Joseph and
the ass are borrowed from the engraving. The Madonna and Child are
related to various pictures assigned to the Master of the Magdalen Legend
to whom this panel has been reasonably attributed.[3]

References: (1) Max Lehrs, *Katalog der Kupferstiche Martin Schongauers,* Vienna, 1925;
the same, *Martin Schongauer,* Vienna 1914, pl. VI. (2) Julius Baum, *Martin Schongauer,*
Vienna 1948, p. 37. (3) for a detailed discussion, see *Corpus Melbourne.*

Illust. 79a   Right wing obverse: **The Raising of Lazarus**

Total height 111.3 cm; width 36 cm.

Comment: The story occurs only in *S. John* XI, 1-44. In the foreground
Lazarus stands upright in a grave, looking up at Christ; a man unwinds
the grave clothes; on the displaced gravestone are illegible marks of
lettering. In the background, to the r., small figures of Christ with some
Apostles and Mary and Martha.
Attributed by Friedländer to the Master of Embroidered Foliage,[1]
perhaps on account of the castle in the middle distance which recurs
very similarly in the *Virgin and Child* in the Johnson collection,
Philadelphia, ascribed by Friedländer to his master.[2] The figures and
the landscape in the picture here differ however markedly from those in
the Johnson collection picture. For further discussion, see
Corpus Melbourne.

References: (1) M. J. Friedländer, *Die Altniederländische Malerei,* Vol. IV, 1926, p. 137/8
(no attribution); Vol. XII, 1935, p. 18. (2) *Ibid.,* 1926, No. 85, pl. LXIV.

Illust. 79b   R. wing reverse: **S. Peter**

Comment: S. Peter holds two keys (to "bind" and to "loose", *Matthew*
XVI, 19). Reasonably connected by Friedländer with the Master of
The Embroidered Foliage.[1] Certain plants in the *Martyrdom of SS Crispin
and Crispinian* at Warsaw are almost identical with some in *S. Peter.*[2]

References: (1) M. J. Friedländer, *Die Altniederländische Malerei,* Vol. XII, 1935, p. 18.
(2) J. Bialostocki, *Les Musées de Pologne (Les Primitifs flamands* I, *Corpus de la peinture
flamande des anciens Pays-Bas méridionaux au quinzième siècle,* 9, Brussels 1966,
No. 113.

Flemish   16th Century

Illust. 80   4560/3 **The Descent from the Cross**

panel, ogee shaped top, 71.5 x 106 cm. (panel size). Unsigned, undated;
painted about 1520.

Condition: panel split; cradled; broad priming cracks, particularly in the sky and in the lower centre; old discoloured varnish; some retouches but on the whole in sound condition.

Comment: Attributed by Friedländer to a master of the *Antwerp Mannerists* whose style is close to the *Adoration* in the collection van Groote.[1] Antwerp, between 1500 and 1530 was the leading art centre in Belgium, where painters from all parts of the Netherlands practised a "modish", eclectic style which aimed at an agitated expression of emotion. The Composition of 4560/3 continues a type seen in Gerard David's *Descent from the Cross* of about 1511 in the Frick Collection;[2] the landscape on the left recurs similarly in an *Adoration* in the collection van Groote;[3] the kneeling Magdalen has its counter part in a *Lamentation under the Cross* by the same master;[4] the fainting Virgin supported by one of the Maries goes back in type to Rogier van der Weyden's *Deposition* in Madrid.[5]

Provenance: Owned by Lucy Smith, Melbourne; probably brought to Victoria in 1846. Offered by the owner and acquired under the Felton Bequest in 1931.

References: (1) Correspondence Felton 31/1243, letter from Dr. Friedländer, 30 Dec., 1931; M. J. Friedländer, *Die Altniederländische Malerei,* Vol. XI, 1933, p. 35. (2) *Ibid.,* Vol. VI, 1928, pl. LXXXIX, No. 192. (3) *ibid.,* Vol. XI, 1933, pl. XVIII, No. 27. (4) *ibid.,* pl. XXII, No. 33. (5) *op. cit.,* Vol. II, p. 92, No. 3, pls. II-VI.

Flemish School   16th century

Illust. 81   4590/3 **S. Jerome**

panel, 42.7 x 31.4 cm. Unsigned, undated; inscribed *Homo Bulla* (Man is a bubble).

Condition: a crack runs vertically through the left half of the panel.

Comment: Formerly listed as School of Dürer.[1] The composition goes back to the *S. Jerome* by Dürer, painted for a Portguese in Antwerp, 1521, now at Lisbon,[2] which was perhaps inspired by a composition of Quentin Massys. A frequently repeated theme. 4590/3 resembles a painting by Joos van Cleefe formerly in the Duke of Fife collection.[3] The landscape is additional.

Provenance: In 1931 in the possession of Miss J. Davies, Camberwell, Melbourne. The picture had belonged to her father, Robert Boyle Davies, a solicitor in early Melbourne. Acquired for the Felton Bequest by Bernard Hall in 1932.

References: (1) *Cat. N.G. Victoria,* 1948. (2) E. Panofsky, *Albrecht Dürer,* 1943, Vol. II. Paintings No. 41, w. bibl. (3) M. J. Friedländer, *Altniederländische Malerei,* Vol. IX, 1931, pl. XXVIII, pp. 46f., 132, No. 39a, Duke of Fife Auction, 19 July 1924. No. 110 and Vol. XII, 1935, p. 70, no. 163 (for the same motif in the work of Marinus van Reymerswaele). Also W. Cohen in *Les Arts Anciens de Flandres,* Vol. II, 1906/7, p. 153; J. Held, *Dürer's Wirkung aut die Niederländische Kunst seiner Zeit,* 1931, pp. 81 ff., (for Massys, Marinus van Reymerswaele and Joos van Cleefe).

Flemish, Antwerp   16th Century

Illust. 82/83   3660/3 **Carved Retable of the Passion of Christ**

The Wings,

four panels, 203.2 x 100.3 cm; unsigned, undated, painted after 1511.

Condition: the panels are cut and filled in around the edges; crudely over painted, flaking in various places; in poor condition.

left wing obverse: 1. *Pentecost.*   2. *Ascension of Christ.*
left wing reverse: 1. *Abraham and Melchisedek.*   2. Part of the *Mass of S. Gregory.*

right wing obverse: 1. *Christ before Pilate.*   2. *The Betrayal of Christ.*
right wing reverse: 1. *The Last Supper.*   2. Part of the *Mass of S. Gregory.*
small upper left wing obverse: *Christ in Limbo.*
small upper left wing reverse: Part of the *Mass of S. Gregory.*
small upper right wing obverse: *Christ shown to the People.*
small upper right wing reverse: Part of the *Mass of S. Gregory.*

Comment: With closed wings the panels combine to a representation of the *Mass of S. Gregory,* accompanied on the left by *Abraham and Melchisedek* and on the right by the *Last Supper.* Melchisedek, king of Salem offers bread and wine to Abraham (Genesis, 14, 18-24); this scene is a traditional Old Testament prefiguration of the Last Supper.[1] When S. Gregory celebrated mass, one of the bystanders doubted the presence of Christ in the host. At the prayer of the saint, Christ descended on the altar showing his stigmata and surrounded by the Instruments of the Passion.[2] When opened up, the scenes on the painted panels expand the *Passion of Christ,* which, together, with scenes from his *Infancy,* form the subject matter of the carved centre. Most of the larger paintings bear a distant resemblance, though much simplified, to corresponding scenes in the *Small Woodcut Passion* by Dürer of 1511. *The Christ Shown to the People* is closer to the same scene B.9 of about 1498 in Dürer's *Large Woodcut Passion.* The panels are later in style than the carved centre which is dated by Michel into the 1490's.[3] They appear to have been stuck into the old frame at a later date.

Provenance: In 1912 in the possession of Count van der Straeten Ponthoz.[3] Acquired for the Felton Bequest on the advice of Sir Sydney Cockerell from Durlachers, London, 1937.

References: (1) *Lexikon der christlichen, Ikonographie,* ed. E. Kirschbaum, Freiburg i/Br. 1971, III, 241-2. (2) Réau, *op. cit* III, *Iconographie des Saints,* II, 1958, p. 614. (3) A. Michel, *Histoire de l'Art,* 1912, Vol. V, 1, pp. 325 f, fig. 198. See under Sculpture.

Prospero Fontana   1512-1597

Italian. Born at Bologna. Pupil of Innocenzo Francucci. 1528 assistant
to Perino del Vaga in Rome. Collaborated with Vasari in Rome
and Florence. After a short stay in France in 1560 returned to Bologna.

Reference: *Th.B.*

Illust. 84   839/5 **Holy Family with S. Jerome, a Female Martyr,
and the infant S. John**

panel, 102.2 x 82.8 cm, signed lower right *PROSPER. FONTANEUS;*
painted probably in the 1550s.

Comment: The composition is of the type known as "Santa
Conversazione". A feature more usually associated with the
Annunciation is the workbasket on the lower right, containing a ball of
purple wool, a white cloth, the edge of which is embroidered in purple, a
yellow cushion; a pair of shears is leaning against the basket on
the left. The contents of the basket characterise the Madonna as one
of the Virgins entrusted with the task of producing a new curtain for the
Temple at Jerusalem.

J. A. Gere has identified some frescoes in the Villa Giulia in Rome,
documented to have been executed between April 1553 and March
1555 by Fontana, by comparing the head of the female martyr in
839/5 with that of a satyress in the Villa Giula frescoes.[1] The similarity
suggests that 839/5 was executed during the same period. Dr. Herman
Voss has drawn attention to the relation between 839/5 and a small
Holy Family in Dresden also given to Fontana.[2] Another painting,
comparable to that at Dresden, is in Verona,[3] described by Voss as
early, raphaelesque phase of Fontana (attributed to Bernard. India in
Verona). The composition bears a distant resemblance to Correggio's
The Madonna of S. Jerome of 1527-28[4] which was greatly praised by
Vasari in his Vite.[5]

Provenance: Duncombe Park Cat., 1812, p. 10 and app. (seat of the Fevershams).
Yorkshire Fine Arts Exhibition, York, 1879, No. 49, owner the Earl of Feversham; Catalogue
Exhibition of Paintings of Old Masters, P. & D. Colnaghi, London (1960) No. 2 repr.; bt.
Jeudwine. Acquired for the Felton Bequest from W. R. H. Jeudwine, London, on the advice
of A. J. L. McDonnell, 1961.

References: (1) J. A. Gere, *The Decorations in the Villa Giulia,* in: *Burl. Mag.,* Vol.
CVII, 1965, pp. 201 f, fig. 46. (2) letter A. J. L. McDonnell, No. 172, 12 February, 1961,
archives National Gallery of Victoria; the picture is listed in Karl Woermann, *Catalogue of
the Royal Picture Gallery,* Dresden 1905, p. 29, No. 115, 29½ in. x 25⅝ in. (Photograph in
archives National Gallery of Victoria) and in H. Posse, *Die Gemäldegalerie zu Dresden,
Katalog der alten Meister,* 1930, Nr. 115 (where an attribution to Giovanni Francesco Bezzi,
called Nosadella, is mentioned). (3) Thieme Becker's *Dictionary,* Vol. XII, 1912, p. 186, in
poor condition, photo Gall. Archives. (4) Corrado Ricci, *Correggio,* London, New York,
1930, pp. f, pl. CLIX. (5) Giorgio Vasari, *The Lives of the Painters, Sculptors and
Architects,* Everyman's Library, London, 1927, Vol. I', 173-4.

French (?) 18th Century

Illust. 85   305/1 **Portrait of a Gentleman in Green Coat**

canvas, 60 x 45.2 cm.

Condition: heavy craquelure in the face.

Comment: The sitter wears a short grey wig and ruffled waistcoat.

Provenance: Acquired by the Trustees on the advice of E. von Guérard in 1876.[1]

Reference: (1) *Illustrated Catalogue of the National Gallery*, 1918, p. 112, No. 15.

Thomas Gainsborough   1727-1788

British. Born Sudbury, Suffolk. The years 1740-1748 were spent in London, where he does not seem to have served out a regular apprenticeship, but came into contact with Gravelot, for whom he almost certainly worked, and Hayman. After returning to Sudbury moved to Ipswich, where he practised as a portrait painter. In the autumn of 1759 moved to Bath. In 1774 went to London, where he was recognised as the chief rival of Reynolds until his death. Exhibited at the Society of Artists 1761-1768, and at the Royal Academy, of which he was a Foundation Member, 1769-1772, and 1777-1783.

His early works include landscapes painted under the influence of Wynants and Ruysdael. In Ipswich evolved a style of portraiture combining the traditions of the conversation piece and Dutch landscape, but abandoned this after the middle fifties. During his Bath period aimed at an elegance inspired by Van Dyck, and developed his characteristic landscape style influenced by the work of Rubens. Most of his fancy pictures (some known only from engravings) were painted after 1781.

Elizabeth Wrottesley, later Duchess of Grafton, was painted in Bath after he had refined his style under the influence of Van Dyck. The *Portrait of an Officer of the 4th Regiment of Foot* illustrates his occasional practice of wedding a likeness taken *ad vivum* with a figure painted from another model or lay figure. *The View at the Mouth of the Thames* belongs to his final phase of the eighties, when his style developed in a highly creative and original manner, although never losing touch with his observation of reality.

References: W. H. Whitley, *Thomas Gainsborough,* 1915; Ellis Waterhouse, *Gainsborough,* 1958.

Illust. 86   4727/3 **Elizabeth Wrottesley, later Duchess of Grafton**

canvas, re-lined, laid on panel, 76.1 x 63.5 cm in painted oval. Unsigned, undated; painted 1764/5.

Condition: excellent.

Comment: The sitter was the third daughter of the Rev. Sir Richard Wrottesley, Bart. Elizabeth was born in 1745; in 1769 she married Augustus Henry Fitzroy, 3rd Duke of Grafton, who was Lord Bute's opponent and succeeded Pitt as Prime Minister in 1768.[1] Ellis Waterhouse comments that the date of the portrait must be 1764/5 "as the Bedford-Wrottesleys seems to have been at Bath that winter and all sitting to Gainsborough";[2] a related picture in a different pose is at Woburn Abbey.[3]

Provenance: Lady Elizabeth Fitzroy, the sitter's daughter, gave the picture to her sister Frances and her husband the 1st Baron Churchill (1837); inherited by Francis George, 2nd Baron Churchill, sold Christie's 12 May, 1888, lot 23. Bought Mrs. William Agnew, d. 1892; (exh. R.A. 1892, No. 29); Sir George Agnew, Bart., 1910; Sir William Agnew, 1928; bought Count John McCormack, 1931, acquired for the Felton Bequest from Sir William Agnew on the advice of Randall Davies in 1933.

References: (1) D.N.B. (2) Ellis Waterhouse, Gainsborough, 1958, No. 738 and correspondence Burke, Waterhouse (N.G. Victoria files); Walpole Society, XXXIII, 1953, p. 115 (2). (3) Waterhouse, Walpole Society, op. cit., p. 115, No. 1, and Gainsborough, No. 737, 1. See also Walter Armstrong, Gainsborough, 1898, p. 120, p. 196; Mortimer Mempes and J. Greig, Gainsborough, 1909, p. 86.

Illust. 87   1223/3 **An Officer of the 4th Regiment of Foot**

canvas, 230.2 x 156.1 cm. Unsigned, undated; painted between 1776 and 1780.

Condition: cleaned prior to purchase in 1922; yellow varnish taken off by Harley Griffiths in 1960. In excellent condition.

Comment: The portrayed wears the dress of officers of the Grenadier and Light Companies of the 4th Foot in the campaign in America between 1776 and 1780. The hat shown in the portrait was worn on ordinary occasions.[1] Various attempts at identification of the sitter have been rejected by Ellis Waterhouse.[2]

Provenance: According to the catalogue of the New Assembly Rooms, Brighton, 1867, Oil Paintings, No. 69*, the portrait was in 1867 in the possession of Mr. Tarner.[2] As Professor Waterhouse pointed out, the picture was for about thirty years in a warehouse in Marylebone prior to being sent for sale at Christie's on 18 March, 1921, lot 35; bought W. L. Peacock and A. H. Buttery; acquired in 1921/22 on the advice of Frank Rinder for the Felton Bequest.[3]

References: (1) L. E. Buckell, Journal of the Society of Army Historical Research, Vol. XXVII, 1949, p. 159. (2) Correspondence Ellis Waterhouse—A. J. L. McDonnell—Joseph Burke, Dec. 1953, Jan. 1954, copy on N.G. Victoria files. (3) Rinder corr. 1 Dec., 1924; see also: Ellis Waterhouse, Walpole Society, XXXIII, 1953, p. 90, the same, Gainsborough, 1958, No. 772, pl. 138.

Illust. 88   1840/4 **A View at the Mouth of the Thames**

canvas, 156.2 x 190.5 cm. Unsigned, undated; painted about 1783.

Condition: satisfactory.

Comment: The composition recurs in reverse on a small glass painting which Gainsborough made for his Eidophusikon, a box in which he placed a candle and then showed transparencies. These transparencies are now in the Victoria and Albert Museum.[1] They consist of a series of twelve scenes, two of which are variations on 1840/4; No. 1 of these is closer to 1840/4 than the other.

A similar composition occurs on a drawing in the Department of Prints and Drawings, British Museum (formerly in the possession of William Pearce of Cadogan Gardens).[2]

Ellis Waterhouse points to the unusual nature of the group of seapieces painted by Gainsborough during the last years of his life which foreshadow a tradition later taken up by Morland and Turner.[3]
M. Woodall refers to the affinity of 1840/4 with Dutch marine painting.[4]

Provenance: Exhibited by the artist at the R.A. 1783, No. 240 (as *A Seapiece, a Calm*); probably passed from Robert Palmer (d. 1787) to his daughter, Lady Beauchamp Palmer; exh. R.A. 1878, No. 288, by Sir Reginald Proctor Beauchamp, Langley Park, Norwich, and again by the same owner at the Grosvenor Galleries, 1885, No. 178; sold at Sotheby's, 11 June, 1947, lot 23, bt. Agnew; acquired by the Felton Bequest from Arthur Tooth's on the advice of A. J. L. McDonnell and Sir Kenneth Clark, 1947-8.

References: (1) Ellis Waterhouse, *Gainsborough*, 1958, p. 32, fig. 266, Cat. No. 976; Jonathan Mayne, "Thomas Gainsborough's Exhibition Box," in: *Victoria and Albert Museum Bulletin*, I, 3, 1965, pp. 17-24, fig. 9. (2) Dr. Mary Woodall kindly drew attention to this drawing. (3) Waterhouse, *op. cit.*, pp. 31-2. The same, *Painting in Britain, 1530-1790*, 1953, p. 189. (4) M. Woodall, *Thomas Gainsborough*, London 1949, pp. 99, 101. Waterhouse, *Gainsborough*, 1958, No. 964. Other references: *Quarterly Bulletin N.G. Victoria*, 1949, III, (3), 2; W. Armstrong, *Gainsborough*, 1904, p. 284.

Illust. 89   1204/5 **The Rt. Hon. Charles Wolfran Cornwall**

canvas, 228 x 148.5 cm. Unsigned, undated, painted 1785/6.

Condition: cleaned by Horace Buttery 1961, condition of high standard.[1]

Comment: The sitter was born at Berrington, Herefordshire. Called to the Bar at Gray's Inn, but soon retired from professional life. Member of Parliament from 1768; Lord Treasurer 1774-80; Chief Justice and Privy-Councillor. 1780 Speaker of the House of Commons until his death.[2] Wraxall wrote of him: "Cornwall possessed every physical quality requisite to ornament the place—a sonorous voice, a manly as well as imposing figure and a commanding deportment."[3] Gainsborough shows him wearing the robes of his office and holding a snuff box. The identification of the sitter is traditional and undoubted. Records of the sittings occur in April 1785.[4] Gainsborough painted only two state portraits, this one and that of John, 4th Duke of Argyle, S.A. 1767, in the Scottish National Portrait Gallery.[5]

Provenance: Exhibited by Gainsborough at Schomberg House in 1786;[6] remained in the family of the sitter at their seat at Moccas Court, Herefordshire; included in sale by Sir Geoffrey Cornwall Bt. at Moccas Court by Russell, Baldwin and Bright, 17. VII 1946 (328) bt. in. in recent years on loan to the Shire Hall of Hereford.
Acquired on recommendation of Lord Rennell of Rodd and A. J. L. McDonnell under the terms of the Everard Studley Miller Bequest, 1961/62.[7]

References: (1) *Corr.* N.G. Victoria. (2) *D.N.B.* (3) Sir Nathanial William Wraxall, *The Historical and the Posthumous Memoirs,* London 1884, Vol. I, p. 260. (4) William T. Whitley, *Thomas Gainsborough,* London, 1915, p. 237. (5) Ellis Waterhouse, *Gainsborough,* 1958, No. 164, 62. (6) Whitley, *op. cit.* p. 257. (7) Gallery archives. (8) See also: W. Armstrong, *Gainsborough and his place in English Art,* London, 1898, 193; T. Woodward, *A Picture History of British Painting,* London, 1962, 68 *repr.*; Harley Procton, "Some Recent Acquisitions under the Terms of the Everard Studley Miller Bequest," in *Annual Bulletin, N.G. Victoria,* 1963, 21, *repr.*

Arent (Aert) de Gelder   1645-1727

Dutch. Born Dordrecht. 1660 became pupil of Samuel van Hoogstraten.
In 1661 in Amsterdam as a pupil of Rembrandt's on whose later manner de Gelder based his style. He continued to live in Dordrecht. A drawing by de Gelder is in the Print Room.

Reference: *Th.B.*

Illust. 90   216/4 **King Ahasuerus Condemning Haman**

canvas, 80.5 x 96.5 cm. Signed *A. de Gelder f.* u.r., undated; painted about 1680.[1]

Condition: satisfactory; some repairs at upper left.

Comment: The story of Ahasuerus and Haman is related in the *Book of Esther,* Chs. II-VII. A table with golden cup and a fruit dish indicates the banquet to which Queen Esther had bidden Ahasuerus and Haman. King Ahasuerus, front left, dressed in rembrandtian fancy dress and holding a dagger, is about to rise in wrath against Haman (VII, 7) who is covering his face with his hands, in fear (VII, 8); behind Ahasuerus Queen Esther, who has revealed to the King Haman's plot to destroy the Jewish people in Babylon. The painting is similar in style to de Gelder's *Esther and Mordechai* in the Budapest Museum, which is inscribed 1685.[2]
The subject was much favoured by Rembrandt and his school. For Rembrandt's early treatment of this theme see the article by Seymour Slive.[3]

Provenance: Said to have come from a private owner in Paris; exhibited by Messrs. Douwes, Amsterdam, May 7-June 2, 1934, Cat. No. 19. Acquired on the advice of Bernard Hall for the Felton Bequest in 1934.

References: (1) Dr. H. Gerson gave the suggestion of the date. (2) Dr. Karl Lilienfeld, *Arent de Gelder,* The Hague, 1914, No. 38. (3) Seymour Slive, *The Young Rembrandt* in *Allen Memorial Art Museum Bulletin,* Oberlin, Vol. XX, 1963, No. 3, pp. 139-141.

Jean-Louis-André-Théodore Géricault 1791-1824

French. Born Rouen. In 1808 pupil of Carle Vernet, and later of Pierre Guérin. Studied old master paintings and classical sculpture in the Louvre. 1816-17 in Italy, 1818-19 painted *The Raft of the 'Medusa'*, his most famous work. In London from 1820-22 where he came into contact with Thomas Lawrence and Wilkie, and discovered the landscapes of Constable. Géricault aimed to reconcile the monumental element of classical art with the rendering of reality. Topical subjects, scenes from the Napoleonic wars, horse races, oriental figures painted in a dramatic chiaroscuro which grew freer towards the end of his career, exercised a strong influence on the Romantic movement and particularly on Delacroix (q.v.)

References: Klaus Berger, *Géricault, 1952*; Fritz Novotny, *Painting and Sculpture in Europe, 1780-1880,* 1960.

Illust. 91   3028/4 **The Entombment**

canvas, 80.2 x 64.5 cm. Unsigned, undated.

Condition: very good, except for old damage, u.r.

Comment: Unpublished before 1928.[1] Sir Anthony Blunt calls it "strangely close to an early . . . subject by Guérin at Montpellier",[2] this is reproduced by Antal as *Pietà* 1787 by A. L. Girodet (1767-1824), Musée Fabre, Montpellier.[3] Professor Bernard Smith has investigated the relation between 3028/4 and traditional Entombments and discussed its dating and significance. He reproduces a related preliminary drawing at Besançon.[4]

Provenance: The seal P.D. and the label with the full name of P. Dubaut on back of canvas. Exhibited at Peintres normands, Galerie Hodebert, Paris, 1928 (owner Dubaut); Marie Sterner, New York, Nov., 1936, No. 2 (owner Dubaut); Bernheim-Jeune, Paris, 1937, No. 32 (owner M. P. Dubaut); Marlborough Galleries, London, Oct.-Nov., 1952, No. 4, from where is was acquired by A. J. L. McDonnell and Daryl Lindsay for the Felton Bequest, 1952-3.

References: (1) *L'Art Vivant,* 1 February, 1928, No. 75, p. 116, illus. p. 117; *Géricault,* ed. Braun, pl. 25; Courthion, *Trésors de la Peinture Française,* XIX Siécle, Skira, 1948, pl. 14; *Catalogue, Marlborough Galleries,* 1952, pl. 2; *Quarterly Bulletin, N.G. Victoria,* 1953, VII, (3). (2) A. Blunt, *Géricault at the Marlborough Galleries, Burl. Mag.,* Vol. XCV, 1953, p. 24. (3) F. Antal, *Burl. Mag.,* Vol. LXVIII, 1936, p. 130, pl. la. (4) Bernard Smith, *The Melbourne Géricault* in *Art Bulletin of Victoria,* 1967-68, pp. 5-12; 1968-69, pp. 16-23.

Luca Giordano 1632-1705

Italian. Born Naples; son and pupil of Antonio Giordano. 1665 member of the painters' guild in Naples. Active in Naples, Rome, Florence, Venice and Bergamo. In 1692 he went to Spain to become court painter to King Charles II. 1702 returned to Naples. Painter of mythological, religious and historical subjects.

Reference: *Th.B.*

Illust. 92   214/4 **S. Sebastian**

canvas, 141.7 x 195.2 cm. Unsigned, undated.

Condition: in poor condition, old varnish; numerous re-paints in the background and in some places on the figure of the Saint.

Comment: Previously catalogued as by Ribera. Professor José Milicua of Barcelona and Prof. Martin Soria, Michigan, regard this as an early work of Ribera's pupil Luca Giordano. The picture interprets very freely the compositions of this subject by Ribera in a style characteristic of Luca Giordano. [1]

Provenance: In the possession of Sir Edward Charles Nugent, West Harting Hall, Norfolk;[2] acquired for the Felton Bequest by Bernard Hall from Cecil Rae's Studio in 1934.

References: (1) Correspondence Milicua-Hoff, 4 Jan., 1961, N.G. Victoria files. (2) Felton correspondence, letter 9/1934.

Francisco Goya   1746-1828

Spanish. His full name was Francisco José de Goya y Lucientes. Born at Fuendetodos, near Saragossa. Studied under José Luzán in Saragossa, 1760 and under Francisco Bayeu, 1766 in Madrid. In 1771 in Rome from where he returned to Saragossa in the same year. In Madrid in 1775, worked for the Royal tapestry works until 1791. Deputy director of the Academia of San Fernando, 1785. Appointed *pintor del rey* in 1786 and *pintor de cámara* 1789. In 1799 he became *primer pintor de cámara* and continued in the appointment in the succeeding reigns. Moved to Bordeaux in 1824 where he lived until his death. Goya carried on a decorative and monumental style of painting which he developed under the influence of G. B. Tiepolo *(q.v.).* His use of tonality owes much to his study of Velasquez. Many of his sharply satirical paintings and etchings were inspired by the fight for liberalism in Spain and by the guerrilla warfare of the Spaniards against the invading armies of Napoleon. A set of the 1st edition of the Tauromachia etchings is in the Print Room collection.

References: V. van Loga, *Francisco de Goya,* 1903; *C.N.G.*

Attributed to Goya

Illust. 93   1963/3 **Portrait of a Lady**

canvas, 85 x 70.5 cm. Unsigned, undated.

Condition: satisfactory; old varnish removed by Mr. Holder, London, in 1925.

Comment: The portrait is obviously Goyaesque in character and had been offered by the owner as a Goya to the London National Gallery in 1925. Since the Gallery already possessed a portrait of a woman by Goya, purchase was declined. After acquisition for Melbourne the picture was exhibited at the London National Gallery as by Goya. The owner was not able to furnish documentary evidence of the provenance stated below, and the portrait has not been included in the standard literature on Goya. In the opinion of present-day Goya experts, Signor Enrique Lafuente Ferrari of Madrid and Professor Martin Soria of Michigan University, U.S.A., the detail of handling is uncharacteristic of the master.[1] The portrait is not a copy of a known original by Goya.

Provenance: Acquired for the Felton Bequest in 1925/6 on the advice of Frank Rinder. According to information received at the time of purchase, Count de Pradere had this picture from his godmother, an ancestor of whom had obtained it directly from Goya. The picture was exhibited at the London National Gallery, 19 Oct., 1925 16 Jan., 1926, in the Spanish Room XVII.[2] Arrived in Melbourne March 1926.

References: (1) Correspondence 1955, 1959 N.G. Victoria files. (2) Felton correspondence Rinder, 1925.

El Greco, real name Domenicos Theotocopoulos, 1541-1614

Greek-Spanish. Born probably at Fodele, Crete; presumably had some local training; the style of the 16th century Cretan school, carrying on the Byzantine tradition, is shown in our No. 1980/4 (p. 18). About 1565 El Greco was in Venice where he worked in the studio of Titian and became acquainted with the paintings of Jacopo Bassano (q.v.), Tintoretto (q.v.), Veronese (q.v.); in 1569 documented in Rome. In 1577 in Toledo where he remained until his death. The portrait listed below shows well the mannerist style of the artist with its use of distortion and anti-naturalistic colour and tone.

Reference: Th.B.

Illust. 94   2253/4 **Portrait of a Cardinal**

Condition: originally a three-quarter length portrait, 102.9 x 84 cm. described by Cossio in 1908: "All has been redone without character, except the face which, although overcleaned, remains more true; the eyes, the nose and, above all, the ear."[1] At some time after 1908 the picture was cut down, relined and cleaned. There is evidence of rubbed condition in the face and particularly on the cape where the first three buttons at the top have disappeared.

Comment: As can be seen from the photograph taken in 1902 by Vicente Moreno,[2] the original portrait showed the cardinal near a desk at the left, holding in his right hand a pen over an ink-stand and placing his left hand on an open manuscript. Cossio described the sitter as "S. Bonaventure (?)" and gave the date as 1576-84; Prof. Martin Soria regards it as a portrait from life and, on its stylistic resemblance to the S. Bernardino, Toledo[3] (the date of which is documented as 1603[4]) dates it 1603-4.[5] Harold Wethey calls it "School of El Greco, S. Bonaventure".[6]

69

Provenance: According to Cossio[1] the portrait of the Cardinal was part of the estate of Dalborgo di Primo, Baron del Asilo; it was purchased in 1858 from this estate by the first Marquis de Pidal; in 1902 it was exhibited in the El Greco exhibition in Madrid as No. 2 and as owned by the succeeding Marquis de Pidal, and was still in the Pidal family in 1908 (see Cossio); acquired for the Felton Bequest on the advice of A. J. L. McDonnell and Sir Kenneth Clark from Tomas Harris, London, in 1950.

References: (1) Manuel B. Cossio, *El Greco*, 1908, Vol. I, pp. 572-3; catalogue No. 122. (2) Professor Martin Soria first drew my attention to the Cossio reference and the existence of the old photograph; a print from the Moreno cliché 191, 192, was made available by Senior José Gudiol, Instituto Amattler de Arte Hispanico, Barcelona. (3) Ludwig Goldscheider, *El Greco*, 3rd ed., 1954, pls. 151, 153. (4) See F. de B. de San Roman, *Greco*, 1900, pp. 43-48. (5) Correspondence Soria-Hoff, 1954, N.G. Victoria files. (6) Harold E. Wethey, *El Greco and his School*, 1962, Vol. II, No. X, 243; figs. 243-244. See also: *Quarterly Bulletin, N.G. Victoria*, 1950, IV, (2), 1 *repr.* A. G. Xydis, *A Cardinal by El Greco* in *In Honour of Daryl Lindsay, Essays and Studies*, edited by Franz Philipp and June Stewart, Melbourne, 1964, pp. 62-66.

Francesco Guardi   1712-1793

Italian. Born at Venice, the son of Domenico Guardi. His early works were figure paintings in which he collaborated with his brother Gian Antonio. In 1764 he exhibited Vedute paintings in the Piazza San Marco and from then on gaining a growing reputation for this style of work. The chronology of his work is still tentative.

References: *ThB., C.N.G.*

Illust. 95   3432/3 **Gates of Venice (View of the Venetian Lagoon with the Tower of Malghera)**

panel, 24.3 x 34.9 cm. Unsigned, undated; painted probably in 1770s. Condition: excellent; old varnish removed by Harley Griffiths.

Comment: The gondoliers in the centre are dressed à la Vallona, a kind of livery which indicates that this is a private gondola. Another version in the London National Gallery (No. 2524). Michael Levey identifies the tower as a relic of the ancient Venetian fortifications near Mestre and follows Goering in dating the picture between 1770 and 80.[1] Goering grouped the London National Gallery painting together with Nos. 491, 494, 503, 508 in the Wallace collection.

There is a drawing of the same subject by Guardi in the collection of M. Hippolyte Worms, Paris, but it is certainly derived from Canaletto's etching (Pallucchini-Guarnati 8), whereas the Melbourne picture seems to be an independent view. A drawing at Hamburg[2] is somewhat similar in composition, but is not of the same tower.[3]

Provenance: Acquired from P. M. Abercrombie, Hobart, Tasmania, on the advice of Bernard Hall for the Felton Bequest, 1927.

References: (1) Michael Levey, *The Eighteenth Century Italian Schools,* C.N.G., p. 60. M. Levey, *The Seventeenth and Eighteenth Century Italian Schools,* National Gallery Catalogues, London, 1971, No. 2524. (2) J. Byam Shaw, *The Drawings of Francesco Guardi,* London, 1951, pl. 68. (3) Information supplied by Mr. J. Byam Shaw.

Illust. 96   229/4 **The Lock at Dolo on the Brenta: Cappriccio**

canvas, 39.5 x 32.5 cm. Unsigned, undated; painted late 70s or 80s.[1]

Condition: excellent

Comment: Previously known as *Canal Scene with Bridge*.[2] The following other versions of this composition are known:
(1) Oblong drawing in the Museo Correr (Pallucchini 90).[3] It is inscribed, apparently in G's own hand, *Veduta delle Porte del Dolo p(per) andar a Padova* (View of the lock gates at Dolo on the way to Padua). 26.6cm x 38.4cm.

(2) Oblong oil belonging to Mr. Dudley Tooth, corresponding, with only minor variations in the figures, to the Correr drawing. 24.1cm x 33.7cm.[4]

(3) Oblong oil in the Fauchier-Magnan Sale, Sotheby, 4 Sept., 1935, lot 81 (bought by Mrs. Assheton Bennett). 19.4cm x 24.5cm.[5]

(4) Oblong oil, National Gallery, Budapest, 14.5cm x 18.5cm.[6]

(5) Upright small oil, Gulbenkian Foundation, Lisbon. 18cm x 14cm.[7]

(6) Upright oil ascribed to an imitator of G. Guardi.[8]

In the Melbourne and Gulbenkian versions the composition is concertinaed to fit the upright format. The lighting is more dramatic, and there are further variations in the figures; but the figures on the bank in the left foreground correspond more or less to those in Nos. 1 and 5 above, whereas there are no figures at this place in any of the other paintings.

The inscription on the Correr drawing suggests that this is a *real view* but it bears no resemblance to Canaletto's well known etched view of the subject,[9] and Pallucchini describes it as a cappriccio.[10]

Provenance: An old label on the back shows that the picture was in the possession of P. and D. Colnaghi, Comp., before 1890. According to N.G. Victoria files, 1934, owned by W. Wilkes of Leamington. Acquired for the Felton Bequest on the advice of Bernard Hall 1934/5, from Messrs. Asscher and Welker, London.

References: (1) Listed by Pallucchini among works of this period. R. Pallucchini, *Note alla Mostra dei Guardi* in *Arte Veneta,* Vol. XIX, 1965, p. 234, No. 138. (2) *Catalogue of the National Gallery of Victoria,* 1948, p. 62. (3) Pallucchini, *I disegni del Guardi al Museo Correr de Venezia,* Venice, 1943, (not seen). (4) R. Pallucchini, 'Note alla Mostra dei Guardi' *Arte Veneta,* Vol. XIX, 1965, p. 234. (5) *Catalogue of Paintings and Drawings from the Assheton Bennett Collection,* City of Manchester Art Gallery, 1965, No. 82, pl. XXIII, *The*

Bridge over the Brenta at Dolo, closely related to 229/4; cf. under No. 81; Pallucchini *op. cit.* (8) G. Fiocco, *F. Guardi,* 1922, pl. CXX, fig. 141 and *Pallucchini, op. cit.* (9) Information Budapest, 1967, p. 295 (not seen). (7) Gulbenkian Catalogue No. X and Pallucchini, *op. cit.* (8) G. Fiocco, *F. Guardi,* 1922, pl. CXX, fig. 141 and Pallucchini, *op. cit.* (9) Information kindly supplied by Mr. J. Byam Shaw. (10) Pallucchini, *op. cit.*

Benjamin Robert Haydon   1786-1846

British. Born at Plymouth. In 1806 became an evening student at the R.A. schools. Aimed at being a history painter but found little support. His friends included most of the major writers of his time and the two Landseers, Eastlake, Bewick and Harvey were among his pupils. Always in financial difficulties, he was deeply disappointed at his failure to obtain the commission for the decoration of the Houses of Parliament in 1841. When an exhibition of his cartoons for this project met with public indifference, he committed suicide.

Reference: *Th.B.*

Illust. 97   40/2 **Marcus Curtius**

canvas, 76.5 x 63.5 cm. Signed on back and dated 1843.

Condition: badly blistered near lower margin. Two holes.

Comment: The picture was listed in the 1948 catalogue as "Mettus" Curtius; it represents however Marcus Curtius, who "mounted on a horse . . . plunged fully armed into the gulf" which had opened up in the middle of the Forum in Rome.[1]

From Haydon's journal we know that he was working on a picture of Curtius on 27 January, 1842;[2] this (large) picture was exhibited at the British Institution of 1843 and at the Pantheon in 1846[3] and hung later in the billiard room of Gatti's Restaurant in the Strand: it is now in the Royal Albert Museum, Exeter.[4]

A sketch of the Curtius together with a portrait of Wordsworth was sent by Haydon to Miss Elizabeth Barrett (Browning) in January 1843.[5] After the completion of the big picture he sent her another sketch;[6] both sketches are referred to by Elizabeth Barrett in a letter of 1 January, 1843: "Curtius fulfills my idea from your first sketch—and it strikes me that you have happily seized the balance of the moment when the horse begins to sink, losing its muscular command and power of animal life—while the man-will reigns right royally unto death".[7] Our picture which is a small and rather close repetition of the large painting may well be the second sketch sent to Elizabeth Barrett.

Provenance: It is possible that the picture was taken to Australia by R. Twentyman, a London businessman who—together with Bennock—was a patron of Haydon in his last years. Twentyman came to Australia in 1846 or 47 and brought with him several of Haydon's paintings.[8] The Curtis sketch may have been among them. It was acquired on the advice of Bernard Hall from the Robert Wallen estate, sold 15 Dec., 1897, at Gemmell and Tucketts in Melbourne.

72

References: (1) Livy, *History of Rome,* Book VII, ch. VI. (2) *The Autobiography and Memoirs of Benjamin Robert Haydon,* ed. A. P. D. Penrose, 1927, pp. 552, 563. (3) *ibid.,* pp. 565, 566, 619. (4) Clarke Olney, *Benjamin Robert Haydon,* 1952, p. 259, fig. 284. (5) *Autobiography, op. cit.,* p. 563. (6) This is possibly the sketch referred to in the *Autobiography, op. cit.,* p. 570. (7) *Letters from Elizabeth Barrett to B. R. Haydon,* ed. Hale Shackforth, 1939, p. 12. (8) Eric George, *The Life and Death of Benjamin Robert Haydon,* 1948, preface.

Jan Davidsz de Heem   1606-1683-84

Dutch-Flemish. Born at Utrecht; pupil of Balthasar van der Ast, 1625-c. 1629 in Leyden. In 1030 admitted to the guild of St. Luke in Antwerp. After 1050 the records show that he was often absent from Antwerp. Member of the Guild of St. Luke in Utrecht from 1669-1672; returned to Antwerp where he remained until his death. His early works resemble the simple plates with fruit and bowls of flowers by van der Ast. Most of the extant work of the Leyden period consists of Vanitas paintings. From 1628-30 date some still lifes in the manner of the Haarlem School. Sandraert suggests that de Heem went to Antwerp: "Since one could have there rare fruits of all kinds."

Tables laden with exotic fruits on precious dishes of silver and Delft ware, accompanied by Venetian type and Dutch glasses and Delft ware of silver cups and goblets form one of de Heem's frequent subjects after his removal to Antwerp. The painting listed below belongs to the simpler type of compositions painted by the artist in the 40s. Other types that occur in his later works are: cartouche frames decorated with flowers or fruit; garlands and hanging bouquets; flowerpieces. In these works Dutch and Flemish traditions mingle.

Reference: Ingvar Bergström, *Dutch Still Life Painting,* 1956, pp. 191-214.

Illust. 98   231/4 **Still Life with Fruit**

canvas, 67 x 78.8 cm. Signed upper right *J. D. de Heem f.* Undated; probably painted in the sixteen-forties.

Condition: in good condition.

Comment: The following objects appear in the picture from left to right; vessels: a *roemer,* Dutch, 17th century, green glass, cylindical stem with two rows of four large flat prunts, the stem supported on a short, coil-wound foot. A similar glass is in the Jerome Strauss Collection, New York;[1] *flute,* a tall drinking glass, Venetian type, Dutch, 17th century; this resembles in shape the glass with portrait of Frederick Henry of Orange (1625-47) in the Rijksmuseum, Amsterdam;[2] cup with cover, silver gilt, German, 17th century. The dish and bowl are Delft ware, 17th century. A similar *roemer* and *flute* appear in a painting by de Heem in the Royal Castle, Stockholm, painted probably in the late 40s;[3] a similar German covered cup, together with a *flute,* and a dish of Delft ware in a painting at Koetser's in 1960.[4]

G

Provenance: In the Comte deL'Espine and Princesse de Croy Collections, Paris;[5] acquired on the advice of Bernard Hall for the Felton Bequest from O. Hirschmann, Amsterdam, in 1934/5.

References: (1) *Glass Drinking Vessels from the Strauss Collection. The Corning Museum of Glass,* New York, 1955, Exh. Cat. No. 96, 6⅜ in. h. (2) N. Hudson Moore, *Old Glass, European and American,* 1926, p. 76, fig. 32. (3) Ingvar Bergström, *Dutch Still Life Painting,* 1956, fig. 171. (4) Photograph in N.G. Victoria files. (5) Felton Correspondence, Hall, 1934.

Egbert van Heemskerk   1634/5-1704

Dutch. Apparently born at Haarlem; said to have been a pupil of Pieter de Grebber in Haarlem; 1663 (28 years of age) in The Hague; 1665 (31 years of age) in Amsterdam; later settled in London under the patronage of Lord Rochester. In England he painted satirical recruiting scenes, concerts, picture auctions and other subjects from popular life; Antal claims him as an important link between the Dutch school and Hogarth. According to Walpole died 1704 in London.

References: A. v. Wurzbach, *Niederländisches Künstlerlexikon,* Vienna, Leipzig 1900. F. Antal, *Hogarth and His Place in European Art,* London, 1962, pp. 55, 61-2.

Illust. 99   1444/5 **Family Group in a Landscape**

canvas, 87.6 v 102.3 cm (stretcher) signed with monogram and dated 1966 lower right.

Condition: good.

Comment: The attribution was confirmed in 1930 by Dr. Hofstede de Groot.[1] Remarkable are the elements of playfulness and intimacy: the mother, exchanging a glance with her husband, amuses the baby on her lap with what appears to be a rattle. The elder daughter, held by the hand by her father, tries to attract the baby's attention with two cherries; the younger daughter to the left smilingly teaches the dog to sit on his hind-legs. A children's toy cart lies in the right foreground. The informality of the group in a natural setting foreshadows the English 18th century conversation piece.

Provenance: Collection Count Zoubov, Leningrad; transferred to Berlin after 1918; after 1924 owner coll. Dr. Maurice Laserson, Berlin, who brought the picture to Sydney in 1940; Contemporary Art Society Loan Exhibition, Sydney 1950, owner Dr. Maurice Laserson; acquired from Mrs. M. Laserson for the Felton Bequest on the advice of Dr. Ursula Hoff in 1965.[2]

References: (1) Archives N.G. Victoria; corr. Westbrook-Laserson 1965. (2) *ibid.*

John Frederick Herring   1795-1865

British. Born at Meopham Park near Tunbridge Wells, Kent. Worked as sign and coach painter for his father, an American merchant of Dutch origin.

Drove a mailcoach between Wakefield and Lincoln, later between Doncaster and Halifax and finally between York and London. Continued to paint, mainly horses. Pupil of the horse painter, A. Cooper, in Doncaster. 1830 moved to Newmarket, 1833 to London. Exhibited at the R.A. from 1818, also at the British Institution and the Society of British Artists of which he became a member from 1841-1852. Became court painter to the Duchess of Kent. Also painted hunting scenes for William Taylor Copeland, owner of the Spode Potteries, which were reproduced on Spode china and earthenware.

Reference: Th.B.

Illust. 100   300/1 **Horses and Pigs, 1864**

canvas, 35.6 x 61.5 cm. Unsigned, undated.

Condition: cleaned by Harley Griffiths 1960, excellent.

Comment: One of the group of eleven paintings which were the first to be acquired for this Gallery.[1]

Provenance: Purchased by Sir Charles Eastlake, President of the Royal Academy, from exh. at the R.A. 1864, No. 248.[2]

References: (1) *Quarterly Bulletin N.G. Victoria,* 1948, III, (1), 2. (2) Fine Arts Commission, receipt 31 June, 1864. State Library of Victoria Archives; picture listed in Th.B. 1923.

Illust. 101   1741A/4 **Cleveland Bays**

canvas, 86 x 111.4 cm. Signed and dated *J. F. Herring snr. 1852,* left, on stable partition.

Condition: good, but some flaking in lower centre.

Provenance: Purchased by Daryl Lindsay in 1947 in London.

Reference: Daryl Lindsay, *Quarterly Bulletin N.G. Victoria,* 1952, VI, (2) 5.

Joseph Highmore   1692-1780

British. Born at London. His uncle, William, was Sergeant Painter to King William, but did not teach him. Articled as clerk to an attorney in 1707;[1] in 1713 left the law to study painting, and joined Kneller's Academy about 1714-15.[2] In 1715 he established himself in the city of London as a painter;[3] Vertue and Walpole relate that he was "much employed there for family pieces".[4] His first dated portrait is from 1721.[5] In 1720 and later he must have studied at the St. Martin's Lane Academy, conducted by Chéron and Vanderbank and there met Hogarth, who joined this academy in the same year.[6] In 1723-4 he moved from the city of London to Lincoln's Inn Fields.[7] In 1726 he drew the procession of the *Knights of the Bath* to be engraved by John Pine. Walpole and *The Gentleman's Magazine* also refer to some painted portraits of the Knights carried out at the same time.[8] According to *The Gentleman's Magazine* he made, together with friends, a journey to Düsseldorf and Antwerp in 1732, where he saw the work of Rubens on whom he later wrote two articles.[9] According to the same source went to Paris in 1734. His Pamela series 1741-5 through which he later met the author, Samuel Richardson,[10] reveals his close scrutiny of the work of Gravelot who was in England 1732-45. On the marriage of his daughter to the Rev. John Duncombe of Canterbury in 1761, Highmore gave up his Lincoln's Inn residence and moved, in 1762, to Canterbury, where he spent the remainder of his life.[11]

Highmore's portraits impressed his contemporaries by their naturalness; Vertue noted that he painted his faces at one sitting, his hands and drapery from life: "If any thing is wanting tis painting in a greater stile."[12]

References: (1) *Vertue Note Books, Walpole Society,* Vol. XXII, 1934, p. 17; *The Gentleman's Magazine,* Vol. L, 1780, p. 176 (quoted as G.M. below). Prof. Joseph Burke supplied the reference to the sources used in this entry. (2) Vertue, *loc. cit.,* p. 17 (no year given), p. 29, "came into the Academy under Sir G. Kneller about ye 3rd or fourth Year after it was set up" (1711); *G.M. loc. cit.,* implies that he entered the Academy while still a clerk "where he drew 10 years"; "on June 13, 1714, his clerkship expired"; H. Walpole, *Anecdotes of Painting in England,* ed. R. N. Wornum, 1888, Vol. II, p. 322, "under whom (Kneller) he entered the Academy." (3) *G.M., loc. cit.,* "March 26, 1715"; *Vertue, loc. cit.,* p. 29. (4) *Vertue, loc. cit.,* p. 29; *Walpole, op. cit.,* p. 323. (5) J. W. Goodison, *Burl. Mag.,* Vol. LXXII, 1938, p. 125. (6) British Museum Add. Ms. 23082. Other evidence for connections between Highmore and Hogarth is to be found in Hogarth's scheme for presenting works of art to the Foundling Hospital, for which Highmore painted *Hagar and Ishmael,* exhibited in 1747; R. H. Nichols, F. A. Wray, *The History of the Foundling Hospital,* 1935; p. 251; *Vertue, loc cit.,* p. 135. (7) *Vertue, loc. cit.,* p. 29, 39; no date; *G.M., loc. cit.,* "1723-4." (8) *Vertue, loc. cit.,* p. 29/30, 37; *Walpole, op cit.,* p. 323; *G.M., loc. cit.* (9) Remarks on some Passages in Mr. Webb's Enquiries into the Beauty of Painting, *G.M.,* 1766, p. 353; note to an Epistle to an Eminent Painter, *G.M.,* 1778, p. 526. (10) W. T. Whitley, *Artists and their Friends in England,* Vol. I, 1928, p. 47. (11) *G.M., loc. cit.,* p. 178. (12) *Vertue, loc. cit.,* pp. 17, 29.

Illust. 102   398/5 **Samuel Booth, Messenger of the Order of the Bath**

canvas, 126.8 x 101.3 cm. Unsigned, undated; painted 1732.

Condition: excellent. Cleaned prior to purchase.

Comment: The sitter, d. 1737, was Steward to the Duke of Montague, who was the first (and only) great master of the Order of the Bath, as revived in 1725. Booth was the first to be appointed messenger to the Order of the Bath. He wears over his ordinary clothes the esquire's white surcoat with a badge of three crowns upon a plain blue shield and seems to be carrying a flat hat in Tudor style.[1]

Provenance: Descended through the Booth family of Glendon Hall, Northants, to Mrs. Gompertz; sale 22 May, 1953, lot 66, as T. Hudson, bt. Leadbeater; exhibited at Leggatts, 1956; R. A. Winter Exh. 1956/7, No. 193 (anon. owner); acquired on the advice of A. J. L. McDonnell from Messrs. Gooden and Fox, for the Everard Studley Miller Bequest 1959/60.

References: (1) J. L. Nevinson, *The Connoisseur,* Vol. CXXXIV, 1954, p. 153 *seq.*; p. 159, fig. 12 *(as unidentified gentleman by Th. Hudson).* Sitter identified in Cat. R.A. 1956/7, *British Portraits* No. 193 (Ellis Waterhouse); see also *Annual Bulletin N.G. Victoria* 1960, Vol. II, p. 17.

Illust. 103   1760/4 **Self Portrait**

canvas, 126.4 x 101 cm. Unsigned, undated; painted between 1745-47.

Condition: very good.

Comment: Antal[1] compared this self portrait with the one in *Mr. Oldham und his Friends* in the Tate Gallery which from stylistic evidence he dates "in the 40s or even 50s." Highmore appears to be considerably younger in the Melbourne portrait.[2]

Provenance: See under 1761/4.

Exhibitions: *Paintings by Joseph Highmore 1692-1780,* The Iveagh Bequest, Kenwood, London County Council 1963, No. 3.

References: (1) F. Antal, *Burl. Mag.,* Vol. XCI, 1949, p. 131, fig. 7. (2) The dating adopted was suggested by Prof. Ellis Waterhouse. See also: *Quarterly Bulletin, N.G. Victoria,* 1947, II, (4), 4.

Illust. 104   1759/4 **Anthony Highmore** (1718-1799)

canvas, 126.4 x 101.3 cm. Unsigned, undated; painted between 1745-47.

Condition: very good.

Comment: Anthony Highmore, a legal writer, was the only son of Joseph Highmore; the identification, traditional in the family, is not quite certain. The picture bears a close resemblance to the portrait of a young man in the Tate Gallery dated 1747. Dating suggested by Prof. Ellis Waterhouse.

Provenance: See under 1761/4.

Reference: See *Quarterly Bulletin, N.G. Victoria,* 1947, II, (4), 4 repr.

Illust. 105   1761/4 **Portrait of a Young Girl**

canvas, 91.5 x 71.1 cm. Unsigned, undated; painted between 1745-50.

Condition: very good.

Comment: The girl is represented with her favourite possessions: she holds up a miniature of a girl in fancy dress; on the Queen Anne side table a scrap book with cut-outs of a lady and a gentleman in fashionable attire and a tortoiseshell cat; at the back a bookcase; above, a black and red parrot in a ring. The portrait may perhaps be said to resemble in type the self-portrait of George Vertue, who holds a miniature of Lord Oxford in his hand and has represented himself with the emblems of his profession.[1]

Provenance: The three portraits 1759/4, 1760/4, 1761/4 have descended through the Highmore family. Mr. Highmore King of London, Mr. Morgan Payler, Melbourne, and Mr. Gordon Thomson provided the following information: Joseph Highmore's son, Anthony Highmore (1718-1799), had a son (4th child), John Field Highmore (30 June, 1749-June, 1794), whose daughter, Maria (b. 12 June, 1783), married the Rev. William Payler,[2] rector of Patricksbourne and Bridge, Kent, on 12 May, 1806, at St. Mildred's, Canterbury; she died on 18 June, 1814. Their daughter, Charlotte Clara (b. 7 January, 1809), married the Rev. F. Morgan of Biddelsden Park, Bucks, who took the name Payler in addition to his own, the surname becoming Morgan Paylor. One of his sons, Frederick Morgan Payler, was the father of Frederick Trafford Morgan Payler, 1872-1954, Archdeacon of Ballarat, Victoria, Australia. The three portraits were inherited by him together with other paintings by Highmore; the portraits were acquired for the Felton Bequest on the advice of Daryl Lindsay in 1947.

Exhibitions: *Paintings by Joseph Highmore, 1692-1780,* The Iveagh Bequest, Kenwood, London County Council 1963, No. 14, pl. III B.

References: (1) Vertue Notebooks, I, *The Walpole Society,* 1929/30, Vol. XVIII, frontispiece. See also: *Quarterly Bulletin, N.G. Victoria,* 1947, II, (4), 4 repr. (2) It is of interest to note that already in 1780 *The Gentleman's Magazine,* Vol. L, p. 178, mentions a painting by Highmore as *"now in the possession of Thomas Watkinson Payler Esq. at Ileden in Kent."* Theodore Crombie, *Highmore at Highgate, Apollo,* Vol. 78, 1963, 135 repr.

Illust. 106   1114/3   1. **Pamela Fainting**
                            No. 3 of series.
                            63.5 x 76.2 cm.

Illust. 107   1115/3   2. **Pamela Preparing to go home**
                            No. 4 of series.
                            63.5 x 76.2 cm.

Illust. 108   1116/3   3. **Pamela Greets Her Father**
                            No. 8 of series.
                            63.5 x 76.2 cm.

Illust. 109   1117/3   4. **Pamela and Lady Davers**
                            No. 10 of series.
                            63.5 x 76.2 cm.

canvas. Original frames; unsigned, undated; painted 1741-5.

Condition: good, old varnish.

Comment: The pictures are illustrations to Richardson's novel, *Pamela.* Pamela Andrews is a servant maid in an English country house. Her mistress has died; her new master, young Squire B, makes repeated attempts to seduce her. In No. 1 the Squire has entered the bedroom in which the housekeeper, Mrs. Jervis, and Pamela sleep together. Pamela has fainted and Mrs. Jervis exclaims "my poor Pamela is dead for certain" (Shakespeare Head Press ed. 1929, Vol. 1, letter XXV, p. 80). The Squire, apparently tired of her resistance, pretends to send her home. Pamela (No. 2), in the simple clothes she made for herself, carrying

the *Shepherdess* hat of the period stands in the green room before
Mrs. Jervis; at her feet the clothes her mistress and her master gave her;
she refuses to take them with her: the former because they did not befit
her, the latter because they were meant as "the price of shame". The
third parcel contains her own modest belongings: "Come to my Arms,
my dear third parcel, the Companion of my Poverty and the Witness of
my Honesty . . . so I hugg'd my third bundle" (Vol. I, p. 99, 102, letter
XXIX). The Squire, however, has Pamela sent to another of his residences,
and after further fruitless attempts at seduction, decides to marry her.
Pamela's father, worried about the fate of his daughter, goes to visit her
and is kindly received by the Squire who introduces him to a party of
guests. Pamela is called down to participate in a card game. Unaware
of her father's presence, she sits down. Presently "I knew his Voice and
lifting up my Eyes and seeing my father, gave a Spring, overturn'd the
Table without Regard to the Company and threw myself at his feet"
(No. 3). (Vol. II, p. 73).

The Squire secretly marries Pamela. During his absence from home,
his sister, Lady Davers, who disapproves of the marriage on account
of Pamela's low social origin, arrives with her nephew. After a long
conversation in which Pamela bravely holds her own, "she gave me
a slap on the Hand and reached to box my Ears; but Mrs. Jewkes
(householder) hearkening without, and her Woman too, they both came
in at that Instant" and interposed themselves between Lady Davers and
Pamela (No. 4), (Vol. II, p. 195-216).

The first edition of Richardson's novel was published in 1741.[1] Highmore
made twelve illustrations; Nos. 2, 5, 6, 12 are in the Fitzwilliam Museum,
Cambridge. Nos. 1, 7, 9, 11 are at the Tate Gallery, London.[2] On 22
February, 1744, Highmore advertised prints illustrating the novel;[3] he
quoted the subscription price and continued: "ten of the pictures being
already finished and may now be seen at Mr. Highmore's house, the Two
Lions, in Lincoln's Inn Fields, where subscriptions are taken in".
The engravings were made by A. (or C. L.) Benoist[4] (1st half 18th century),
and L. Truchy (1721-1764); they are dated 1 July, 1745 (a set of the 1762
ed. in the Print Room collection).

Highmore's pictures show a general resemblance to the illustrations
engraved by F. Hayman and Gravelot for the 6th edition of Richardson's
novel in 1742. Nos. 2 and 3 show similar disposition of figures and
comparable types. Highmore illustrates the narrative more closely and
more dramatically, and character heads in No. 3 (the old man in wig in right
background) and No. 4 (Mrs. Jewkes) reflect the influence of Hogarth. The
rococo lightness of touch, as Ellis Waterhouse has pointed out, is evidence
of the influence of Gravelot.[5] No. 2 compares with Gravelot, *Le Lecteur*
(York Art Gallery).[5a]

Provenance: The original series of 12 paintings was still in Highmore's house in
February, 1750;[6] they were listed as *Illustrations to Clarissa Harlowe by C. Troost,* from the
collection of Major Dermont McCalmont, Cheveley Park, Newmarket, at Christies, 26 Nov.,

1920, lot 130; bt. Peacock for A. H. Buttery; they were identified by C. H. Collins Baker prior to sale[7] and through Frank Rinder were divided between the London National Gallery, the Fitzwilliam Museum, Cambridge and the Felton Bequest in 1921.

Exhibitions: *Paintings by Joseph Highmore,* The Iveagh Bequest, Kenwood, London County Council, 1963, Nos. 17, 18, 22, 24.

References: (1) The date of publication is wrongly given as 1744 in the *Gentleman's Magazine,* 1780, Vol. L, p. 177. (2) Tate Gallery Catalogue, 1953, p. 95, Nos. 3573-3576. (3) *London Daily Post and Advertiser,* February 22, 1743-4. (4) The engraver signs his name A. Benoist on the engravings; in the article on Truchy in Thieme Becker, Vol. XXXIII, 1939, p. 446, Truchy's collaborator on the Pamela engravings is referred to as C. L. Benoist; Nagler, *Künstlerlexikon,* Vol. I, 1835-1852, p. 416, says that C. L. "Benoit" went to London in 1712, and returned later to Paris. (5) Ellis Waterhouse, *Painting in Britain, 1530-1790,* 1953, p. 136. (5a) *Paintings by Joseph Highmore,* Iveagh Bequest Kenwood. London County Council, 1963, Cat. p. 23. (6) *Correspondence of Samuel Richardson,* ed. A. L. Barbauld, Vol. IV, 1804, p. 362; Richardson to Lady Braidshaigh, 15 Feb., 1749-50, *"Mr. Highmore told me that a promise of another visit was made, against which he was to take out the historical paintings of Pamela."* (7) *Times Literary Supplement,* 16 Dec., 1920; *The Connoisseur,* Vol. LX, 1921, pp. 39, 40. For the glassware in No. 4 see G. Bernhard Hughes, *English, Scottish and Irish Tableglass,* London 1956, pp. 292/3.

Meindert Hobbema   1638-1709

Dutch. Born at Amsterdam. Apprenticed to Jacob van Ruisdael. Established in Amsterdam but painted also around Haarlem, Deventer, Middleharnis and the eastern provinces of Holland. In 1668 became one of the winegaugers in Amsterdam and retained this post until his death. His painting activities continued after 1668 but grew noticeably less.

Reference: *C.N.G.*

Illust. 110   2252/4 **The Old Oak**

canvas, 101 x 144 cm. Signed and dated *M. Hobbema f* 1662 lower left.

Condition: excellent, cleaned prior to purchase.

Comment: 2252/4 also often referred to as *The Swamp*[1] marks the year of Jacob van Ruisdael's strongest influence on Hobbema. As Stechow has shown, the artist's early pictures, dating from 1658-1661, consisting of river scenes and spindly trees, were light in tone. The heavy dark browns seen in 2252/4 are characteristic of the first impact of Ruisdael's work.[2] The composition closely reflects Ruisdael's etching, *The Travellers* (B.4). Rosenberg has quoted documents to show that Hobbema had been Ruisdael's pupil at one time.[3] Stechow refers to another version of 2252/4 in the collection Schloss Rohoncz, Lugano, with different figures and small differences in the landscape motifs, which is signed but not dated.[4]

Provenance: According to notes in the Heris sale catalogue of 25 March 1841, the picture and its companion piece (Hofstede 100) were painted by Hobbema for the ancestor of Jonckheer Alberda, Castle Dijksterhuis near Pieterburen (Groningen); since 1834 owned by van Arnhem and Gockinga in Groningen;[5] auctioned by Heris (Biré) in Paris, 25 March, 1841, lot 1 (bt. in);[6] owner Col. Biré of Brussels. Lauters, who lithographed the painting for the sale catalogue, states that he made the collection for Col. Biré;[7] reproduced in an engraving by Tamisier in Dr. J. van Vloten, *Nederlands Schilderkunst voor het nederlandsche Volk geschechtst,* Amsterdam, 1874, p. 327; sale Paris (Drouot) 25.5.1945, A. repr.;[8] acquired from Thomas Agnew and Sons on the advice of A. J. L. McDonnell and Sir Kenneth Clark for the Felton Bequest in 1949/50.

References: (1) Thus in W. Stechow, *Dutch Landscape Painting of the Seventeenth Century, London 1966, p. 78, Jacob Rosenberg, Seymour Slive, E. H. Ter Kuile, Dutch Art and Architecture, The Pelican History of Art, Hardmondsworth, 1966, p. 157.* (2) W. Stechow, *The Art Quarterly,* 1959, Vol. XXII, p. 10 f. (3) J. Rosenberg, *Jahrbuch der Preussischen Kunstsammlungen,* Vol. 48, 1927, pp. 139 *seq.* No. 11. (4) *Stechow, 1966 loc. cit.; Catalogue Sammlung Thyssen-Bornemisza,* exh. Museum Folkwang, Essen, 1960, No. 84 pl. 91 and bibl. (5) Hofstede de Groot, *Verzeichnis der Holländischen Maler,* 1911, Nos. 100, 132, and bibl. *Catalogue of Dutch Paintings,* 1912, Vol. IV, Nos. 100, 132 and bibl. (6) *ibid.* No. 132. (7) 2252/4 must have been mentioned in an article in *La Renaissance,* Vol. II, 1839 (not seen). (8) See also G. Broulhiet, *Meindert Hobbema, Paris,* 1938, No. 224 (Thyssen) repr.; No. 225 (Melbourne) repr.; *Quarterly Bulletin, N.G. Victoria,* 1950, IV, (2), 3.

Melchior de Hondecoeter   1636-1695

Dutch. Born at Utrecht. Grandson of the landscape painter, Gillis de Hondecoeter; son and pupil of the landscape and bird painter, Gysbert de Hondecoeter (d. 1653); nephew of Jan Baptist Weenix (1642-1719) whose Italian scenes are believed to have exerted an influence on Hondecoeter. Worked at The Hague by 1659; settled in Amsterdam in 1663. Specialised in the genre of birds.

Reference: *C.N.G.*

Illust. 111   1067/3 **The Poultry Yard**

canvas, 148.2 x 170.3 cm. Signed *M. D. Hondecoeter* behind cock on stone in centre; undated.

Condition: excellent; old varnish removed in 1920.

Comment: In the entry for this picture in the Lansdown Tower sale of 1841, reference was made to "the magnificent landscape, evidently by Both" (see under provenance). While there is no reason to assume that the landscape is by a different hand, it is certainly Italianate in character, giving a grand manner setting to the rare fowl depicted in the foreground

J. B. Decamps relates an anecdote that Hondecoeter had trained a cock to stand model; the artist could bend the cock's head with the mahlstick this way and that; open his wings etc. and he remained like this until the master got up.[1]

A canvas of similar subject, 81½ cm. x 103 cm.; was at P. de Boer's, Amsterdam, in 1963-4, *Wintertentoonstelling,* Cat. No. 15, Illust. 20; architecture and distance are similar, the big flying bird, the hen crouching on the sill, the fighting cock lower left are comparable.

Provenance: The picture was seen by Waagen "at Mr. Beckford's Tower in Bath" in 1838;[1a] it was listed in the Lansdown Tower sale, 4 Jan., 1841, lot 17 (size given as 5 ft. 6 in. x 4 ft. 9½ in.), £111; no purchaser's name is recorded here; it was listed again in the Lansdown Tower sale, 20 November, 1845, lot 324 (size 57 in. x 66 in.), buyer Labouchère, £185; in 1850 it was seen by Waagen at Quantock Lodge, the home of Henry Labouchère, afterwards Lord Taunton;[2] the same owner exhibited the picture at the Manchester Art Treasures Exhibition, 1857, No. 863. It was acquired on the advice of Frank Rinder from A. H. Buttery, who acted as agent for the family of the late Lord Taunton, in 1920 for the Felton Bequest.

References: (1) J. B. Decamps, *la vie des peintres flamands, allemands et hollandais,* Paris 1660, Vol. 3, quoted in: Melchior de Hondecoeter, *Gemäldegalerie der Akademie der bildenden Künste in Wien,* XVI, Sonderausstellung, Wien 1968, (booklet). ([1a]) G. F. Waagen, *Works of Art and Artists in England,* Vol. III, 1838, p. 115; William Beckford, 1759-1844, the author of "Vathek." (2) G. F. Waagen, *Treasures of Art in Great Britain,* Vol. II, 1854, p. 422 (seen on his visit to Quantock Lodge in 1850). See also: *Quarterly Bulletin N.G. Victoria,* 1945, 1, (3), 4; *Masterpieces,* pp. 50, 51 repr.

John Hoppner   c. 1758-1810

English. Born at Whitechapel. Pupil at the Royal Academy in 1775. Became painter to the Prince of Wales in 1793; R.A. 1795. Hoppner was the follower of Reynolds *(q.v.)* and the rival of Lawrence *(q.v.).*

Illust. 112   4659/3 **Portrait of a Lady**

canvas, 76.9 x 63.5 cm. Unsigned, undated. Painted about 1795[1]

Condition: satisfactory; some re-paints in the background.

Comment: A large coloured mezzotint by Percy Martindale of this picture is in the Print Room collection.

Provenance: John James Robert Manners, 7th Duke of Rutland, d. 1906, who acquired the portrait at a small dealer's sale in Worthing about 1876/7;[2] Lady Victoria Manners, from whom the portrait was acquired for the Felton Bequest on the advice of Randall Davies in 1931/32.

References: (1) W. McKay, W. Roberts, *John Hoppner,* 1909, p. 289; *The Connoisseur,* Vol. XXIV, 1909, p. 78 repr. The dating kindly suggested by Professor Ellis Waterhouse, letter to Hoff, 2. IX, 66. (2) Waterhouse *ibid.*

Attributed to Hoppner

Illust. 113   541/2 **Mrs. Mary Robinson, "Perdita" (?)**

canvas, 76.8 x 63.8 cm stretcher size, unsigned, undated, painted about 1785-6.[1]

Condition: cleaned about 1909;[2] darkened varnish; re-lined; painting cut noticeably at the lower edge.

Comment: The presumed sitter, Mary Derby (1758-1800), married to Thomas Robinson in 1774, was an actress at the Drury Lane Theatre. In her last role as Perdita in the *Winter's Tale* she attracted the attention of the Prince of Wales who corresponded with her under the name of Florizel and made her his mistress.[3]
While the picture was in the Pleydell-Bouverie collection the sitter was known as *Mrs. Abington*; this was changed to *Mrs. Robinson* after the sale of the Pleydell-Bouverie collection in 1907; according to Ellis Waterhouse this identification of the sitter is not convincing.[4] This picture was listed by McKay and Roberts as an original by Hoppner,[5] but this was disputed by Bernard Hall on grounds of quality;[6] the attribution to Hoppner is doubted by Ellis Waterhouse.[7]

Provenance: Bought by Walter Pleydell-Bouverie of Market Lavington, Wilts., about 1870-71 as *Mrs. Abington* by Romney;[8] sold by him in 1907 to Trevalyn Turner; in the possession of Sir William Bennett from whom it was acquired for the Felton Bequest in 1911, on the advice of Charles Ricketts and Frank Gibson.

References: (1) I am indebted to Prof. Ellis Waterhouse for the date. (2) Bernard Hall, *The Connoisseur*, Vol. XLII, 1915 (August), p. 232; (3) *D.N.B.* (4) *Report Bernard Hall*, No. 30, 1911 National Gallery Director's Papers, Latrobe Archives. *Corr.* Waterhouse-Hoff, Sept. 2, 1966. (5) W. McKay, W. Roberts, *Supplement and Index to John Hoppner, R.A.*, 1914, p. 44, pp. 217-18. (6) Leading article in the Melbourne *Argus*, April 24, 1915; partly reprinted in *The Connoisseur, loc. cit.*, p. 231 f.; this article was answered by F. Gibson, *op. cit.* Vol. XLIII, 1915 (December), p. 231 f.; (reprinted in *Victorian Artists Society Journal*, July 1, 1916, p. 5). B. Hall, *The Connoisseur*, 1916, Vol. XLIV (April), p. 217 f. (reprinted in Vivtorian Artists Society Journal, August, 1916, p. 5). (7) *Corr.* Waterhouse-Hoff, Sept. 2, 1966. (8) *Corr.* Bernard Hall-Miss Pleydell-Bouverie as recorded in *Report Bernard Hall*, Nov. 30, 1911, National Gallery Director's Papers, Latrobe Archives.

John Jackson   1778-1831

British. Born London; studied at the Royal Academy Schools where he became a friend of Wilkie's. His style was influenced by Thomas Lawrence. Travelled with the sculptor Chantery *(q.v.)* to Rome in 1818.

Reference: *Th.B.*

Attributed to   Jackson

Illust. 114   306/1 **Sir David Wilkie**

canvas, 76.3 x 63.5 cm. Unsigned, undated; painted about 1815.[1]

Condition: satisfactory; an old tear visible on lower right.

Comment: The sitter has fair to reddish hair, grey-blue eyes, a fair skin with pink cheeks; he weans a brown coat. His features show a certain resemblance to those in T. Phillips' portrait of David Wilkie in the Scottish N.P.G. Professors Waterhouse and Miles suggest John Jackson as the painter.[2]

Provenance: Purchased in 1878 in London,[3] on the advice of the Agent-General, Sir A. Michie.[4]

References: (1) I am indebted to Professor H. A. D. Miles for the dating, *corr.* Miles, Hoff, 1.12.71. (2) (See note 1). (3) Purchase reported by E. von Guérard, 30 Nov. 1877, in State Library of Victoria Archives. (4) *Illustrated Catalogue of the National Gallery* (Victoria), 1918, p. 112, No. 17.

Italian Florentine   15th Century

Illust. 115   557/4 **Madonna and Child**

panel, ogee shaped top, 121.7 x 67.3 cm. Unsigned, undated; painted about 1420-40.

Condition: not good, paint layer thin; few fleshtones in the face of the Madonna; several fill-ins and repairs.

Comment: Shorr refers to a painting by the master of the Griggs Crucifixion, active 1420-40 (in turn based on a Madonna of the Giotto School in the Washington National Gallery), which shows the Child Christ grasping the finger of the Madonna with his left hand and reaching out for a flower with his right hand.[1] According to Howard Spensley 557/4 is related to the Madonna by the Griggs Master.[2] Attributed to the Griggs Master whom Bellosi has identified with Giovanni Toscani (1370-1430).[3]

Provenance: Acquired by Howard Spensley from R. E. A. Wilson, Ryder St., London, and bequeathed in 1939.

References: (1) D. C. Shorr, *The Christ Child in Devotional Images in Italy during the XIV Century,* 1954, p. 111, type 17, Florence 3, repr.; for the master of the Griggs Crucifixion, see Thieme Becker, Vol. XXXVII, 1950, p. 127 and lit. (2) *Howard Spensley Mss.,* Book I, p. 78, Cat. No. 543. (3) L. Bellosi, *Paragone* No. 193/13, 1966, p. 47.

Illust. 116   2124/4 **St. George Slaying the Dragon**

wood, with inscribed arch, 62.2 x 38.8 cm. Unsigned, undated. Probably painted c. 1440-50.

Condition: good; the silver armour of St. George has darkened.

Comment: The legend illustrated here occurs in the *Legenda Aurea,* which tells that St. George "came to the province of Lybia to a city which is said Silene". In order to appease a dragon, the people of Silene sacrificed their children to him. When the lot fell on the King's daughter, St. George resolved to save her and "rode heartily against the dragon and smote him with his spear''. The wounded dragon was then led in triumph into the city by the Princess who had tied her girdle around his neck.[1] In another version of the story, by Petrus de Natalibus, however, St. George ''swinging his lance wounded him (the dragon) gravely and threw him to the ground; he then drew his sword and cut off his head with one blow''.[2] The latter version is illustrated here. St. George has dismounted; his sword is poised to pierce the open jaws of the dragon.[3]

The iconography of the picture is unusual. In Italian art St. George is more often depicted on horseback attacking the dragon with his lance. (So in the Lanckoronski Uccello, N.G., London, and the ''Uccello'', Musée Jacquemart André, Paris.)[4]

The dragon, standing high on two legs, with large bat wings on which appear round markings, is reminiscent of Uccello's dragon. The bent and rounded neck of the horse, the stylized cave on the left and the rock formations in the middle distance also appear in Uccello's picture. The city of Silene at the back, often filled with spectators, occurs in Byzantine renderings of the scene.[5] God the Father, protecting the town like a patron saint,[6] lends divine aid to the fight.[7]

R. Longhi had given the panel to the school of Paolo Uccello and later to Uccello himself.[8] Van Marle and Kenneth Clark, followed by the author attributed it to Domenico di Bartolo.[9] Both attributions are unsatisfactory. Certain features of the picture recur in *The Annunciation* attributed by Berenson to Pietro Giovanni Ambrosi (Ambrogi).[10] Comparable details are: the God the Father with very long grey beard and grey curly locks, wearing a papal tiara; the incised long rays and the haloes impressed into the gold ground; the grey and white ermine used for collar and cuffs in the garment of the Virgin, for cuffs in that of the Princess; the curvilinear shape of the light coloured rocks and the small buildings dotting the hillsides in the distance. Further resemblances have been found in the work of Domenico di Michelino, in *The Departure of John V Paleologus,* attributed to the Florentine school c. 1440 and in *The Resurrection of Lazarus* of the Museum of Pisa.

Provenance: Sold to T. Agnew & Sons in 1949 by the 11th Earl of Southesk who, as Sir Charles Alexander Carnegie, b. 1893, exhibited it at the National Gallery of Scotland in 1927 as by Orcagna; possibly purchased by his grandfather, the 9th Earl (James Carnegie, b. 1827). Acquired from T. Agnew & Sons on the advice of A. J. L. McDonnell and Sir Kenneth Clark for the Felton Bequest in 1949.

References: (1) Jacobus de Voragine, *The Golden Legend, as englished by Caxton, Temple Classics ed.* Vol. III, 1900, p. 126 seq. (2) Petrus de Natalibus, *Heiligenleben,* c. *1370, fol. LIV.* (3) Early 15th century northern engravers often represent the dismounted St. George; see the Master of the Playing Cards (M. Lehrs, *Geschichte des Kupferstichs,* 1908, Vol. 1, p. 92, No. 35 and pl. 3, No. 4) the Master of Kalvarienberg (ibid. p. 255, No. 5A, pl. 37, No. 93), Master E.S. (ibid. Vol. II, p. 205, No. 144, and pl. 53, No. 131), and discussion in W. F. Volbach, *Der Heilige Georg,* Strassburg 1917 (Studien zur Deutschen Kunstgeschiche) p. 15, 80, seq. In all these northern representations, St. George kneels on the back of the dragon and pierces him with his sword, his pose resembling that of the classical Mithras (W. H. Roscher, *Lexikon d. Griechischen und Römischen Mythologie,* 1894-7, Vol. II, p. 305—fig. 6). (4) Van Marle, *op. cit.,* Vol. X, 1928, p. 207, fig. 132 and p. 209, fig. 133; M. Davies, *Burl. Mag. 1959,* Vol. CI, pp. 309-15. (5) For example *St. George,* Stare Nagoricino, photogr. Warburg Institute. (6) For example *St. Ginesius protecting his town,* Marchigan School, 1st half 15th century, S. Agostino, San Ginesio, in van Marle, *op. cit.* Vol. VIII, 1927, p. 305, fig. 191. (7) M. Davies, *op. cit.* p. 310. (8) R. Longhi, Researches on Giovanni di Francesco in *Pinacotheca,* 1928, pp. 34-38; re-printed in *"Me pinxit"* Florence 1968, p. 25 and fig. 61. (9) R. van Marle, *The Italian Schools of Painting,* Vol. IX, 1927, pp. 544, 546, fig. 342 and Felton correspondence 1949; previously known as by *Orcagna.* (10) I am indebted to Mr. Christopher Lloyd of the Ashmolean Museum Oxford and Professor Carlo Volpe for having drawn my attention to the connection between the Ashmolean picture and 2124/4. (11) Professor Volpe kindly brought these pictures to my attention (*corr.* Volpe-Hoff, 7.4.1971 Gallery files).

Illust. 117   1731/5 **The Adoration of the Magi**

tempera on wood, 18 x 52 cm; unsigned, undated, painted about 1420-30.

Condition: infra-red and ultra-violet photographs taken at the London National Gallery show minor damages only; in very good condition.

Comment: 1731/5 has the shape of a predella panel.[1] The Madonna, enthroned, is seated under a thatched roof, indicating the stable; wise men of the East *(S. Matthew* II, 1-12) were, as here, represented as kings since the 8th century.[2] In the *Legende Aura* they were called Melchior, Balthazar and Caspar.[3] Melchior, the old king, has set aside his crown and prostrates himself on the ground to kiss the Child's foot, a motif inspired by a passage in Pseudo-Bonaventura,[4] which is found earlier in the work of Giotto and the Pisani. The two standing kings are dressed in fashionable garments, the elder one wearing a turban.

1731/5 is credibly connected by *Bellosi* with the *Griggs Crucifixion* Metropolitan Museum, New York, so-called after its former owner Mr. F. Maitland Griggs.[5] The Griggs Master may be regarded as belonging to the circle of Masaccio. *Bellosi* identifies him with Giovanni di Francesco Toscani documented in Florence as a member of the guild of S. Luke, d. 2.5.1430; no works survive which can be attributed with certainty to Toscani. 1731/5 has a certain resemblance to Masaccio's predella of the same theme in Berlin;[6] the figures stand on a "stage space", their feet marking their position on the ground, but they do not form an arc shape as emphatically as they do in Masaccio's work[7] and do not cast shadows. The costume of the two younger kings is ornate in the international gothic manner; *Bellosi* likens their style of execution to Gentile da Fabriano. For another work in the collection attributed to the Griggs Master, see Italian School, Florentine, 15th century, 557/4.

Provenance: Professor Sellars, of Edinburgh; Archibald Anderson; inherited by his nephew Archibald George Blomefield Russell (Lancaster Herald); sold 1946 to Herbert Bier, London; undisclosed private owner; Schaeffer Galleries, New York; Herbert Bier, from whom it was acquired in 1966/67 for the Felton Bequest on the advice of Dr. M. Woodall, supported by Mr. Martin Davies and Mr. Michael Levey of the London National Gallery.

References: (1) Luciano Bellosi, *Il Maestro della Crocifissione Griggs: Giovanni Toscani* in *Paragone,* 1966, No. 193/13, col. repr. and fig. 28, pp. 49 ff. (2) J. J. Timmers, *Symboliek en Iconographie Der Christelijke Kunst,* Roermond-Maaseik, 1947, p. 219. (3) L. Réau, *l'Iconographie de l'Evangile, II, Nouveau Testament,* Paris 1957, p. 238. (4) Réau, *op. cit.,* p. 248. (5) Bellosi, *op. cit.,* pp. 49 ff. (6) R. van Marle, *The Development of the Italian Schools of Painting,* Vol. X, 1928, fig. 169. (7) Millard Meiss, *Masaccio and the Early Renaissance: the Circular Plan,* in: *Studies in Western Art,* Vol. II, 1963, pp. 123-144.

Inust. 118   1641/4 **Profilo Portrait of a Lady**

panel, 42.6 x 20.5 cm. Unsigned, undated, painted between 1450-75.

Condition: cleaned prior to purchase. In good condition.

Comment. The sitter's hair is done up in mitre head dress; it consists of yellow material; the hair hanging down at the end is false. Crowe and Cavalcasella and Borenius disproved the traditional identification of the sitter as Isotta da Rimini.[1]

1541/4 has been attributed to various masters;[2] it was acquired as by Uccello, but the edgy outline, the colour scheme, the sharp definition of detail do not coincide with Uccello's style. It does not seem possible to connect 1541/4 with the work of a known master. The dating towards 1475 proposed by Lipman[3] places it slightly later than the more flatly designed profile portraits at the Kaiser Friedrich Museum, Berlin (Antonio Pallaiuolo),[4] in the Brera, Milan (Antonio Pollaiuolo),[5] or the National Gallery, London (Baldovinetti),[6] and earlier than the more animated and realistic portraits, often with architectural and landscape backgrounds by the school of Botticelli, Mainardi and Piero di Cosimo.[7]

Provenance: Exhibited, British Institution, 1858, No. 17 (owner Alexander Barker) as *Piero della Francesca: Isotta da Rimini;* R.A. 1873, No. 195 (owner Francis Cook) as *Piero della Francesca, Profile Portrait;* Burlington Fine Arts Club. Winter Exh., 1902, No. 14 (owner Sir Frederick Cook, Bart., withdrawn prior to exhibition) as: *painter uncertain; said to be Isotta da Rimini.* Acquired for the Felton Bequest on the advice of Daryl Lindsay in 1946.

References: (1) J. A. Crowe and G. B. Cavalcaselle, *Italian Painting, 1864,* Vol. II, p. 543. H. Cook, *A Catalogue of Pictures at Doughty House, Richmond,* Vol. I. *Italian Schools,* by T. Borenius, 1913, No. 19, p. 25, pl. IV, quoted as Borenius, *Cook Catalogue.* (2) G. F. Waagen, *Treasures of Art in Great Britain, Supplement,* 1857, p. 74: as by *Piero della Francesca;* Crowe and Cavalcaselle, *op. cit.:* as *not Piero della Francesca;* H. F. Cook, *Les Arts,* No. 44, 1905, p. 10, as *Piero della Francesca;* B. Berenson, *Central Italian Painters,* 1909, p. 170; as *Francesco di Giorgio;* so also in *Pitture Italiane,* 1936, p. 174; Borenius, *Cook Catalogue:* as *possibly Piero Pollaiuolo;* R. van Marle, *Development of the Italian Schools of Painting,* Vol. X, 1928, p. 236, fig. 154: tentatively as *Uccello;* I. Lipman, *The Art Bulletin,* Vol. XVIII, 1936, p. 96, fig. 41: as *Florentine School;* R. W. Kennedy, *Alesso Baldovinetti,* 1938, p. 131, note 280: as *Florentine School;* Goldscheider in J. Burckhardt, *The Civilization of the Renaissance in Italy,* 1945, pl. 50: as attributed to *Lorentino d'Arezzo;* John Pope Hennessy, *Paolo Uccello,* 1950, p. 150, fig. XIV; as *Florentine School, "Lippesque."* (3) Lipman, *op. cit.,* p. 101, *1450-75.* (4) Lipman, *op. cit.,* fig. 12. (5) Van Marle, *op. cit.,* Vol. X, 1928, opp. p. 326 repr. (6) Lipman, fig. 36. (7) *ibid.,* figs. 26, 37, 39. See also *Quarterly Bulletin, N.G. Victoria,* 1947, II, (3), 1; 1956; X (1), 7 repr.

87

Italian   16th Century

Illust. 119   1587/5 **Portrait of a Youth**

poplar panel, oval, 74.5 x 57.2 cm. Unsigned, undated; inscribed on cartellino in gold lettering CLARIOR HOC PVLCRO REGNANS IN CORPORE VIRTUS. (Brighter [than beauty] is the virtue residing in this beautiful body.)

Condition: cleaned prior to purchase; apart from a few superficial paint losses around the edges and in minor parts of the picture the preservation is unusually good for the period. The tunic of the young man is supposed to have had first a purplish cast which has faded. It was probably originally not an oval (an unusual shape in the Renaissance).[1]

Comment: The sitter is unidentified; the picture is assumed to have been painted about 1520; formerly attributed to Raphael, then to Paolo Morando.[2] None of these attributions are now accepted. Mr. Cecil Gould places it in the Parma area.[3] Professor Waterhouse has suggested a painter from Verona, and compared the picture with a portrait of a Lady in the Hermitage in Leningrad,[4] regarded by Longhi as by Correggio and dated 1518, previously attributed to Lorenzo Lotto.[5] The tree at the back appears to be myrtle (Mirtus communis, L.).[6]

Provenance: Prince de Canino (Lucien Bonaparte, died 1841) as by Raphael. W. Buchanan, *Memoirs of Painting,* London, 1824, Vol. II, p. 289, No. 25 as Raphael. Portrait of F. Penni (list of Bonaparte's paintings). Exhibited Grafton Galleries, Old Masters, 1911, No. 79 as "Paolo Morando . . . (hitherto described as a Portrait of 'Lucretia') . . . At one time in the possesion of Farrer, the picture dealer and subsequently in the collection of Th. Woolner, the sculptor (fl. 1843-1893). Not previously exhibited, lent by Sir George Donaldson." Viscount Lascelles (later 6th Earl of Harewood), Harewood House, Green Drawing Room; The Rt. Hon. The Earl of Harewood, sale Christie, July 2, 1965, No. 85 (as by Morando); acquired for the Felton Bequest on the advice of Dr. M. Woodall from P. and D. Colnaghi, in 1965/6.

References: (1) Felton letter No. 17, M. Woodall 24.XI.65; report from John M. Brearley attached; also Woodall 7.I.66. (2) *see* under Provenance. (3) Woodall letter 7.I.66. (4) *ibid.* (5) Roberto Longhi, *Le Fasi del Correggio Giovane e l'Esigenza del suo Viaggio Romano,* in *Paragone, Arte,* IX, No. 101, 1958, 43 f, fig. 20. (6) Identified by the Royal Botanical Gardens, Kew, London. (7) T. Borenius, *Catalogue of Harewood House, London,* 1936, (42) (called Portrait of a Young Woman; attributed to Paolo Morando).

Italian   17th Century

Illust. 120   4564/3 **Study of a Man's Head**

canvas, 48.8 x 37.5 cm. Unsigned, undated.

Condition: paint losses and retouches in background. Covered with old yellow varnish.

Provenance: Lucy Smith, Castlefield Collection, Melbourne; Sale Leonard Joel, 1 September, 1931—acquired for the Felton Bequest.

Italian   18th Century

Illust. 121   1210/5 **Portrait of Luigi Boccherini**   1743-1805

canvas, 133.3 x 90.7 cm. Unsigned, undated. Probably painted 1764-7.
Condition: satisfactory.

Comment: Luigi Boccherini, famous composer and 'cellist, was born in
Lucca in 1743. He was taught the 'cello by his father, Leopoldo, by the
Abbate Vannucci of Lucca, and by Costanzi, a celebrated 'cellist in Rome.
'Cellist in the orchestra of the Imperial Theatre in Vienna from 1757;
appointed 'cellist by the Grand Council of the City of Lucca in 1764;
settled in Madrid in 1768/9 where he increasingly devoted himself to
composing, and where he died in 1805.[1] For identification the features
of the sitter may be compared with those in an anonymous engraving
reproduced by Piquot in his *Notice sur la vie et les ouvrages de Luigi
Boccherini,* Paris 1815;[2] the engraving is not recorded, nor is the name
of the sitter vouched for except by Picquot. An engraving by
Bourgeois de la Richardière, reproduced by Rothschild,[3] and a lithograph
in the B.M. by or after Mazas[4] both show the sitter at an older age and
do not help with the identification.

Boccherini is here portrayed as a 'cellist; a point worth noting is the
position of the 'cello, held between the legs instead of resting, as now,
on an end pin. The end pin, according to Anthony Baines,[5] was
introduced after Boccherini's lifetime by the Belgian musician
Adrien François Servais (1807-1866).

Traditionally ascribed to Longhi, the portrait was given by Hermann Voss
to Pompeo Batoni;[6] this attribution is rejected by recent critics; Francis
J. Watson suggests a North Italian or German origin;[7] Anthony Clark
gives it to be the Roman painter Sebastiano Ceccarini (1703-1783).[8]

Provenance: Berlin, art market (Ch. de Burlet) 1942; private collection, Berlin (see note
6); private owner, Munich; M. Widler, Zürich;[9] acquired on the advice of A. J. L. McDonnell
from Rowland, Browse and Delbano, London, under the terms of the Everard Studley
Miller Bequest in 1961.

References: (1) Germaine de Rothschild, *Luigi Boccherini,* London, 1965. (2) *ibid.* fig. 2
and p. XI. (3) *ibid.* 2, p. XI. (4) Information supplied by A. J. L. McDonnell (letter to
Ingvar Bergström, *Dutch Still Life Painting,* 1956, pp. 260-285.
Hoff, 13.VII.62). (5) Anthony Baines, *Musical Instruments through the Ages,* London, 1961,
p. 147. (6) Thus in: Ernst Emmerling, *Pompeo Batoni, sein Leben und Werk,* Darmstadt
1932, p. 98, No. 8. (7) Letter A. J. L. McDonnell—E.W. (8) Letter to H. Preston, Dec. 7, 1964;
archives N.G. Victoria. (9) Emmerling, *loc. cit.* (10) See also John Kennedy, *Luigi Boccherini,
1743-1805,* in *Annual Bulletin N.G. Victoria,* IV, 1962, 16 ff, *repr.*

Jacob Jordaens   1593-1678

Flemish. Born Antwerp. 1607 pupil of Adam van Noort. 1615 master in the
Guild of St. Luke where he was registered as a painter in watercolours.
His earliest oil paintings date before 1616. The influence of Rubens can be

89

H

seen in his work from the beginning. After Ruben's death in 1640 Jordaens became the leading painter in his country and received commissions from Charles I of England, Christina of Sweden and the Regent of the Netherlands for whom he decorated the Huis ten Bosch in the Hague.

Reference: Dr. Fr. R. A. d'Hulst, *De Tekeningen van Jacob Jordaens,* Brussels, 1956.

School of Jordaens

Illust. 122   183/4 **The Satyr and the Peasant**

canvas, 117.6 x 151.7 cm. Unsigned, undated; original painted 1618.

Condition: fair, rubbed.

Comment: The subject is taken from Aesop, *Fables* (ed. Francis de Furia, 1810, Fab. XXVI), the picture is a repetition of the painting of the same subject in the gallery at Kassel with slight variations.[1]

Provenance: Acquired on the advice of Bernard Hall from Rev. Patrick Gorry, County Kildare, Ireland, for the Felton Bequest in 1934. Said to have been bought at the Doyne Sale, Dublin, 1867, and subsequently belonged to Mrs. Fitzmaurice, Everton, Carlow.[2]

References: (1) For Kassel painting Max Rooses, *Jacob Jordaens,* 1908, p. 19 f and Dr. Fr. R. A. d'Hulst, *De Tekeningen van Jacob Jordaens,* Brussels, 1956, p. 80, fig. 40.
(2) Felton correspondence No. 6, Hall, 1934.

Willem Kalf   1619-1693

Dutch. Born Rotterdam where his family were wealthy burghers: pupil of François Ryckhals (after 1600-1647) who painted still lifes of precious objects in the Flemish manner. In 1638 left Rotterdam; his presence in Paris is recorded in 1642, where he seems to have lived until 1646. In 1651 in Hoorn; between 1653-1693 lived in Amsterdam. Kalf also seems to have been a dealer in *objets d'art* and in engravings. His work comprises landscapes, interiors, game pieces and, for the greatest part, still lifes, composed of precious objects. His still lifes fall into two groups:

1. Works of the French period containing many objects, tilted and overturned vessels and a light tonality;

2. The works of his second Dutch period, in which the number of objects is greatly reduced, are painted in chiaroscuro with sparing colour contrasts which reveal the influence of Rembrandt.

Reference: Ingvar Bergström, *Dutch Still Life Painting,* 1956, pp. 260-285.

Illust. 123   1251/3 **Still Life**

canvas, 53 x 43.7 cm. Unsigned, undated; painted probably in the 1650s.

Condition: satisfactory.

Comment: A similar *roemer* and richly wrought silver dish set on a marble table whose edge is bevelled as in 1251/3, appear in a picture by Kalf formerly at Messrs. Duits, dated 1659 (?);[1] an octagon Venetian (or Venetian-type) glass of the kind seen in 1251/3, grouped together with a similar *roemer* and *flute* and accompanied by a (smaller) silver dish, lemon and orange can be found in another still life by Kalf in the collection of Dr. Hugo Engelson, Lund (not dated).[2] The composition and colour scheme of the work show the characteristics of Kalf's second Dutch period.[3]

Provenance. Acquired from Alexander Reid, Glasgow, for the Felton Bequest on the advice of Mr. Frank Rinder in 1922.

References: (1) Ingvar Bergström, *Dutch Still Life Painting*, 1956, fig. 228. (2) *ibid*, pl. VII. (3) *ibid., p. 282, seq.*

Sir Godfrey Kneller   1646 or 49 - 1723

German-British. Born Lübeck; trained under Rembrandt's pupil, Ferdinand Bol, in Amsterdam and perhaps also under Rembrandt. In the 1660s he visited Italy, and studied in Rome and Venice. In 1674 in London; was made Principal Painter jointly with Riley in 1688; knighted in 1692; baronet in 1715. In 1711 became the first Governor of the first Academy of Painting to be set up in London. His best work is the series representing members of the Kit Kat Club done between 1702-1717.

Reference: Ellis Waterhouse, *Painting in Britain, 1530-1790,* 1953, pp. 97-100.

Illust. 124   1900/4 **Sir Thomas Aston**

canvas, 242.5 x 150.4 cm. Signed and dated, *G. Kneller, Eques, 1711,* ¾ in. down on right.

Condition: satisfactory, cleaned prior to purchase.

Comment: Sir Thomas is shown leaning against a fountain, his right hand is pointing into disance towards a rearing horse, led by an ostler. The sitter was Sir Thomas Aston, who wedded Catherine, daughter of William Widdrington Esq.; died 16 January 1724. Succeeded to the title in 1702, at the death of his father, Sir Willoughby Aston, who had erected Aston Hall, Warrington (Cheshire).[1]

Provenance: The Aston property descended to Brigadier-General Hervey Talbot, Sale Aston Lodge, Brown & Co., Chester, 27 April, 1927[2] (no catalogue available). According to a note on a photograph of the portrait in the Witt Library, Courtauld Institute, London, the picture was in the possession of Leggatts in 1928. Listed as from the Aston collection in sale of pictures, belonging to the Hon. Lady Ward. Christie's, 17 May, 1946, lot 54, bt. Wallis. Acquired for the Felton Bequest from Messrs. Leggatt on the advice of A. J. L. McDonnell and Sir Kenneth Clark in 1948.

References: (1) Prof. Ellis Waterhouse identified the sitter; and gave the reference to the sale of 1927 (see provenance). See also J. Burke, *The Extinct and Dormant Baronnetcies of England,* 1841, p. 26. (2) Advertisement in *Chester Chronicle,* 2 April 1927, p. 6; reference supplied by the City Libarian, Chester Public Library.

Nicolas de Largillière   1656-1763

French. Born Paris but spent his youth in Antwerp where he studied from 1668 under Antoni Goubau, 1674 went to England and became assistant to Sir Peter Lely at the court of Charles II. 1678 to Paris. His brilliant palette and lightness of touch reveal his Flemish training and particularly the influence of the work of Anthony van Dyck. 1704 Professor, 1728-32 Director, 1743 Chancellor of the *Academie.* Together with Rigaud *(q.v.)* the leading French portaitist of his time.

Reference: *Th.B.*

Illust. 125   1819/5 **Frederick August of Saxony, King of Poland**

canvas, 135.5 x 102.5 cm. Unsigned, undated; painted 1714.

Condition: cleaned prior to purchase; excellent.

Comment: Frederick August, Elector of Saxony and King of Poland (August III) 1697-1763, was one of Europe's noted collectors and patron of the arts. One of his agents, Count Algarotti, acquired for him Tiepolo's *Banquet of Cleopatra* (see no. 103/4) which hung in his hunting castle, Hubertusburg, and was sold by auction at Amsterdam in 1765.[1] 1819/5 was painted when Augustus, as a young man, stayed in Paris

in 1714. It seems to have been intended as a pendant to the portrait of his father, August the Strong, now in Kansas City,[2] painted about 1697. This may be one of the reasons why he is shown wearing the Danish Order of the Elephant conferred on him in 1711, and not the Polish Order of the White Eagle more suitable for the Prince Royal of that country, but which did not yet exist, when Largillière portrayed his father. Thinking in terms of a pendant, it is obvious that the painter followed in the son's portrait, the details of costume appearing in that of the father.[3]

Exhibitions: Höfische Bildnisee des Spätbarock, Schloss Charlottenburg, Berlin, September-October, 1966, Cat. No. 50 (not seen).

Provenance: Princess von Hohenlohe, Paris; Baron d'Huart, Paris; Huart sale, Paris, Hotel Drouot, 7.12.1938, lot 38 (repr.), Heim Galleries, Paris and London. Acquired under the terms of the Everard Studley Miller Bequest on the advice of Dr. M. Woodall, Mr. Kenneth Hood, 1968, from Heim Galleries, London.

References: (1) See p.   of this catalogue. (2) August the Strong, oil on canvas, 57 in. x 45½ in.; *Nelson Gallery of Art, Atkins Museum, Kansas City, Handbook of Collections,* 1959, p. 108, illus. August points towards a distant landscape. Information kindly supplied by Mr. Harley Preston. (3) *Antiques,* (London), 1968, p. 438 repr.; *The Connoisseur,* Jan. 1968, 30, repr. 1; *Annual Bulletin of Victoria,* 1968-9, p. 50, illus.

Sir Thomas Lawrence   1769-1830

British School. Born Bristol; an infant prodigy, he began a career as portrait draughtsman at the age of ten. Received some instruction in oil painting in Bath by Thomas Barker in 1780. Settled in London in 1786 where he spent three months as a student of oil painting at the R.A. School. Painter to the king at the death of Reynolds in 1792; R.A. 1794; P.R.A. in 1820. Lawrence was a portraitist of international renown and portrayed many of the great personalities of his day. His collection of old master drawings, many of which are now in the Ashmolean Museum in Oxford, was one of the finest ever made.

Reference: Kenneth Garlick, *Sir Thomas Lawrence,* 1954.

Illust. 126   314/5 **Robert Hobart, Bt., 4th Earl of Buckinghamshire**

canvas, 128.8 x 103 cm. Unsigned, undated; painted about 1795

Condition: cleaned prior to purchase. Heavy cracks in background, extensively restored.

Comment: Robert, Lord Hobart, succeeded his father George, 3rd Earl of Buckinghamshire as 4th Earl of Buckinghamshire in 1804 and in the baronetcy; after that date his title in full was shown as in the title of 314/5. Born 6th May, 1760, educated at Westminster School. 1 May 1776, became a Lieutenant in the 7th Regiment; rose to the rank of Captain in 1778; a member of parliament 1787-88 and in 1790. In 1788 and 89 acted as Inspector of Recruiting in Ireland and was made an Irish Privy Councillor. English Privy Councillor in the same year. In 1793 became Governor of Madras. In 1801 appointed Secretary of State for the Colonial War Department. In 1804 Hobart Town, Tasmania, was founded and named after him. In 1812 he was appointed President of the Board of Control for Indian Affairs, which post he held until his death on 4 Feb. 1816.[1]
The portrait was engraved by T. Grozer in 1796.[2] The pose, setting and composition are based on Reynold's portrait of *Charles James Fox, R.A.* 1784.[3]

Other Versions: A bust portrait closely related to 314/5 is in the National Library, Canberra; it came from the Hulbert family, Tilshead Manor, Wiltshire; later Overton House, Codfrod Wiltshire, residence of Mrs. Fanny Hulbert; Rex Nankivell Collection, No. 5632. Regarded by Kenneth Garlick as 'studio of L'.

Provenance: In the possession of the sitter. Since 1816 owned by Sarah Albinia Louisa Hobart, Countess Ripon, the daughter of the sitter. National Portrait Exhibition, 1868, No. 174 (owner Earl de Grey and Ripon); a private collector, London; P. Jackson Higgs, N.Y., 1930; brought from America to London by Messrs. Frank Partridge and acquired on the advice of A. J. L. McDonnell for the Everard Studley Miller Bequest in 1958.

References: (1) *D.N.B.,* Vol. IX, p. 928/9. (2) Kenneth Garlick, *Sir Thomas Lawrence,* London, 1954, p. 29, and previous literature. See also *Annual Bulletin N.G. Victoria,* 1960, Vol. II, 19 repr. (3) Kindly pointed out by Mr. Harley Preston. cf. Ellis Waterhouse, *Reynolds,* 1941, p. 246.

After **Lawrence**

Illust. 127   1208/4 **Arthur Wellesley, 1st Duke of Wellington**

panel, 30.4 x 23.9 cm. Unsigned, undated.

Condition: in very good condition.

Comment. This is a version of a portrait exhibited by Lawrence in 1822 which was painted for General Arbuthnot and is now in the collection of W. V. Goodbody, Scotland.[1] The engraving by Cousins of the Duke of Wellington is based on the Arbuthnot version.

Provenance: Presented by the Duke of Wellington about 1830 to Colonel Theo Anderson, grand uncle of Mr. Edgar Anderson. Purchased from the latter via Joshua McClelland, Melbourne, in 1943.[2]

References: (1) For Arbuthnot version Kenneth Garlick, *Sir Thomas Lawrence,* 1954, p. 62, No. 5.
(2) Correspondence N.G. Victoria files 1943.

Illust. 128   659/2 **George IV of England**

canvas, 90.4 x 71.3 cm. Unsigned, undated.

Condition: In poor condition; heavy cracks, the tendency to flake.

Comment: King George is represented in the robes of the Order of the Garter. The portrait is identical with part of the portrait in the Vatican, Rome,[1] which is described by Kenneth Garlick as a replica of the portrait by Lawrence exhibited at the R.A. in 1818, No. 61, and is now at Buckingham Palace. The replica was commissioned by Pope Pius VII in 1819.[2]

Provenance: Presented by John Connell 1914.

References: (1) Information received from Mr. Kenneth Garlick, correspondence 1953, N.G. Victoria files. (2) Kenneth Garlick, *Sir Thomas Lawrence,* 1954, p. 38, pl. 87.

Frederick Richard Lee   1798-1879

British. Born Barnstaple, Devonshire; studied at the R.A. from 1818. R.A. 1838. Painter of landscapes, marine pieces and still lifes. Died at Viesch Bank Farm, South Africa.

Reference: *Th.B.*

Illust. 129   303/1a **Ben Lawers**
board, 35.4 x 45.5 cm.

Provenance: Presented by the artist, during a visit to Victoria in 1872.[1]

Reference: (1) *State Library of Victoria* Room Catalogue, 1879, p. 2.

Illust. 130   303/1b **River, Mill and Farm**
canvas, 112.4 x 183 cm.

Provenance: Commissioned by the Commission of Fine Arts,[1] 1868.

Reference: (1) Art Gallery correspondence, Nos. 94, 95; State Library of Victoria archives.

John Linnell   1792-1882

British. Born London.[1] In 1805 became a student at the Royal Academy under Benjamin West; he also studied with John Varley; with William Hunt, his fellow pupil at Varley's, sketched in the country around London and made drawings at Dr. Munro's house in the Adelphi. Also came under the influence of Mulready.[1] Until 1846 worked mainly as a portraitist; after this date returned to landscape painting. Linnell is now best known as a patron of William Blake whom he met in 1818.[2] Blake helped Linnell with the engraving of his portraits;[3] Linnell called Blake's attention to the works of Albrecht Dürer, Marc Antonio Raimondi and Bonasone[4] which were responsible for a marked development in Blake's style of engraving. Dr. Thornton, whose *Virgil (Eclogues)* Blake illustrated with woodcuts in 1821, was Linnell's family doctor.[5] In 1823 Linnell commissioned a set of watercolour drawings from the set made by Blake for Thomas Butts in 1820, and asked Blake to engrave the series.[6] In 1824 he ordered from him a series of designs in illustration of Dante's *Divine Comedy*[7] and found buyers of Blake's works.[8]

36 of the 103 watercolours of the *Divine Comedy*, two watercolours to Milton's *Paradise Lost,* a set of engravings of the *Book of Job* and of the woodcuts to Thornton's *Virgil,* all by Blake and from the collection of John Linnell are in the Print Room collection.

References: (1) Laurence Binyon, *The Followers of William Blake,* 1925, p. 6. (2) A Gilchrist, *The Life of William Blake,* 2nd ed. p. 265. (3) Gilchrist, p. 265. (4) Gilchrist, p. 303. (5) Binyon, p. 7. (6) Gilchrist, p. 302. (7) Gilchrist, p. 351. (8) Gilchrist, p. 354, 377.

Illust. 131   312/1 **Wheat**

canvas, 94.2 x 140.6 cm. Unsigned, undated; painted 1860.

Condition: fair; cracking and paint losses.

Comment: Inscribed on back: "Red Stone Wood, Red Hill, Surrey, April 1860, John Linnell sen." Exhibited by the artist R.A. 1860, No. 199.

Provenance: Purchased by Thomas Agnew from the artist;[1] exhibited at the Paris Universal Exhibition, 1867, No. 66, owner J. Chapman, Esq., Hill End, Mottram, Cheshire; Royal Jubilee Exh. Manchester, 1887, No. 896, as "A Corn Field," owner Charles Chapman, Thurlestone, Penistone, Yorkshire. Recommended by Sir James McCulloch, London; purchased 1888 by Sir George Verdon from T. Agnew & Sons for the N.G., Victoria.

Reference: (1) State Library of Victoria Archives, 88/430, in letters.

Simon Marmion   active 1449, died 1489

French (French-Flemish). 1449-1454 mentioned at Amiens. From 1458 in Valenciennes; 1468 member of the Guild of S. Luke at Tournai. Renowned as "The Prince of Illuminators". His work remained unknown until the last decade of the 19th century, and none of it can be connected to the master by documentary evidence. The S. Bertin panels, some of which are in the London National Gallery, the others in the Berlin Gallery, are usually accepted as the key works of the master. Marmion's style is very close to that of the Flemish Primitives.

References: *Th.B.; C.N.G.*

Illust. 132　3079/4 **The Virgin and Child**

panel, 38.1 x 28 cm; painted surface, 37.6 x 27.7 cm. Unsigned, undated; painted 1465-75.

Condition: in excellent condition; fine priming craquelure; cleaned prior to purchase.

Comment: The picture which at one time was described as a replica of the Kleinberger version[1] has been accepted as the original by recent authorities.[2] The attribution to Marmion rests on the similarity of the facial type of the Madonna, of certain architectural and landscape motifs to other works usually associated with this master's name. The steep rock, resting on a sloping base in the left background is similar to one in fol. 388 of Ms. 9232 of the Bibliothèque Royale in Brussels (before 1460)[3] and also to the rock in *S. Jerome and a Donor* in Philadelphia.[4] In fol. 388, quoted above, we also find the rocks set in water and the characteristic combination of delicate atmospheric blues with greys and greens. This illumination also shows the octagonal or round church tower on top of which sits a narrower round tower crowned by a small pointed spire; this tower is also to be found in 3079/4. Another connection between 3079/4 and the work of Marmion is established by the Kleinberger version which is nearly identical with 3079/4 but for a brocade hanging filling the space between the columns behind the Madonna. This brocade hanging has exactly the same pattern as one behind the donor of the *S. Bertin altarpiece* by Marmion (1459).[5]

Iconography: The type of Madonna represented in 3079/4 is based on that of Rogier van der Weyden's *Madonna of S. Luke* of c. 1435[6] and the several single half-figure adaptions of this type made by Rogier and by his workshop towards 1460.[7] Rogier's *Madonna and Child* at Caen shows the Virgin joining her hands in prayer in a manner from which stems Marmion's variation in 3079/4.[8]

Rogier never seems to have placed his half-figure Madonnas against a landscape background. This is done however in early works by Memling in the 1460s.[9] The balustrade used by Marmion echoes the balustrade in Rogier's *Madonna of S. Luke.*

Provenance: The picture is not listed in the Catalogue of the Czartorisky collection in Cracow,[10] which later became the Czartorisky Museum. It is first referred to as in the possession of the Czartorisky family by F. Winkler in Thieme Becker, Vol. XXIV, 1930, p. 123; again by G. Ring, *A Century of French Painting*, 1949, p. 220, No. 176 (both Winkler and Ring describe it as a replica of the Kleinberger version, see note 1). The picture was taken by Count Czartorisky to Paris in 1939 and exhibited in *La Vierge dans l'Art Francais*, Petit Palais, 1950, Cat. No. 39, pl. 46. Acquired in 1954 on the advice of A. J. L. McDonnell through the Marlborough Galleries, London, for the Felton Bequest.

References: (1) E. Michel, *Gazette des Beaux Arts,* VI. XVI, 1927, p. 142; repr. opp. See also under provenance. (2) E. T. Hoffman, *Simon Marmion* 1958 (Thesis, Ms. Courtauld Institute, London). A certificate was given by M. Friedländer. (3) *La Miniature Flammande,* Palais des Beaux-Arts, Brussels, 1959, p. 66, Cat. No. 59. (4) G. Ring, *A Century of French Painting,* 1959, pl. 98. (5) E. Michel, *op. cit.,* p. 142, and Ring, *op. cit.,* pl. 104. (6) E. Panofsky, *Early Netherlandish Painting,* 1953, p. 252-4 quotes the Boston version as the best replica of a lost original. (7) *ibid.,* Vol. II, p. 295, fig. 368 (*Madonna,* formerly Renders coll. Bruges). (8) *ibid.,* Vol. II, fig. 372. (9) An adaptation of Rogier's *Madonna of S. Luke* as a half figure placed against a landscape background in the Museum of Fine Arts, Boston, was ascribed to "Memling's youth" by M. J. Friedländer, *Burl. Mag.,* Vol. LXXV, 1939, p. 124, pl. A. A similar painting in the Brussels Gallery, also described as Memling, repr. by Friedländer, *op. cit.,* pl. B. (10) I am grateful to Dr. Bialostocki for having given me this information. See also; *Quarterly Bulletin N.G. Victoria,* 1954, (D), p. 2-3. For full discussion see U. Hoff, M. Davies, *The National Gallery of Victoria, Melbourne (Les Primitifs flamands, I, Corpus de la peinture flamande des anciens Pays-Bas méridionaux au quinzième siécle,* 12) Brussels 1971, No. 133, p. 51.

Ben Marshall   1767-1835

British. Born London. Studied portraiture under L. F. Abbot. Seeing Gilpin's *The Death of the Fox* in 1793, he took up sporting subjects *(The Sporting Magazine).* In 1812 he moved to Newmarket. From 1796 his work was reproduced in the *Sporting Magazine* for which he later wrote articles on the turf under the pseudonym of *Observator.*

Reference: W. Shaw Sparrow, *George Stubbs and Ben Marshall,* 1929.

Illust. 133   3255/4 **Lord Jersey's Middleton**

canvas, 72.2 x 91.5 cm. Signed and dated *1825;* inscribed *Middleton* l.l.

Condition: satisfactory; apparently cleaned prior to purchase.

Comment. Middleton was bred by George Child Villiers, the 5th Earl of Jersey (1773-1859). He was foaled in 1822 by Phantom, dam Webb by Waxy. He won the Derby Stakes of £1,950 with James Robson up on 19 May 1825. A description of the race is to be found in *Sporting Magazine,* Dec. 1825.

Provenance: 1st Baron Revelstoke 1828-1897; inherited by his daughter, Elizabeth, married 5th Earl of Kenmare, 1867-1944; Alfred H. Caspary, U.S.A., sold 29 April, 1955; acquired by A. J. L. McDonnell for the Felton Bequest from Messrs. Frank Partridge and Sons in 1955.

References: (1) T. H. Taunton, *Portraits of Celebrated Race Horses,* 1887, Vol. II, opp., p. 238 repr. engr.; further literture W. Gilbey, *Animal Painters,* 1900, Vol. II, p. 95. W. Shaw Sparrow, *British Sporting Artists,* 1922, p. 177, No. 23. G. A. Gannan, *Quarterly Bulletin,.. N.G. Victoria,* 1955, IX, (3), 6.

Hans Memling   active 1466, died 1494

Flemish. Born Seligenstadt, near Frankfort on Main. May have been trained at Cologne and seems to have entered the workshop of Rogier van der Weyden in Brussels about 1459-60. Became a citizen of Bruges on 30 January, 1465. Formed hs style under the influence of Rogier and Bouts. Swags of fruit and flowers and putti in his later work point to an Italian source.

Reference: M. J. Friedländer, *Die Altniederländische Malerei,* Vol. VI, 1928.

Illust. 134   1335/3 **The Man of Sorrows in the Arms of the Virgin**

panel; gold ground; 27.4 x 19.9 cm.
Unsigned; inscribed *1475* on capital of column to left.

Condition: excellent; very fine priming crackle; cleaned prior to purchase.

Comment: Christ, with the wound marks of the Crucfixion, yet with eyes open, alive, with his left hand under the side wound, and collecting the blood in his right hand, is held by the Virgin in a linen sheet. This image of Christ, known as the Gregorian Man of Sorrows, is a symbolic representation showing Christ, with the signs of his death, yet upright and alive, as an image of sacrifice; it is frequent from the late 13th century onward.[1]

Behind the Virgin appears the cross from which hangs a purple cloth (? the garment worn by Christ during the scourging). Against the left arm of the Cross lean the spear and the reed with sponge. On the extreme left of the panel the pillar to which Christ was tied during scourging; the pillar is tied around with cords which hold the scourge of three thongs, and a bunch of twigs. On the capital appears the label from Christ's Cross. Above the column the head of Judas with the rope around his neck, to which his purse is attached; higher up the heads of S. Peter and the maid servant face to face; below them two male heads which may be the high priests Annas and Caiaphas, and lower again three hands: one an open right hand, "striking" (S. John, XVIII, 22); two other hands, one clenched, "hitting"; one as if holding the staff which was offered to Christ during the mocking (staff not depicted). On the other side the heads of Pilate (with turban) and Herod (with crown); below a hand in a mocking gesture (fica gesture) the hammer, the mocking face of a soldier, a hand holding hair that had been torn from Christ's head, a kicking foot and the three nails with which Christ was nailed to the Cross.

Discovered by James Weale in 1905 and attributed to "a master of Tournai".[2] Attributed to Memling by Justi before 1908,[3] attribution taken up by Panofsky,[4] Friedländer,[5] and Hulin de Loo.[8] The features of the Madonna resemble closely the features of the Madonna lamenting (in Granada) of about 1475;[7] both wear a blue mantle over the head with white kerchief underneath; on one of the assisting women in Granada a double frill appears in the kerchief which returns in the kerchief of the Madonna of 1335/3. The Dead Christ in the second panel at Granada resembles the Christ of 1335/3 in the slant of the head, the slight growth of beard, the regular pattern of the drops of blood formed by the pressure of the crown on the forehead, the narrow shoulders and thin arms, etc.

In the inventories of the art treasures belonging to Margaret of Austria (died 1530; Regent of the Netherlands), drawn up in 1516, a picture of a similar subject is described thus: "A small picture of a God of Pity in the arms of Our Lady; the painting has two wings in each of which there is an angel . . . the painting is by the hand of Rogier, and the aforesaid wings are by the hand of Hans."[8] The 1956 edition of Friedländer, *From van Eyck to Brugel* suggests two possible explanations: (i) that this inventory reference does in fact refer to the picture in Melbourne, and that there was no painting by Rogier, (ii) that the Melbourne painting reflects a version by Rogier. The provenance of 1335/5 is insufficiently known to establish the first point. The second point, namely that it reflects a version by Rogier, is likely since a number of such versions is in existence, one of which at least is not derived from the Melbourne picture.

Versions: 1. Engraving by the Master f., date uncertain, possibly about 1470, position of arms similar to Melbourne picture. The instruments of the passion do not decorate the background but are contained in heraldic shields.[9]

2. Capilla Real, Granada.[10] The group of Christ and the Virgin resembles that in Melbourne, except that the position of Christ's arms is reversed: the right hand lies under the side wound, the left hand is lower down still with the cupped hand; this motif has become senseless since it no longer serves to collect the blood. Instead of the gold ground, clouds; the instruments of the passion, heads and other details are differently distributed; all is more realistically rendered. Friedländer dates it earlier, Panofsky later than the Melbourne version; Burger dates it about 1490. The change in the position of Christ's arms, reverting to the traditional position but leaving out of account the purpose of the cupped hand, would seem to argue for a later date.

3. Church of Cormatin Saône-et-Loire; exhibited in *La Verge dans l'Art Français,* Petit Palais, Paris, 1950, No. 44, pl. 50; date given as end of 15th century, h. 0.75cm. (29½ in.) x w. 0.60cm. (23⅝ in.). More closely related to the foregoing picture than to the Melbourne one; described in the catalogue as "rather Burgundian than Flemish".

4. Two other versions are quoted by Friedländer, *op. cit.,* No. 37, b, c; one of these may be identical with the picture in the church of Cormatin. The iconographic tradition on which the Melbourne picture is based has been analyzed by Panofsky and Berliner.[11] The representation of the instruments of the passion resembles most nearly that on the painting of the S. Gregory's Mass, from the School of the Master of Flémalle, where the head of Judas also appears in the unusual position above the capital of the column.

Purchased by Theodore Griveau of Connérée, Sarthe, France from a "brocanteur" (second hand dealer) in Caen, c. 1900-05. Acquired from Thomas Agnew London in 1924 on the advice of Frank Rinder under the terms of the Felton Bequest.

References: (1) Erwin Panofsky, *Imago Pietatis,* in *Festschrift für Max J. Friedländer,* 1927, p. 275, fig. 20; Rudolf Berliner, *Arma Christi* in *Münchner Jahrbuch,* 3rd series, Vol. VI, 1955, pp. 35-152; reference to the Melbourne picture on p. 76, and note 437. (2) W. H. J. Weale, *Burl. Mag.,* Vol. VII, 1905, p. 75, and pl. 11. (3) Referred to by M. Gomez Moreno, *Gazette des Beaux Arts,* Vol. XL, 1908, p. 305. (4) Panofsky, *op. cit.,* p. 275. (5) M. J. Friedländer, *Altniedländische Malerei,* Vol. VI, 1928, No. 37, p. 17, pl. XXVII. (6) Hulin de Loo saw the picture prior to cleaning at Agnews and called it "a characteristic work of Memling and of high quality"; see Rinder correspondence 21 May, 1924, N.G. Victoria files. (7) Friedländer, *op. cit.,* No. 13, pl. XV, XVI. (8) Full text in original French re-printed in Franz Bock, *Memling Studien,* 1900, p. 3. (9) Max Lehrs, *Geschichte und Kritischer Katalog des deutschen, niederländischen und französischen Kupferstichs im XV Jahrhundert, Vienna,* 1908-34, Vol. VII, p. 353, No. 1; J. D. Passavant, *Le Pentre Graveur,* 1860, Vol. II, pp. 290, 1, describes the version formerly in the duc d'Arenberg collection, Brussels (now at Colnaghi's), and says "perhaps based on a good original by Roger van de Weyden". F. W. H. Hollstein, *Dutch and Flemish Etchings, Engravings and Woodcuts,* Vol. XII, 1949 seq., p. 139. An impression of the original engraving was offered for sale at Craddock and Barnard, Catalogue No. 86, No. 409, and is now in the Print Room collection, N.G. Victoria. Another impression was at Colnaghi's in 1959 as noted above. (10) M. Gomez Moreno, *Gazette des Beaux Arts,* Vol. XL, 1908, p. 305; W. Burger, *Die Malerei in den Niederlanden,* 1925, pl. 95, pp. 77/8; Friedländer, *op. cit.,* No. 37a; Panofsky, *op. cit.,* p. 274. (11) Panofsky, *op. cit.;* Berliner, *op. cit.* (see note 1). See also: Roger van Schoute, *La Chapelle Royale de Grenade,* Brussels, 1963 *(Les Primitifs Flamands I, Corpus de la peinture des anciens Pays-Bas Méridionaux au quinzième siècle* 6) review J. Bruyn, *Oud Holland,* LXXX, 1965, 133-7. U. Hoff, M. Davies, *The National Gallery of Victoria, Melbourne (Les Primitifs flamands, I, Corpus de la peinture flamande des anciens Pays-Bas méridionaux au quinzième siècle,* 12) Brussels, 1971, No. 134, p. 61.

Antonis Mor (Antonio Moro) ca. 1517-21—1576-7

Dutch. Born Utrecht; pupil of Jan Scorel; his earliest dated work is the portrait of two Pilgrim Canons of Utrecht in Berlin. 1547 moved to Antwerp where he became a member of the guild; 1549 in Brussels in the service of Cardinal Granvella, through whom he came in contact with the Spanish-Hapsburg court. 1550 in Rome; 1552 in Lisbon in the service of the Queen of Portugal; after a short stay in Utrecht visited England 1553/4 where he painted Queen Mary of England (Madrid, Prado). Back in Brussels in 1555; in 1559 he seems to have accompanied Philip II to Madrid; 1568 recorded in Antwerp where he enjoyed the patronage of the Duke of Alba. Mor portrayed many of the reigning heads and other leading personalities of the Hapsburg courts. The nobility of his work shows his knowledge of the portraits of Titian but his meticulously realistic style is Dutch.

Reference: Th.B.

Illust. 135   1823/4 **Portrait of a Lady**

panel, 100.3 x 72.1 cm. Unsigned, undated; painted 3rd quarter 16th century (?).

Condition: excellent, in 16th century frame. The panel has two vertical cracks, secured by two old and one modern fastenings.

Comment: Previously known as a portrait of Queen Mary I but the features show no resemblance to Mor's portrait of this Queen in the Prado; an undescribed portrait: the costume, with its puffed-out shoulders, its long waist and the type of lace work in the lady's cap suggests that the sitter is Flemish.[1]

Provenance: Prof. Ellis Waterhouse informed me that the picture descended in a younger branch of the Beckford family which came from Francis, 6th son of Peter Beckford, Governor of Jamaica. It may have come through his second wife (married 1755), Susannah, daughter and heiress of Richard Love of Dacing Park. The Beckfords inherited Basing Park, and lived there until the property was sold in the last century.[2] Exh. D.I., 1853, 42 (as *Queen Mary,* owner W. Beckford); R.A. 1879, 156 (as *Portrait of Queen Mary,* owner Mrs. William Beckford, Orford House); anonymous sale, Christie's, 10 May, 1879, lot 120; exhibited by Mrs. H. Kirby at Winchester in 1938.[3] Somerset Society of Artists, Old Master Exh. Taunton, May, 1946; acquired on the advice of A. J. L. McDonnell and Sir Kenneth Clark from T. Agnew and Sons, for the Felton Bequest in 1948.

References: (1) J. L. Nevinson, N.P.G. London, correspondence 10 Oct., 1958, N.G. Victoria files. (2) Correspondence N.G. Victoria files 1960. (3) Colin Agnew, correspondence 22 Jan., 1954, *ibid.;* see also *Quarterly Bulletin N.G. Victoria,* 1949, III, (3), 1, repr.

George Morland   1763-1804

British. Born London, the son of the genre and portrait painter Henry Robert Morland. Worked as portraitist in Margate and St. Omer. In 1786 he married, in London, the sister of the painter and mezzotint engraver William Ward, who engraved many of the genre and animal subjects which made Morland popular. Died in the debtor's prison in London.

Reference: *Th.B.*

Illust. 136   542/2 **The Farmyard**

canvas, 71.5 x 91.7 cm. Signed, *G. Morland pinxt* on the paling; undated.

Condition: satisfactory; some re-paints in the sky.

The picture was in the Wynn Ellis Sale, Christie's, 6 May, 1876, lot 66; and in the Sir Frederick Thorpe Mappin sale (late of Thornbury, Sheffield), Christie's, 17 June, 1910, lot 50. It was exhibited at the Annual Exhibition, Artists' General Benevolent Fund Institution, at Agnews, 1910, No. 10 (copy of this exh. cat. at Knoedlers, London,[1] has the printed entry for No. 10, Turner, *Pas de Calais* crossed out and *Morland Farmyard* written in by hand). The picture is referred to in *Art Journal,* April 1911, p. 126, as "recently on view at Messrs. Agnews", p. 128 as "having gone to Melbourne". Acquired for the Felton Bequest on the advice of Frank Gibson from T. Agnew and Son in 1911.

Reference: (1) The above provenance made available by Mr. Frank Simpson of Knoedlers.

Bartolomé Esteban Murillo 1617-1682

Spanish. Born in Seville, he became a pupil of Juan de Castillo. His early work shows the influence of Zurbaran and Ribera. Throughout his life Murillo's compositions often reflect his knowledge of Flemish, French, Italian and German engravings. He established his fame with a cycle of Franciscan themes for the Franciscan monastery in Seville in 1645-6. He soon surpassed Zurbaran in popularity and became the leading painter in Seville, painting for churches and religious institutions and portraying the local aristocracy. In 1660 he founded the Seville Academy of which he became the first President. Murillo's work, including religious subjects, low-life genre, landscape and portraiture exemplifies the late baroque style in Spanish painting.

Reference: *Th.B.;* Georg Gubler, Martin Soria, *Art and Architecture in Spain and Portugal, 1500-1800,* 1959, p. 273 *seq.*

Illust. 137 1826/4 **The Immaculate Conception**

canvas, 235 x 208 cm. Unsigned, undated; painted between 1660-70.

Condition: in excellent condition.

Comment: The meaning of the Immaculate Conception as given by Mâle is that the Virgin was created by God before all the world and free from the law of sin.[1] Francisco Pacheco (1564-1654), in his *The Art of Painting, its Antiquity and Greatness,* first published in Seville in 1649 describes in Book III, Chapter XI, *How to Paint the Immaculate Conception of Our Lady;* the excerpt given here shows that Murillo followed several of the precepts of Pacheco.[1a] "In this most lovely mystery the lady should be painted in the flower of her youth, twelve or thirteen years old, as a most beautiful young girl, with fine and serious eyes, a most perfect nose and pink cheeks wearing her most beautiful golden hair . . .
She should be painted with a white tunic and a blue mantle . . . Under her feet is the moon. Although it is a solid planet (I took the liberty to make it) light and transparent above the landscape as a half moon with the points turned downward." Pacheco quotes the opinion of Father Luis del Alcazar on the necessity of depicting the moon in this way and continues, "Seraphim or entire angels holding some of the attributes may be introduced."

Though sometimes described as a replica of the *Esquilache Madonna* in the Hermitage, most authorities regard the Hermitage picture as a workshop piece and accept the Melbourne version as authentic.[2] In its strongly accentuated diagonal composition, 1826/4 resembles the *Small Conception* at Bowood House (1665-75)[3] and the *Purissima* in the Louvre (about 1665).[4] The pose of the Madonna, with the mantle bunched over her praying hands appears similarly in the *Conception with the Mirror,* London, Earl of Northbrook (1660-78).[5]

Provenance: The picture has been referred to alternately as a *Conception* or an *Assumption*. In 1759 called a *Conception, painted for an Altarpiece,* by Murillo, size 7 ft. 8 in. x 7 ft. 1 (18) 8 in., it was listed in Dodsley's *London and its Environs,* Vol. I, p. 274, as in the Belvedere, near Erith, Kent, the seat of Sampson Gideon; this is repeated in *The English Connoisseur* 1766, p. 14, owner Sir Sampson Gideon (1774-1824) and also in *The Ambulator,* 1774, p. 12; E. W. Brayley, *The Beauties of England and Wales,* vol. VII, 1808, p. 546 (as *Conception*). Sir Sampson Gideon assumed the name of Eardley and was created Lord Eardley in 1789; after his death Belvedere was inherited by his son-in-law Lord Saye and Sele (1789-1844). It figures in a Ms. Catalogue of Belvedere (copy N.G. London in 1856, p. 10) (as *Assumption*); Sir Culling E. Eardley (Lord Eardley's second son-in-law) put it as an *Immaculate Conception* up for sale at Christie's, 30 June, 1860, lot 17, 7 ft. 8 in. x 6 ft. 8 in., bt in; the remaining pictures from Belvedere were removed to Bedwell Park in the same year (Ms. note in Dodsley's *London,* N.G. London copy); the picture was exhibited B. I, 1862, No. 1 (as *Assumption*); at the Manchester Art Treasures Exhibition 1857, No. 641 as *Madonna in Glory*; owner Sir Culling E. Eardley; his eldest daughter, Mrs. Culling Hanbury exhibited it as an *Assumption* at the R.A. 1871, No. 259; the picture was inherited by Sir C. E. Eardley's second daughter, Mrs. W. H. Fremantle, and passed by inheritance to Sir Francis the Hon. Edward Fremantle (d. 1943); sold after his death by his son, Lieutenant Col. F. D. E. Fremantle as *Immaculate Conception* at Christie's 14 Dec., 1945, lot 26, bt. Roland. Acquired for the Felton Bequest in 1947-8, on the advice of A. J. L. McDonnell and Sir Kenneth Clark, from Roland, Browse and Delbanco.

Reference: (1) E. Mâle, *L'Art Religieux de la fin du XVIe, Siècle, du XVII Siècle* . . . 1951, pp. 41-45. (1a) See Elizabeth Gilmore Holt, *A Documentary History of Art,* Vol. II, 1958, pp. 221-4. (2) The following authorities accept the painting: W. Burger, *Trésors d'Art,* Manchester, 1857, p. 128; G. F. Waagen, *A Walk through the Art Treasures Exhibition* (Manchester) 1857, p. 25, No. 641; *Art Treasures in Great Britain, Suppl.* 1857, p. 275/6 letter V; H. von Tschudi, *Die Kaiserliche Gemäldegalerie der Ermitage in St. Petersburg,* n.d., p. 25, quotes Justi as regarding the *Esquilache Madonna* as a school copy (w. additions) of the Melbourne picture. Carl Justi, *Murillo,* 1904, p. 52; Prof. D. Angulo-Iniguez, Madrid (verbal discussion 1959); Prof. Martin Soria (correspondence, 1954, N.G. Victoria files) and Prof. Ellis Waterhouse (verbal discussion 1959) support the authenticity of the painting. The following authorities have rejected the painting: Ch. B. Curtis, *Velasquez, Murillo,* 1883, p. 135, No. 45, "a replica of the Esquilache Madonna"; Neil MacLaren, *The Spanish School, National Gallery Catalogues,* London, 1952, p. 44, note 9, "a repetition" of the *Esquilache Madonna,* "by a follower". MacLaren notes that in most *Conceptions* by Murillo, the Madonna stands on a crescent moon with upturned horns. The *Esquilache Madonna* was not included in the current catalogue of the Hermitage Museum since it is regarded as a schoolpiece and is earmarked for transfer to a provincial gallery. (Information received from Mme. Nemilova, The Leningrad Hermitage, through Miss Mary Chamot. Tate Gallery, London, correspondence 1959, N.G. Victoria files.) (3) A. L. Mayer, *Murillo,* 1913, p. 75. (4) *ibid.,* p. 76. (5) *ibid.,* p. 165. See also: *Quarterly Bulletin, N.G. Victoria,* 1948, III (2), 2.

Daniel Mytens the Elder   c. 1590-before 1648

Dutch. Born Delft, probably trained under Mierevelt (1567-1641), member of the guild at the Hague in 1610. Was working for the king of England soon after 1618. Painter to Charles I in 1625. After 1632 he was eclipsed by van Dyck and returned to Holland in about 1635.

Reference: *Th.B.*

Illust. 138   E1/1972 **Sir John Ashburnham**

oil on canvas, 224.8 x 134.6 cm. Unsigned, undated, painted probably in the late 1620s.

Condition: two patches at back, some re-paints; in good sound condition.
An alteration of the contour of the r. hand leg is visible under the landscape.

Comment: John Ashburnham 1603-1671 began his court career under
the patronage of the Duke of Buckingham. In 1628 he was elected M.P.
for Hastings and in the same year made groom of the bedchamber.
His two functions as member of Parliament and servant to the king became
incompatible; when his attendance on his master prevented his obeying
the summons of the house he was proceeded against for contempt and
"discharged and disabled" in 1642. He became treasurer and paymaster
of the king's army. Involved in an unsuccessful plot to assist Charles
in flight Ashburnham was unjustly suspected of disloyalty by the Royalists
and suffered great hardship under the Commonwealth. At the Restoration
he came back to his old place of groom of the bedchamber. He and his
brother William shared in an enterprise for reviving the manufacture
of tapestry at Mortlake in 1667.
The full length figure is portrayed in a green slashed doublet with sleeves
paned and buttoned on the inside of the forearms in the manner current
between 1620 and 1635. The wings encircling the sleeves became a fashion
after 1625. The straight lower edge of the doublet is also to be met with
usually after 1630. The baldrick replaced the waist belt after 1625. The
breeches style also points to a period after 1628. The soft tight fitting boots
have hose tops of linen edged with lace. The shape of the spur leathers
suggests a date before 1630. The costume thus leads to the assumption
that the portrait was painted in the very late 1620s or c. 1630. Through the
mist a river, trees and a cornfield visible on the right.
Engravings: three quarter length by Robert Graves (1798-1873) as
frontispiece for John Ashburnham's *Narrative,* ed. Lord Ashburnham 1930.

Provenance: Ashburnham collection; Sale Sotheby, London July 15, 1953, lot 91, bt.
Lord Wilton, Ramsbury Manor; sold to the late Lord Rootes; acquired from his son under
the terms of the Everard Studley Miller Bequest on the recommendation of Eric Westbrook,
Dr. Roy Strong, Professor Ellis Waterhouse and Dr. Woodall from Leggatt's London,
1971; arrived 1972.

Patrick Nasymth   1787-1831

British. Born Edinburgh, son and pupil of Alexander Nasmyth (1758-1840).
Followed the manner of his father; also influenced by 17th century Dutch
paintings. Moved to London about 1807 where he became a foundation
member of the Royal Society of British Artists.

Reference: *Th.B.*

Illust. 139   695/2 **River and Trees**

panel, 17.7 x 26.7 cm. (sight measurements). Unsigned, undated.

Condition: covered with old varnish.

Provenance: Presented by John Connell, 1914.

William Owen   1769-1825

British. His early work is painted in the manner of Reynolds. R.A. 1806. Portrait painter to the Prince of Wales in 1810, Principal Portrait Painter to the Prince Regent in 1813. Painted many of the leading scholars, ecclesiastics, lawyers and statesmen of his day in a sober, recording style, eschewing flattery.

References: M. H. Spielmann, *British Portrait Painting to the Opening of the 19th century*, Vol. II, 1910, p. 76; T. S. R. Boase, *English Art, 1800-1870*, 1959, p. 14.

Illust. 110   3267/4 **Rachel, Lady Beaumont**

canvas, 214.3 x 136.1 cm. Painted 1808, inscribed (later): *Rachel Lady Beaumont aged 91. Born 1718. Died March 9th* (?illeg.) l.l.

Condition: very good.

Comment: Rachel, Lady Beaumont, was the mother of Sir George Howland Beaumont 1753-1827, painter friend and patron of painters and poets of his era, famous collector and John Constable's[1] lifelong friend. Allan Cunningham attributed Sir George's achievements to the influence of his mother: "his mother observed the progress of her son in learning and taste with no little pleasure; her powers of mind were such that she would direct as well as appreciate his studies".[2]

Leslie says that "in about 1792 Mrs. Constable procured an introduction for her son to the Dowager Lady Beaumont, then residing in Dedham". Here Constable met Sir George Beaumont "and began a lifelong friendship".[3]

The portrait is referred to by Farington: "August 9th 1808: Owen called. Had been at Dunmow with Sir G. Beaumont three weeks, in which time he had nearly finished a whole length of old Lady Beaumont now in her 91st year. She rises at 7 and associates with the family and continues up till half-past 9 at night, is cheerful and, Owen said, strong".[4]
The tower of Dedham church can be seen through the window.[5]

Provenance: The portrait remained in the Beaumont family. Exhibited R.A. 1809, No. 78 (owner not stated); R.A. 1825, No. 22 (owner not stated); acquired on the advice of A. J. L. McDonnell for the Felton Bequest in 1955 from Messrs. Colnaghi.

References: (1) *D.N.B.* (2) Allan Cunningham, *The Lives of the Most Eminent British Painters,* 1833, Vol. VI, p. 136. (3) C. R. Leslie, *Memoirs of the Life of John Constable,* ed. Shirley, 1937, p. 5. (4) *The Faringron Diary,* Vol. V, 1808-9, p. 94. (5) T. S. R. Boase, *English Art, 1800-1870,* 1959, pp. 14, 112, pl. 8.

Marco Palmezzano   1458-63—1539

Italian. Born Forlì. Pupil of Melozzo da Forlì, came under the influence of Rondinelli and Cima da Conegliano. Probably stayed in Venice but was resident in Forlì.

Reference: Th.B.

J

Illust. 141   982/3 **The Baptism Of Christ**

panel (cradled), 86.4 x 67.1 cm. Unsigned, undated.

Condition: in fair condition. Re-paints in figures, along two vertical cracks in panel. Very fine priming crackle. Restored 1972 by David Lawrance.

Comment: Berenson refers to documents which prove that Palmezzano was influenced by Giovanni Bellini and regards the Melbourne picture as a copy from a lost Bellini:[1] listed by Grigioni as "undated and undatable".[2]

Provenance: In the collection of Henry Duncan, 2nd Baron Aberconway (1879-1953); said to have been in the family since the last owner's great-grandfather's time. Acquired on the advice of Frank Rinder for the Felton Bequest in 1919-20.[3]

References: (1) B. Berenson, *Pitture Italiane del Rinascimento, Milano,* 1936, p. 357. (2) Carlo Grigioni, *Marco Palmezzano,* 1956, p. 683, No. 91 (aap. IV). (3) Rinder corr. 19.XI.1919, 27.I.1920.

Paolo Veneziano   active 1320, died between 1358-1362

Italian. Fiocco assumes that Master Paolo had made a journey to Constantinople. His presence is documented in Venice, from 1333 to before 1362, by four signatures on altarpieces. He introduces a new impulse toward byzantinism into Venetian painting which he combines with certain western gothic innovations.

References: G. Fiocco, *Dedalo,* June, 1931, p. 877 *seq.;* E. Sandberg Vavalà *Burl. Mag.,* Vol. LVII, 1930, p. 161; *Th.B.*

Illust. 142   1966/4 **The Crucifixion**

panel, arched top, 96.8 x 67.7 cm. Unsigned, undated; painted 1320-30. Condition: in good condition, priming crackle.

Comment: Listed in Catalogue, Appendix 1, 1950, as Venetian School. While in the Muir Mackenzie collection, ascribed to Semitecolo (about 1353-about 1370).[1] Van Marle in 1925 rejected this attribution.[2] When the *Crucifixion* was shown at the Italian Exhibition in London in 1930, Roger Fry pointed out the strongly byzantine features of the composition.[3] Sandberg Vavalà saw its relation to the Chioggia *Crucifixion* and attributed 1966/4 and related compositions to Master Paolo Veneziano and his workshop.[4] Fiocco in 1931 stressed in particular the relation of 1966/4 to the *Crucifixion* from the polyptych in the Cathedral of Pirano, Istria.[5] He grouped the Pirano *Crucifixion* with other works by Master Paolo of a distinctly byzantine style, of which the altarpiece at Dignano is dated 1323. Other variants of 1966/4 are quoted by Sandberg Vavalà: polyptych, San Martino, Chioggia;[6] polyptych from Veglia, Museo Civico, Trieste;[7] altarpiece, Arbe, Dalmatia.[8] Iconographically 1966/4 shows strongly byzantine elements. The Virgin fainting in the arms of supporting women was in the opinion of earlier scholarship of Italian origin.[9] Lasareff however pointed out that this motif can be found in Armenian miniatures of the 13th century "from where it must have passed not only into Byzantium but also into Italy".[10] These illuminations also show the crenelated wall in the background, the lamenting angels above the arms of the Cross, the hillock and cave to be seen in 1966/4.

Provenance: Owned by William Graham (1817-1885),[11] some time M.P. of Glasgow and well known collector of Italian Primitives and English Pre-Raphaelites. Graham exhibited the picture as by Buffalmacco at the R.A. 1884, No. 221; his daughter, Amelia, married in 1874 Kenneth Augustin, 1st Baron Muir MacKenzie of Delvine (1845-1930), who exhibited it at the Burl. F.A.C. 1912, No. 1; R.A. 1930, No. 73; the picture passed from Amelia ʰʰ Ḳⅼⁱⁱ ⁱⁱ her daughter, Mrs. Mark Hambourg, who sold it to T. Agnew and Sons in 1948.[12] Acquired on the advice of A. J. L. McDonnell and Sir Kenneth Clark from T. Agnew & Sons for the Felton Bequest in 1948-9.

References: (1) Exh. as such at Burl. F.A.C. Early Venetian School, 1912, No. 1; R.A. 1930, Italian Art, No. 73, pl. XVIII; Roger Fry, *Burl. Mag.,* Vol. XXI, 1912, p. 47, pl. 1. (2) R. van Marle, *Italian Schools of Painting,* Vol. V, 1925, p. 482/3. (3) Roger Fry, *Burl. Mag.,* Vol. LVI, 1930, p. 83, pl. IV. (4) E. Sandberg Vavalà, *Burl. Mag.,* Vol. LVII, 1930, p. 177, No. 21 and p. 160 *seq.* (5) G. Fiocco, *Dedalo,* Vol. XI, June 1931, p. 877 *seq.,* repr., pp. 888, 889. (6) Sandberg Vavalà, *op. cit.,* p. 177, pl. V, A. (7) *ibid.,* pp. 171, 177, pl. IV, B. (8) Van Marle, *op. cit.,* Vol. IV, 1924, fig. 47. (9) Millet, *Recherches sur l'iconographie de l'Evangile,* 1916, pp. 418-22. See also E. Sandberg Vavalà, *La Croce Dipinta Italiana,* 1929, p. 148 *seq.* (10) V. Lasareff, *Burl. Mag.,* Vol. LI, 1927, p. 62, pl. IV, C & D: Gospel Library of Armenian Patriarchate, Jerusalem, Nr. 2568/13, fol. 88a, between 1259-1284; Gospel, *ibid.* Nr. 2563/8 fol. 362b, of 1272. (11) Stated in Cat. R.A. 1930, No. 73. (12) Information by courtesy of Mr. Colin Agnew, Esq.

Jean Baptiste Perronneau   1715-1783

French. Born Paris. Painter of portraits in pastel and oil; also an engraver. Pupil of Natoire and Laurent Cars. Member of the Academy in 1753. Went to Holland in 1754, 1755 and from 1761-63, where he received many commissions. After an unspecified catastrophe which deprived him of all his wealth, he returned to Amsterdam in 1771 to re-establish his fortune, but came back to Paris in 1772, disappointed in his expectations. Undertook another journey to Amsterdam in 1780, where he remained until his death.

References: L. Vaillat and P. R. de Limay, *J. B. Perroneau,* Paris, n.d.

Illust. 143   3015/4 **Petrus Woortman**

canvas, 78.8 x 61.4 cm. Signed and dated *Perronneau 1771,* upper right (within oval).

Condition: very good.

Comment: Petrus Woortman (1719-1791), Catholic priest at the church of Moses and Aaron in Amsterdam, is depicted in a braided coat, holding a Bible in his hand. A lace collar protects the embroidered stole from the powdered wig.[1]

Provenance: The Church of Moses and Aaron, Amsterdam.[1] Exhibited Burl. Fine Arts Club, 1913, p. 25, No. 13, by C. S. Carstairs; R. A. French Art, 1932, p. 129, No. 260, by Sir Philip Sassoon who left the picture to the Marchioness of Cholmondeley, Houghton Hall; acquired from Th. Agnew and Sons on the advice of A. J. L. McDonnell and Sir Kenneth Clark for the Felton Bequest 1952/53.

Reference: (1) L. Vaillat and P. D. de Limay, *J. B. Perronneau,* Paris (1909), pp. 51, 104, No. 128, pl. 63.

Francesco Pesellino   ca. 1422-1457

Italian. Born Florence. Pupil of Giuliano Pesello, his grandfather and later of Filippo Lippi. Influenced by Masaccio, Fra Angelico and later by Domenico Veneziano. 1447 a member of the Guild of S. Luke.

Reference: *Th.B.*

School of Pesellino

Illust. 144   555/4 **Madonna and Child with Three Angels**

panel, 69.8 x 53 cm. Unsigned, undated.

Condition: cleaned of heavy overpainting after purchase by Howard Spensley.[1] Unfinished; face of Madonna and figure of child only drawn in on white ground; face and hands of angels and hands of Madonna show under paint. Garments laid in in local colours. The background landscape and the sky being the most finished parts.
Everett Fahey, corr. Jan. 1970 (Hoff Fahey) suggests that the unfinished look is due to cleaning down to underpainting.

Comment: Berenson regarded the picture as possibly the work of Fra Diamante; the profile angel on the left shows similarity in type to angels in Fra Diamante's *Death of the Virgin.*[2]

Provenance: Howard Spensley Bequest 1939.[1]

References: (1) Note in Howard Spensley's Ms., Book I, p. 79, Cat. No. 531; (as by Lorenzo di Credi). (2) R. van Marle, *Italian Schools of Painting,* Vol. XI, 1929, fig. 381.

Giovanni Battista Pittoni   1687-1767

Italian. Born Venice. Pupil of his uncle, Francesco Pittoni, influenced by Nic. Grassi and the work or Seb. Ricci, Piazzetta, Tiepolo and other Venetian painters. Worked for the Spanish, French, Polish and other courts as well as for the ruling houses of many Italian cities. 1757, member of the Venetian Academy: succeeded Tiepolo in 1758 as its president. Painter of religious, historical and mythological subjects.

Reference: *Th.B.*

Illust. 145   2360/4 **The Miracle of the Loaves and Fishes** canvas, 120.1 x 178.5 cm. Inscribed in capitals *S. Ricci, 1725,* l.c.; painted about 1720-25.

Condition: very good; cleaned prior to purchase.

Comment: A variant of Pittoni's painting of the same subject in the Accademia at Venice, formerly in the Church of San Cosmo della Guidecca.

This latter picture is mentioned in Zanetti's edition of Boschini's *Guide of Venice* of 1733.[1] Fiocco[2] dates it about 1725 and says that the style in the toning down of local colour and its light brushwork shows the influence of Tiepolo. Max Goering[3] holds that the type of woman used by Pittoni resembles the type used by him in the Rebecca and Eleazar in Bordeaux.[4] Goering dates the Venice picture before 1720.

The inscription S. Ricci in the variant may have been placed on the picture in England where Ricci was better known than Pittoni. There is a close connection between the style of Pittoni and Ricci at this period (cf. *Moses Striking the Rock,* at Hampton Court).[5]

Another version (109.2 x 210.8 cm), differing in certain details from 2360/4, from the collection of Mr. George Rawson, was owned by Messrs. Marshall and Spink in 1952.[6]

Provenance: Owned by the late R. G. A. Palmer-Morewood, Alfreton Park, Derbyshire; acquired from Marshall C. Spink on the advice of A. J. L. McDonnell for the Felton Bequest 1950-51.

References: (1) See Max Goering, *Mitteilungen des Kunsthistorischen Instituts zu Florenz,* Vol. IV, Jan. 1934, p. 238-239, repr. 20 (Accademia version). Rodolfo Pallucchini, *I disegni de Giambattista Pittoni,* Padua, 1945, Nos. 55, 59, 60 lists three drawings, of heads and hands for this picture. I owe this reference to Mr. Harley Preston. (2) G. Fiocco, *Venetian Painting of the Seicento and the Settecento,* 1929, pl. 68, p. 59. (3) Goering, *op. cit.* (4) *ibid.,* fig. 19. (5) A. Blunt, *Burl. Mag.,* Vol. LXXXVIII, 1946, p. 267, pl. IV, V. (6) *Burl. Mag.,* 1952, Vol. XCIV, No 597, pl. XIII, and note. See also: *Quaterly Bulletin, N.G. Victoria,* 1955, IX, (3), 4.

Gaspard Poussin   1615-1675

French. Born Rome, son of Jacques Dughet; adopted the name Poussin from his brother-in-law Nicolas *(q.v.).* Pupil of Nicolas Poussin ca. 1630; also influenced by Claude and others. The main sources are Baldinucci and Pascoli. Landscape painter in and around Rome.

Reference: *Th.B.*

Follower of Poussin

Illust. 146   2968/4 **Landscape with Christ and Mary Magdalene**

canvas, 53.8 x 41.4 cm (sight measurements). Unsighted, undated.

Condition: good.

Comment: The composition of this classical landscape is reminiscent of Gasper Poussin's work but the mauve pinks in the clouds suggest an 18th century artist working in the style of this painter.

Provenance: Private owner, Poland-Australia. Purchased 1952 in Melbourne.

Nicolas Poussin   1594-1665

French School. Born probably at Villiers, Les Andelys (Normandy). Introduced to painting by Quantin Varin; 1612 to 1621 in Paris where he worked under Ferdinand Elle and George Lallemand, and became acquainted with engravings after Raphael and Giulio Romano and with antique scultpure in the Royal Collections. Left for Rome late in 1623 on the invitation of the Italian poet G. B. Marino, who he had met in Paris, spending several months in Venice on the way. Was introduced to Cardinal Francesco Barberini and the antiquary Cassiano del Pozzo who became his most important patron. Together with the Flemish sculptor, Duquesnoy, he drew from classical statues and reliefs; he also studied the paintings of Raphael, Giulio Romano and Titian whose Bacchanalia (Prado, Madrid) were at that time in the Villa Aldobrandini. About 1634-5 his fame was well established. His work, combining mannerist, raphaelesque, baroque and Venetian characteristics often drew its subject matter from Ovid's *Metamorphoses.* Later he turned to the stoic actions of heroes of the Old Testament and Roman History. *The Crossing of the Red Sea,* painted for Amadeo, cousin of Cassino del Pozzo, belongs to this period. In 1638 he received a proposal from Cardinal Richelieu to return to Paris where he arrived in December 1640. He was made first Painter-in-Ordinary to the King and entrusted with the supervision of all paintings and ornament in the Royal Houses. Among his commissions was a series of designs for tapestries, to act as pendants to the *Acts of the Apostles* by Raphael, which did not eventuate at that time. The tapestry of *The Crossing of the Red Sea* (see below) was made for a series of this kind which was later made up from existing paintings by the master who had not supplied the cartoons. Intrigues of the French artists against him, ill health and artistic dissatifaction induced Poussin to return to Rome in September 1642.

The work of his second Roman period achieved a new grandeur and classical severity. Allegorical landscapes became a frequent subject.

References: Charles Sterling, biography in *Cat. Exposition Nicolas Poussin,* Musée du Louvre, 1960, pp. 197-283.

Illust. 147   1843/4 **The Crossing of the Red Sea**

canvas, 155.6 x 215.3 cm. Unsigned, undated; painted in the middle 1630s.

Condition: in good condition; cleaned by A. H. Buttery, London, in 1960, who removed the considerably discoloured varnish and old repairs and over-painting. Mr. Buttery reported that the figures in the background had suffered from earlier cleaning. The "pillar of cloud", red brown in colour is clearly visible on the extreme right.

Comment: The subject is taken from Exodus XIV, 26-31. In Exodus XIII, XIV it is related how the Israelites went out of captivity in Egypt through the Red Sea, led by the Lord who assumed the shape of a "pillar of cloud" by day and a "pillar of fire" by night. They were pursued by Pharaoh with his horsemen and chariots. The Lord caused the sea to recede to let the Israelites pass through. At the command of the Lord, Moses stretched out his hand over the sea and the waters returned and covered the pursuing Egyptians. The traditional title of 1843/4 is inaccurate, since the crossing has been accomplished. The Egyptians have perished "off-stage"; the figures in the foreground salvaging armour and a dead Egyptian are inspired by Josephus, Antiquitates (93 A.D.) II, 16, 6. For opinions on the dating see Blunt.[1] Franz Philipp has discussed the iconographic sources of the composition.[2] Walter Friedländer deals with it in relation to Poussin's theory of the *Affetti*.[3] Poussin intended to repeat the theme in 1648, with twenty-seven figures only, in a painting for Lisle de la Sourdière, but the project was not carried out.[4]

Drawings: Two related groups of drawings are in existence: Group A, in the Hermitage, Leningrad, Friedländer Nos. 17, 18, 19, dated by this author about 1634-5, and Group B, in the Louvre, Paris, Friedländer Nos. 20, 21, which he dated 1635-6.[5]

Copies: A copy described as by Lebrun (1619-1690) was Lot 107 in the catalogue of the Robert Strange collection, Christie's, 6 March 1773.[6] Yvart fils (Joseph Yvart, 1649-1728) copied the composition in a cartoon used for one of a series of Gobelins of the *History of Moses,* after paintings by Poussin and Charles Lebrun. The first weaving took place soon after 1683.[7] A painted copy at Besançon and two drawings after *The Crossing* are listed by Blunt.[7a]

Engravings: Anonymous, published by Etienne Gantrel (1640-1705).[8] The engraving differs from the painting in the absence of the pillar, the shape of the cloud and the wider margin between figure composition and edge of composition. The Strange catalogue suggests that it was based on the copy by Lebrun (see above). An engraving in outline by V. Lignée, in Landon's *Vies et Oeuvres des peintres les plus célèbres,* I, No. 7, Paris, 1809, was apparently made from the Gantrel engraving.

Exhibitions: Royal Academy, 1873, No. 105 (Earl of Radnor); ibid. *French Art,* 1932, No. 142 (Earl of Radnor); Musée du Louvre, *Exposition Nicolas Poussin,* May-July 1960, No. 37.

Provenance: Painted with its companion piece, the *Adoration of the Golden Calf,* London, National Gallery,[9] for Amadeo dal Pozzo, Marquis de Voghera, of Turin before 1640.[10] Sheila Somers Rinehart suggests that the pictures may not have been commissioned by Amadeo, but by Cassiano who sent them to Amadeo.[11] Seen at the Voghera Palace, by Monconys on June 28, 1664.[12] By 1684 the two pictures were owned by the Chevalier de Lorraine (d. 1704), when the *Adoration of the Golden Calf* was engraved by E. de Baudet. Apparently in the possession of Benigne le Ragois de Bretonvilliers, Paris, as ornaments of a room decorated in 1710. Bought through the dealer Samuel Paris in Paris in 1741 by Sir Jacob Bouverie, who was created Viscount Folkestone in 1747; his successor became the Earl of Radnor in 1765. The pictures remained together in the possession of the same family at Longford Castle (*The Passage of the Red Sea* exhibited by the Earl of Radnor at the Royal Academy, 1873, No. 105, and Royal Academy, *French Art,* 1932, No. 142) until 1945 when the *Adoration of the Golden Calf* was acquired for the London National Gallery; *The Crossing of the Red Sea* was acquired for the Felton Bequest, from T. Agnew and Sons on the advice of A. J. L. McDonnell and Sir Kenneth Clark in 1948.

References: (1) Anthony Blunt, *Nicolas Poussin, A Critical Catalogue,* London, 1966, pp. 17 f. (2) and *Nicolas Poussin, The A. W. Mellon Lectures in the Fine Arts,* 1958, London, New York, 1967, Text, p. 128. Franz Philipp, *Poussin's Crossing of the Red Sea* in: *In Honour of Daryl Lindsay, Essays and Studies, Melbourne,* 1964, pp. 80-99, figs. 63-74. (3) Walter Friedländer, *Nicolas Poussin,* London, 1966, pp. 53 f, fig. 43. (4) *Correspondence de Nicolas Poussin* (Archives de l'art Français), 1911, pp. 376, 385. (5) W. Friedländer, *The Drawings of Nicolas Poussin,* Studies of the Warburg Institute, Vol. V, 1939; M. Alpatov, in: *Actes du Colloques Internationaux, Nicolas Poussin,* 1960, Vol. 1, p. 192, fig. 173. (6) Anthony Blunt, *op. cit.* p. 17. (7) M. Fénaille, *Etat Général des Tapisseries des Gobelins, Paris,* 1903, Vol. II, p. 186 fl. repr. R. A. Weigert in *Société Poussin,* 3e cahier, Mai 1950, p. 83 seq. (7a) Blunt, *op. cit.* 1966, pp. 17-20, Nos. 6, 7, 8. (8) G. Wildenstein, *Les Graveurs de Poussin,* Paris 1957, No. 17 repr. (9) Martin Davies, *French School, National Gallery Catalogues,* London, 1957, pp. 177 f. (10) Bellori, *Vite,* 1672, p. 419. (11) *Actes du Colloque Internationaux, Nicolas Poussin,* 1960, Vol. I, p. 19. (12) The remaining account of the provenance is based on Davies, *op. cit.* and Blunt, *op. cit.* (13) For a comprehensive Bibliography see Anthony Blunt, *Nicolas Poussin, A Critical Catalogue,* London 1966, pp. 17 seq.

Mattia Preti   1613-1699

Italian. Born Taverna, Calabria. About 1630 in Rome where he joined his brother, and came under the influence of Caravaggism; he may, however, already have absorbed this in Naples. Between 1630 and 40 probably travelled to Bologna, Parma, Modena and Venice. Documented in Rome in 1641. Between 1642 and 44 carried out commissions in Taverna as well as Rome. 1644-50 executed the ceiling and cupola frescoes in S. Biago in Modena and other North Italian and Venetian commissions. 1650 his name appears in the Congregazione dei Virtuosi al Pantheon in Rome. 1653 member of the Academy of S. Luke in Rome. 1651 carries out choir frescoes of S. Andrea della Valle in Rome. In the sixteen fifties the influence of Guercino shows in his work. 1659/60 in Naples and Malta. 1661 becomes cavaliere di grazia in the order of St. John of Malta. His style combines caravaggesque characteristics with the high baroque of Lanfranco, Pietro da Cortona, Domenichino, to which are added influences from Guercino, Rubens and the Venetian school.

Reference: F. Cummings, R. Wittkower, *Art in Italy 1600-1700,* Detroit Institute of Art, Abrams, New York, 1965.

Illust. 148   1818/5 **Sophonisba receiving the Poison**

canvas, 142.8 x 259.1 cm. Unsigned, undated.

Condition: in good condition; report from restorer H. Lank, London, 4 December 1967; sound old re-lining; a seam runs horizontally along the centre of the picture. There are a few losses and repairs; thinly varnished.

Comment: At its first public showing in 1944-5 the subject was described as *Queen Cleopatra of Cyprus, Poisoned by her Son.*[1] Its close resemblance to the Jerace painting (see under Other Versions below) traditionally known as Sofonisba, and the age of the man pressing her to drink the poison leaves little doubt that the present title is the correct one. Moreover "Cleopatra of Cyprus, poisoned by her son" was not a particularly popular theme in the 17th century while "Sofonisba" was widely represented.[2]

The theme comes from Livy's *History of Rome,* XXX, 12-15. Sofonisba was the wife of the ruler of Carthage and when Masinissa and Laelius under the command of Scipio overthrew Carthage in 203 B.C., Sofonisba took poison, which was, according to Livy's romantic story, sent to her by Masinissa, who, in love with her, wanted to spare her the humiliation of captivity. The subject occurs in the work of Vouet, Guercino and other Caravaggists. 1818/5 had remained unpublished until 1944.[3] Iconographically it is unrelated to Vouet or Guercino but resembles an earlier version of the same theme by Preti which in turn is strongly Caravaggesque,[4] and datable to the 1630s. The Melbourne picture seems to precede the later versions of this subject by Preti, listed below. Stylistic elements link it with Caravaggism and the work of Veronese.

Other Versions: An early version, thought by Nicholson to date from the 1630s was exhibited in 1971 at Gilberto Algranti's exhibition at the Palazzo Serbelloni, Milan.[5] Closely related to the Melbourne picture is the version formerly in the Jerace collection, Naples, probably dating from the early 1640s; upright versions of the theme are in the Museum at Lyon (late 1640s) and in the Pallavicini Gallery in Rome (1650s).[6]

Provenance: From the collections of the principi antichi Mattei, Rome; Conti Gaetani, Rome, exh. *Mostra di Pittore Italiani del Seicento,* Rome, Studio d'Arte Palma, Dec. 1944-Feb. 1945, No. 20. Acquired under the terms of the Felton Bequest from Colnaghi, London, on the advice of Mr. Michael Levi, Signor Carandente and Dr. M. Woodall, Oct. 1967; ar. 1968.

References: (1) Thus in Catalogue of *Mostra di Pittore Italiani del Seicento,* Rome, Studio d'Arte Palma, Dec. 1944-Feb. 1945, No. 20. (2) See A. Pigler, *Barockthemen,* II, 1956, 413-5. (3) M. Woodall 'An unknown version of Mattia Preti's Sophonisba takes the poison' in *Art Bulletin of Victoria,* Melbourne, 1968/69, pp. 10-15, figs. 4-10. (4) B. Nicolson, postscript to Luisa Vertoria 'Five Centuries of Painting at Algranti, Milan' in *Burl. Mag.* Vol. CXII, 1971, pp. 428-29, figs. 90, 92. (5) *ibid.* (6) Letter Woodall-Hoff, 2 Aug. 1971, reporting comments made by Benedict Nicolson.

Sir Henry Raeburn   1756-1823

British. Born at Stockbridge, Edinburgh. Seems to have been largely self-taught, about 1785 probably went to London and met Reynolds;

in Italy 1785-7; returned to Edinburgh where he practised portraiture. R.A. 1815. Knighted and appointed His Majesty's Limner for Scotland in 1822.

Reference: *C.N.G.*

Illust. 149   548/2 **Admiral Robert Deans**

canvas, 90.3 x 71 cm. Unsigned, undated; painted between 1804-1810.

Condition: satisfactory.

Comment: Robert Deans 1740-1815, became Lieutenant on 20 June 1765; Commander 7 Sept. 1778; Captain 9 March 1780; in 1781 he commanded the "Mentor", 20 guns, which was burnt at Pensacola in the American War of Independence. Rear-Admiral of the White 14 Feb. 1799; Rear-Admiral of the Red 1 Jan. 1801; Vice Admiral of the Blue 23 April 1804; Vice Admiral of the Red 9 Nov. 1805. Since he is wearing Vice Admiral's uniform (undress) the portrait must have been painted after 1804 and before 31 July 1810 when Deans became Admiral of the Blue. On 12 Aug. 1812 he became Admiral of the White[1] and died at his seat in East Lothian, Scotland, in March 1815.[2]

Provenance: According to a letter received at date of purchase from Mrs. Blanche Morris, the great-granddaughter of the Admiral, the portrait went from Admiral Robert Deans, son of the man portrayed, to Mrs. R. Deans, his widow who lived in Cheltenham, and from her to her daughter. Acquired for the Felton Bequest on the advice of Frank Gibson from Shepherd Gallery,[3] London, in 1910-11.[4]

References: (1) List of commissioned senior officers of the Royal Navy, by courtesy of National Maritime Museum, Greenwich. (2) *Gentleman's Magazine,* Vol. 85, 1815, p. 283, obituary of Admiral Deans. (3) *Art Journal,* 1911, p. 224 (as at Shepherd Gallery). (4) James Greig, *Raeburn,* 1911, p. 16 repr. (together with portrait of Mrs. Deans), p. 42, listed as owned by N.G. Victoria. See also M. Wood, *The Studio,* Vol. LXVI, 1915-16, p. 229; *Quarterly Bulletin N.G. Victoria,* 1946, I (4), 5.

Illust. 150   1509/3 **James Wardrop of Torbane Hill**

canvas, 30⅜ in. x 25¼ in. Unsigned, undated; painted about 1820?

Condition: Rinder[1] reported in 1924 that bitumen trouble in the two lower corners and above the head had been treated by Ségier in 1898. These bitumen cracks recurred in 1952 when the picture was sent to London to be treated by Mr. Buttery. Otherwise in excellent condition.

Comment: The sitter (1738-1830) inherited Torbane in Linlithgowshire from his family; he sold the estate to reside in Edinburgh. He was father of James Wardrop, surgeon-extraordinary to George IV.[2]

Other Versions: A replica of 1509/3 was described by James Greig as the property of G. S. Davidson Esq., Glasgow. Present whereabouts of this picture unknown.[3]

Provenance: 1509/3 passed from James Wardrop II (1782-1869) to his daughter Mrs. Arthur Shirly,[4] who exhibited it in Edinburgh, 1876, No. 3; R.A. 1877, No. 9; passed to J. C. Wardrop, who exhibited it in Edinburgh, 1886, No. 1588; Grafton Galleries, 1895, No. 38;

1901, No. 183; Whitechapel 1901-2, No. 165. The picture was published in 1908 and 1911 as still in the possession of the same owner,[5] who sold it to the Felton Bequest in 1924-25 on the advice of Frank Rinder.

References: (1) Felton correspondence, 30 October, 1924, F. Rinder. (2) *D.N.B., James Wardrop jnr.* (3) James Greig, *Sir Henry Raeburn,* 1911, pl. 22c. repr. (4) Sir Walter Armstrong, *Raeburn,* 1901, p. 90, pl. 92. (5) *The Masterpieces of Raeburn,* Gowans Art Books, No. 15, 1908, pl. 31; James Greig, *op. cit.,* p. 62, pl. 22c repr. Other publications: W. E. Henley, *Sir Henry Raeburn, 1890,* repr.; W. D. Mackay, *Scottish School of Painting,* 1906, pp. 55-6; J. L. Caw, *Portraits of Sir Henry Raeburn,* 1909, repr.

Illust. 151   230/4 **John Guthrie of Carbeth,** 1768-1834

canvas, 75.5 x 63.2 cm. Unsigned, undated; painted after 1808.

Condition: excellent.

Comment: Born at Baldernock, John Guthrie spent his early life in the West Indies and when he returned to Glasgow he became a partner in the firm of Leitch and Smith. He purchased and built up the estate of Carbeth between 1808 and 1817. Became a magistrate of Glasgow in 1814 and Dean of Guild. Died unmarried in 1834 at Edgcomb Cottage, Devonshire.[1]

Another version of this portrait is in the Lady Lever Art Gallery, Port Sunlight; the sitter is called *James Edgar of Auchingrammont.* No pedigree is given for this picture. R. R. Tatlock expresses doubts about its identity and suggests that the handling is not altogether typical of Raeburn.[2]

Provenance: The estate of Carbeth, renamed Carbeth-Guthrie, was bequeathed by John Guthrie to his cousin William Smith;[3] 230/4 was exhibited by William Smith's son John Guthrie Smith in Glasgow in 1868, No. 118;[4] in 1886 the portrait was stated to be at Mugdock Castle (owner John Guthrie Smith);[5] exhibited 1894, *Old Glasgow Memorial Catalogue* 1896 No. 227[6] (owner Guthrie Smith). John Guthrie Smith died in 1894; after this the picture seems to have been at the Western Club in Glasgow;[7] Greig quotes Mr. Guthrie Smith as owner in 1911.[8]
A reference in the Felton correspondence to Lt. Col. Alexander of Ballochmyle as the last owner seems to be erroneous.[9] While hanging at the Western Club in Glasgow 230/4 was offered to Bernard Hall by W. Norman Scott and acquired for the Felton Bequest in 1934-5.

References: (1) John Guthrie Smith, *The Parish of Strathblane,* 1886, p. 41; the same, *Strathendrick and its inhabitants from early Times,* 1896, p. XVIII, note; *Memorial Catalogue, Old Glasgow,* 1894 (publ. 1896), No. 227. R. R. Tatlock, *The Lady Lever Art Gallery,* Vol. I, 1928, pp. 59, 60, pl. 33. Mr. D. Dutton has brought this version to my attention. (3) *Strathendrick, op. cit.,* p. XIX. (4) Information received from The Scottish National Portrait Gallery. (5) *Strathblane, op. cit.,* p. 45, note 1. (6) *Memorial Catalogue, Old Glasgow, loc. cit.* (7) Felton correspondence 10/1934. (8) James Greig, *Sir Henry Raeburn,* 1911, p. 47. (9) Felton correspondence 10/1934.

Allan Ramsay   1713-1784

British. Born Edinburgh, the son of the poet of the same name. In 1734 in Hysing's studio and Hogarth's Academy in St. Martin's Lane, in London. Went to Italy in 1736-38; worked in Rome with Francesco Imperiali and in

Naples with Solimena, and became acquainted with the art of Batoni in Rome. Settled in London after his return. Introduced into English Portraiture a new "grace" and "style", and was the leading portraitist in Britain before Reynolds.

Reference: Ellis Waterhouse, *Painting in Britain, 1530-17£0*, 1953, p. 151 *seq.*

Illust. 152   983/3 **The Countess of Cavan**

canvas, in a painted oval; 77.2 x 64 cm. Unsigned, undated; painted in 1751.

Condition: satisfactory.

Comment. Traditionally said to represent the Countess of Cavan, Elizabeth Wale of Dublin, who married in 1741 the 5th Earl of Cavan.[1] The companion portrait dated 1751 was exhibited at the Old Master Exhibition of 1903, No. 27, as *The 5th Earl of Cavan.*[2]

Provenance: Lent by Alfred J. Sanders, Holmwood, Chapel Allerton, Leeds, to the Old Master Exhibition, R.A., 1903, No. 25; according to a letter pasted on the back on loan to the Whitechapel Art Gallery, London, in 1912 (Scottish Art and History Exhibition), Upper Gallery, No. 2 (owner Alfred J. Sanders). Also exhibited at Bradford (label on back). On loan to the Scottish National Gallery for several years and returned to the owner on 9 Oct., 1919.[3] Purchased from the owner on the advice of Frank Rinder for the Felton Bequest in 1920.

References: (1) G.E.C.'s *Complete Peerage*—by courtesy of the Scottish National Portrait Gallery. (2) Felton Correspondence, 1920, N.G. Victoria files. (3) Information received from Scottish National Portrait Gallery, Correspondence 1959, N.G. Victoria files. (4) Rinder corr. 18.8.1919, 27.1.1920.

Illust. 153   1554/5 **Richard Grenville, 2nd Earl Temple** (1711-1779)

canvas, 234.3 x 152.4 cm. Signed and dated 1762 lower right; in original eighteenth century carved wooden frame.

Condition: excellent; cleaned prior to purchase; damages sustained in transit on the centre left were repaired by Mr. Harley Griffiths in 1966.

Comment: The identification is traditional. The sitter was the eldest son of Richard Grenville of Wotton Hall, Buckinghamshire.[1] Member for the borough of Buckingham 1734-41 and 1741 to 1752, when, on the death of his mother, the Countess Temple, he succeeded to the House of Lords as Earl Temple. First Lord of the Admiralty 1756-7, Lord Privy Seal 1757-61, Knight of the Garter 1760.[2]

With the inheritance of Stowe from his brother George Grenville in 1770, Earl Temple came into possession of one of the most famous English gardens of the eighteenth century. Created during the ownership of Sir Richard Temple, Viscount Cobham (1669(?)-1749), the garden was planned by Charles Bridgeman, under the direction of John Vanbrugh (1664-1726) with additions by William Kent (1685-1748) and "Capability"

Brown (1715-1783) who had begun as a kitchen gardener at Stowe.
"In 1731 Pope, in his *Epistle to Lord Burlington* uses it (i.e., Stowe) as the
climax of what he has to say on natural gardening . . . Gilpin's very first
publication dealing with his future domain, the Picturesque, was his
anonymous *Dialogue upon the Gardens at Stowe* of 1748."[3]

The sitter is shown in white Garter robes wearing a sword and chain
and badge of the Garter. Like other full length portraits by Ramsay of
this date,[4] 1554/5 reveals the study of Van Dyck; the pose resembles
that of *Charles I* of 1635 (le Roi alle ciasse), Paris, Louvre.[5]

Provenance: Descended in the family to the 2nd Duke of Buckingham and Chandos,
Stowe, 1848; collection Mrs. Alan Palmer (Farley Hall, sold Sothebys 15 July 1964, Lot
105, bt. jointly by Thos. Agnew & Son and Legatt Bros.; acquired 1965 from Loggatt's on
the recommendation of Dr. Mary Woodall under the terms of the Everard Studley Miller
Bequest.

References: (1) For Wotton see N. Pevsner, *Buckinghamshire* (The Buildings of
England), Harmondsworth, 1960, p. 302/3, fig. 44b. (2) *D.N.B.* (3) Pevsner, *op. cit.* 251 ff.,
figs. 46-49. See also: H. Avray Tipping and Christopher Hussey, *English Homes,* Period IV,
Vol. II, London, 1928, pp. 157 ff, reprs. 221-235. (4) Smart, *The Life and Art of Allan
Ramsay,* London, 1952, pp. 109, 213, No. CXXXI. (5) E. Schaeffer, *Van Dyck,* Stuttgart,
Leipzig, 1909, p. 335. See also: Alastair Smart, *Ramsay, The Masters,* 43, Bristol, 1966, p. 6.

Rembrandt Harmensz van Rijn   1606-1669

Dutch School. Born Leyden. A student at Leyden University in 1620. Pupil
of Jakob I. van Swanenburch in Leyden and of Pieter Lastman in
Amsterdam. Until 1632 practised in Leyden, together with Jan Lievens.
The *Anatomy of Dr. Tulp* (1632) established his fame; he moved to
Amsterdam where he married, in 1634, Saskia van Uylenburgh. His wife's
wealth and his own success enabled him to become one of the most
important art collectors of his time and to acquire a large house in the
Breestraat in 1639.

In 1642 he completed the *Nightwatch,* the greatest of his paintings in the
baroque style and often regarded as the turning point in his fortune.
While the stories of the poor reception of this picture have been proved
to be untrue, it is clear that the 1640s were tragic years for the master.
The death of Saskia in 1642 involved him in far-reaching personal
difficulties.

In the 1650s and 60s, when light colours and a light tonality returned
to fashion in Holland, Rembrandt's dark manner was at variance with
official taste. In 1656 he was declared insolvent, yet he continued to
receive important public commissions such as the *Anatomy Deyman*
(1656), the *Staalmeesters* (1661-2) and the *Conspiracy of Claudius Civilis*
(1661); his etchings and drawings were much coveted by collectors all over
Europe and the large number of pupils which had attended his studio
since the 1630s only diminshed after the sale of his house in 1656.

References: Jacob Rosenberg, *Rembrandt,* 1948; Seymour Slive, *Rembrandt and his Critics,* 1953.

Illust. 154   349/4 **The Two Philosophers**

panel, 72.4 x 59.7 cm. Signed and dated *R.L.* (Monogram) *1628,* lower right.

Condition: the paint showed a tendency to blister at time of purchase.[1] The blistering recurred in 1953 and 1958 and was attended to by Harley Griffiths. X radiographs taken with the generous assistance of the Commonwealth X-ray and Radium Laboratory reveal some major paint losses in the lower part of the garment of the Philosopher on the left and minor paint losses in the background. The radiograph also shows that the head and right shoulder and arm of the Philosopher on the left were first about 1½ inches lower down; he had curly hair; the fringes of the tablecloth originally continued further to the right, to the outline of the books.

Comment: *The Two Philosophers* was regarded as a lost painting before 1934, known only from an 18th century engraving.[2] The theme of the painting cannot be determined. In the will of the first owner it was called "Two old men disputing . . . there comes the sunlight in".[2] On the engraving made by Pietro Monaco, it was described as "Elisha predicting the attempt of the King against him".[3] Monaco, as is related under TIEPOLO, *Banquet of Cleopatra (q.v.),* gave biblical titles to non-biblical subjects in order to be able to include certain paintings into his book of Sacred Pictures.[4] Before the original painting had been rediscovered, Kurt Bauch had already suggested that Monaco's engraving was from a painting of disputing philosophers.[5] More recently attempts at closer identification of the subject have been made; Hippocrates and Democritus[6] or Democritus and Heraklitus[7] have been suggested, but without proof. The suggestion of "Peter and Paul" would relate the picture to an engraving by Lucas van Leyden.[6a]
The Philosophers ranks with the very similar *S. Paul in Prison,* at Stuttgart, dated 1627, and the *Simeon in the Temple* at Hamburg, of 1628, as a representative example of Rembrandt's early Leyden manner. The influence of the Caravaggism of Jan Pynas may be discerned in the fall of light, that of the Leyden vanitas still life painters (Jan Dsz. de Heem) can be seen in the old folios, gutted candle and globe.[8] In the following years, 1629-30, the broader handling and the golden brown tone of Rembrandt's mature art came to the fore (*S. Paul,* Nuremberg). The pose of the Philosopher on the right returns in Rembrandt's drawing of *S. Paul* of 1629, preparatory to the etching B. 149.[9]
A drawing of Salomon Koninck of 1649 is clearly related to the Melbourne painting.[10]
George Knox has commented on a possible connection between this picture, its engraving by Pietro Monaco and Tiepolo's *Scherzo* No. 20 (B. de V. 32).[10a]

Drawing: A study for the Philosopher on the left is in the Print Room in Berlin.[11]

Provenance: A picture by Rembrandt of *Two old men disputing . . . there comes the sunlight in* was listed in the inventory of 1641 of Jacob de Gheyn III (1596-1644), Canon of S. Mary's in Utrecht; at de Gheyn's death the picture went by bequest to Joannes Wytenbogaert.[12] Since the picture was engraved by le Fevre, Manaigo and Zucchi and Zucchi died in 1740, it must have been in Venice before that year.[12a] On Pietro Monaco's engraving of 1743 it is stated to have been in the collection of Signor Bertolo Bernardi of San Apollinare. Acquired by the Felton Bequest from Messrs. Hoogendijk, Amsterdam, on the advice of Mr. Bernard Hall in 1934. Arrived 1936.[13]

References: (1) Felton Correspondence, Hall, 1934. (2) Bauch, *Die Kunst des jungen Rembrandt,* 1933, p. 195; W. R. Valentiner, *Burl. Mag.,* Vol. LXVIII, 1936, p. 73, 79; J. Q. van Regteren Altena, *The Drawings of Jacob de Gheyn,* 1936, p. 129. (3) Leblac, *Manuel de l'Amateur d'Estampes,* 1894-97, Vol. III, p. 38, Monaco (Pietro), Nos. 1-99, Battaglia di 99 Ictorio oaoro, Vonioo, 1743; aloo No. 180, Eliooo ohi prodioo i rogni attontato oontro oo stesso. (4) A. Haskell, *Burl. Mag.,* 1958, Vol. C, p. 213. (5) Bauch, *op. cit.* (6) J. G. van Gelder, *Medelingen der Koninklijke Nederlandse Akademie der Wetenschapen,* afd. Letterkunde, N.R., Deel 16, No. 5, 1953, p. 15, illus. 20; K. Bauche, *Der frühe Rembrandt und seine Zeit,* 1960, p. 143 *seq.* stresses that the picture, like other similar work by Rembrandt, isolates figures from a "history"; the author returns, tentatively, to the 18th century title of Elias and Elisha. (6a) Christian Tümpel, *Studien zur Ikonographie der Historien Rembrandts* in *Nederlands Kunsthistorisch Jaarboek,* 20, 1969, p. 181-3, fig. 61, note 149. (7) O. Benesch, *The Drawings of Rembrandt,* Vol. I, 1954, No. 7; *Cat. Rembrandt Exh., Drawings,* Rotterdam and Amsterdam, 1956, No. 7. (8) Valentiner, *op. cit.* See also K. Bauch, *Der frühe Rembrandt,* 1960, pp. 22-24, 248-9. I. Bergström, *Dutch Still Life Painting,* 1956, p. 162, fig. 137. (9) L. Münz, *Rembrandt's Etchings,* 1952, Cat. No. 243. (10) *Rembrandt als Leermeister,* Stedelijk Museum, Leyden, 1956, Cat. p. 62, No. 147; N. McLaren, *Dutch School,* Cat. N.G. London, 1960, p. 338, *seq.,* points out that the picture of *Anna and the Blind Tobit,* by Rembrandt and Gerrit Dou of about 1630 has *considerable* similarity to our painting. (10a) G. Knox, *Catalogue of the Tiepolo Drawings in the Victoria and Albert Museum,* 1960, p. 23. (11) Benesch, *op. cit.* (12) van Regteren Altena, *op. cit.* (13) See note 2 and 3. (14) Felton Correspondence 1936. (B. Hall.) For an account of the protracted negotiations see Leonard B. Cox, *The National Gallery of Victoria, 1861-1968, A Search for a Collection,* [Melbourne 1970], p. 138-9. See also: *Quarterly Bulletin, N.G. Victoria,* 1953, VII (1), 3. U. Hoff, *Apollo,* 1964, Vol. 79, pp. 454 f, fig. 6. Bredius Gerson, No. 423. Horst Gerson, *Rembrandt Paintings,* London 1968, No. 11.

Illust. 155   104/4 **Self Portrait**

canvas, 76.5 x 61.6 cm. Signed and dated *Rembrandt f. 1660,* upper right.

Condition: later inscriptions and thick yellow varnish were removed in 1933, prior to purchase.[1] In good but somewhat overcleaned condition.

Comment: Goulding,[2] Fairfax Murray and Hofstede read the date as 1665. A microphotograph taken in 1933 by Prof. Laurie after cleaning showed the date to be 1660.[3] Holmes related this head to the Louvre *Self Portrait* of 1660: "Rembrandt's face has a similar drawn and wasted appearance".[1] Treatment and features of 104/4 are close to the *Self Portrait with Hat,* (formerly London, undated). A variant of the Melbourne portrait, said to be of lesser quality (57.2 x 44.5 cm) was formerly at Newbattle Abbey, Marquess of Lothian.[5]

Provenance: Fairfax Murray in 1893 established that the picture was at Bulstrode in 1809;[6] came to Welbeck Abbey with the Bulstrode pictures in 1810;[7] acquired from the Duke of Portland on the advice of Randall Davies in 1933 for the Felton Bequest.

References: (1) Fairfax Murray in *Catalogue of the Pictures . . . at Welbeck Abbey,* 1893, p. 2, No. 6, referred to this portrait as "ascribed to Rembrandt", with inscriptions in white letters, "Rembrandt by Himself", above the head and two signatures each in different handwriting on the r. Hofstede de Groot, *Verzeichnis der Werke der Holländischen Maler des 17 Jahrhunderts,* 1915, Vol. VI, No. 579, and Engl. ed. 1916, accepted the picture on recommendation of other connoisseurs (the picture hung in light unfavourable for close inspection) and described the cap as "yellow with a white bandeau". Sir Charles Holmes, *Burl. Mag.,* 1933, p. 103, commented on the thick yellow varnish. This was removed together with the later inscriptions and the genuineness of the second signature was established. A. Bredius, *Rembrandt,* 1935, No. 56, referred to the portrait as "damaged". (2) R. W. Goulding, *Catalogue of the Pictures . . . the Duke of Portland,* 1936, pp. 4-5, No. 6. (3) Note by Prof. Laurie on back of photograph of Self Portrait. "I took the R. I of this picture. The date came out 1660 agreeing with the infra-red photo I took" (Felton file 1934/8). (4) Bredius, *op. cit.,* No. 57; for the Albertina drawing: O. Benesch, *The Drawings of Rembrandt,* 1957, Vol. V, No. 1397, Cat. 1177. (5) W. Bode, Hofstede de Groot, *The Complete Works of Rembrandt,* 1897-1906, Vol. VII (1902), No. 502; Hofstede de Groot, *op. cit.* (see note 1), Vol. VI, No. 561. A Rosenberg, *Rembrandt,* 1909, p. 476; A. Bredius, *Rembrandt,* 2nd ed., n.d., No. 637; Ch. Holmes, *op. cit.,* p. 104. It was exhibited at the Katz Gallery, Basle, 1948, No. 26; Wildenstein, New York, 1950, Cat. No. 23, pl. 25 (lent by the Schaeffer Galleries); N. Katz Sale, Paris, 7th Dec., 1950 (No. 54; present whereabouts unknown. (Photograph in gallery files—by courtesy of the Frick Library, New York). (6) See note 1; Goulding, *op. cit.,* p. XXVIII quotes Pennant's *Bulstrode List,* B.M. Add. Mss. 5726, f.l., pp. 40-6, and *Bulstrode Inventory,* 1809, No. 39. (1) Quoted as at Welbeck Abbey in Fairfax Murray's and Goulding's Catalogues (see notes 1 and 2) and E. W. Moes, *Iconographia Batavia* 1905, Deel 2, p. 315, No. 6693, 67. Other references: *Illustrated London News,* 18 March 1933 repr., p. 379. K. Bauch, *Rembrandt, Gemälde,* Berlin 1966, No. 335. Not in Bredius-Gerson.

Illust. 156   2372/4 **Portrait of a Man**

canvas, 108.9 x 92.7 cm. Signed and dated *Rembrandt f. 1667,* u.c.

Condition: cleaned prior to purchase; restretched soon after arrival in Melbourne in 1951 by Harley Griffiths.

Comment: Sitter unknown; the last dated portrait by Rembrandt; obviously a commission.[1] The sitter, prior to the cleaning usually described as a young man with long fine curls or a blonde man,[2] wears his hair long in the fashion seen in many other Rembrandt portraits from the forties onwards, such at *Gérard de Lairesse* of 1665 or the *Staalmeesters*.[3] He holds a wide brimmed hat under his left hand.

Provenance: Mentioned by Wilson[4] as in the possession of Lord Aylesford (Heneage Finch, 5th Earl of Aylesford, 1786-1859) before 1836; this reference taken up by Vosmaer.[5] Exhibited R.A. 1899, No. 59 (owner Alfred Beit); Burlington Fine Arts Club, 1905, No. 13 (owner Alfred Beit), inherited by the son, Sir Alfred Beit. Acquired for the Felton Bequest on the advice of A. J. L. McDonnell and Prof. Ellis Waterhouse from Marshall C. Spink in 1951.

Exh.: *Rembrandt Tentoonstelling, Schilderijen,* Rijksmuseum, Amsterdam, 1956, No. 99.

References: (1) Rembrandt Tentoonstelling, Amsterdam, 1956, Cat. No. 99. (2) Thus Dutuit, *l'oeuvre complet de Rembrandt,* 1881-5, Vol. III, No. 351; Wurzbach, *Rembrandt Gallerie,* 1886, No. 151; Bode and Hofstede de Groot, *The Complete Work of Rembrandt,* 1897-1906, Vol. VII (1902), No. 500; A Rosenberg, *Rembrandt,* 1909, p. 511; Hofstede de Groot, *A Catalogue of Dutch Painters,* Vol. VI, 1916, No. 743; Bredius, *Rembrandt,* 1935, No. 323; description corrected by J. Rosenberg, *Art Quarterly,* XIX, 1956, p. 387. (3) Bredius, *op. cit.,* Nos. 321, 415. (4) Thomas Wilson, *A Descriptive Catalogue of the Prints of Rembrandt,* 1836, p. 12 (preface) rejects a previous attempt to identify the sitter as the Burgomaster Six. (5) Vosmaer, *Rembrandt,* The Hague, 1877, p. 565. (6) An account of the collections of Sir Alfred Beit by F. B. J. Watson in *The Connoisseur,* Vol. CXLV, 1960, p. 156 *seq.* See also: *Quarterly Bulletin, N.G. Victoria,* 1951, V (2), 1, 3. K. Bauch, *Rembrandt, Gemälde,* Berlin 1966, No. 445, Bredius-Gerson, No. 323; H. Gerson, *Rembrandt Paintings,* London, 1968, p. 130, No. 414; B. Haak, *Rembrandt, His Life, Work and Times,* London, 1969.

Guido Reni   1575-1642

Italian. Born Calvenzano. Pupil of the Fleming Calvaert. About 1595 entered the studio of the Carraccis in Bologna. About 1600-3 went to Rome, where he settled in 1605 until his return to Bologna in 1614. His style combines elements from Caravaggio's naturalism and chiaroscuro with the classicism of the Carraccis.

Reference: *Th.B.*

After Reni

Illust. 157   550a/4 **Eros Destroying the Shafts of Cupid**

canvas, 105 x 139.2 cm. Unsigned, undated.

Condition: satisfactory.

Comment: In the sale from Clumber[1] the picture was ascribed to Guido Reni. According to Gnudi,[2] the original is in the Palazzo spinola in Genoa. A larger variant is in the Museo Communale in Pisa.[3] Frequently repeated composition. Emblem CX in Alciati's *Emblemata* furnishes the subject of this picture: virtuous, celestial, platonic love puts earthly, sensual love in fetters and burns his arrow.[4]

K

Provenance: Pictures from Clumber inherited by Lord Lincoln under the will of the 7th Duke of Newcastle, Christie's, 4 June 1937, lot 78 (together with *Venus and Adonis,* both ascribed to Guido Reni), 16 gns., bt. Adams. Purchased by R. E. A. Wilson, sold to Howard Spensley. Howard Spensley Bequest 1939.[5]

References: (1) See provenance. (2) Cesare Gnudi, Gian Carlo Cavalli, *Guido Reni,* 1955, fig. 16, Cat. No. 12; dated c. 1605-10. (3) *Mostera di Guido Reni,* Bologna, 1954, p. 89. (4) Erwin Panofsky, *Problems in Titian mostly iconographic,* London, New York, 1969, pp. 131-132, fig. 146. (5) Howard Spensley Mss. Vol. I, p. 110, Cat. No. 526.

Illust. 158   308/1 **Christ at the Column**

canvas, 196.9 x 119.4 cm. Unsigned, undated.

Condltion: fair to good; old repairs.

Provenance: Presented by the Hon. Sir J. McBain, 1883.

Niccolo Renieri (Nicholas Regnier in France)   ca. 1590-1667

Franco-Italian. Born in Maubeuge about 1590; pupil of Abraham Janssens in Antwerp; presumably in Italy in 1615, where he came under the patronage of the Marchese Giustiniani. Bartolommeo Manfredi exercised a strong influence on the early Renieri; he also stood in close personal and artistic relations to Vouet. From 1626 resident in Venice. Even after he settled in Venice, Renieri continued to use the caravaggesque tradition of the single half figure but gradually lightened his colour and adopted the more linear style of the Bolognese school.

References: H. Voss, *Zeitschrift für bildende Kunst,* Vol. LVIII, 1924-5, pp. 121-128; H. Voss, *Die Malerei des Barock in Rom,* 1925, pp. 479-480; *Th.B.*

Illust. 159   3262/4 **Hero and Leander**

canvas, 155.3 x 209.5 cm. Unsigned, undated; painted soon after 1626.

Condition: cleaned prior to purchase; in fair condition; the paleness of the tones in the figure of Hero suggests heavy cleaning; extensive craquelure in the body of Leander.

Comment. Attribution by Dr. Herman Voss;[1] Dr. Voss informed us that the painting belongs to Renieri's middle period, when the artist had changed his caraggesque style under the influence of the Bolognese masters.[2] Nicola Ivanoff attributes the painting to Renieri's early Ventian period, about 1626 and relates it stylistically to the same painter's *San Sebastian tended by the Women* in Rouen.[3]

The story goes back to the late antique fable by Musaeus. Hero was a priestess of Aphrodite at Sestos; Leander, from Abydos nightly swam the Hellespont to see her, until a storm put out the light by which she guided him across and he was drowned. "But when she beheld her lover dead, battered upon the rocks . . . she flung herself, face downward, from the lofty tower." Renieri's picture is based on the version of this story which occurs in Ovid, *Heroides,* the relevant passage of which is quoted here from a 17th century English translation by Prince, London, 1647. Leander writes:

> "Yet do I wish I may be wrack't where you
> My mangled body and torne limbs may view;
> For you will weepe and touch the corpse and cry
> The cause of poor Leander's death am I."[4]

Provenance: According to label on back in Lord Lonsdale's collection at Lowther Castle; from the collection of P. D. Nicholls, Gloucestershire; acquired on the advice of A. J. L. McDonnell from P. & D. Colnaghi for the Felton Bequest in 1965.

References: (1) *Felton Correspondence,* 1955. (2) Letter to U. Hoff, 22 Aug. 1969. (3) Nicola Ivanoff, 'Nicolas Regnier' in *Arte Antico et Moderne,* No. 29, 1965, p. 16. (4) Miss June Stewart discovered this quotation.

Sir Joshua Reynolds   1723-1792

British. Born Plympton (Devonshire); 1741-3, pupil of Thomas Hudson in London. Returned to Devonshire but was back in London 1744-6, when he came under the influence of Hogarth and Ramsay. In 1750-52 in Italy where he studied the antique and the masters of the High Renaissance and whence he brought back Giuseppe Marchi, the first of his assistants in painting drapery. After his return he established himself in London where his new style of portraiture met with immediate success; he aimed to unite deliberate allusions to the antique and to old masters with portrait likeness. His emphasis on learning in art, which greatly raised the status of the English 18th century painters, found an eloquent expression in the fifteen discourses delivered to students of the newly founded Royal Academy, of which Reynolds was elected first President in 1768. He was knighted in 1769 and succeeded Ramsay as King's Principal Painter in 1784. After a visit to Flanders in 1781, during which he studied the work of Rubens, Reynolds modified his learned classical manner and adopted a new directness of portrayal.

References: Leslie and Taylor, *Life and Times of Sir Joshua Reynolds,* 2 vols., 1865; Ellis Waterhouse, *Reynolds,* 1941; C.N.G.

Illust. 160   158/4 **Miss Susannah Gale**

canvas, 210.8 x 118.7 cm. Unsigned, undated; painted 1763-4.

Condition: Graves and Cronin[1] report that the picture was immersed in sea water in the 18th century, as a result of which its dimensions had to be reduced. This information repeated by Armstrong.[2] A second, unspecified, injury restored by Frederick Haines.[1] Sir Charles Holmes reports cleaning prior to 1933.[3] The portrait was cleaned again in 1956 by Harley Griffiths, who reported that the picture was relined and on a nineteenth century stretcher. The brushwork of the garment at the lower right runs out of the picture, showing that the canvas has been reduced in size. There are several mends in the canvas; upper left in foliage; lower left in background; left margin centre; general condition good.

Comment: Susannah Hyde, daughter and heiress of Francis Gale of Liguanea in St. Andrews, Jamaica, born 3 May 1749, died London. April 1823. In 1767, in Jamaica, she married Sabine Turner. On 20 May 1769 she took, as her second husband, Captain Alan Gardner, R.N., later created Baron Gardner of Uttoxeter, Co. Stafford.[4] The pocket diaries list the portrait as paid for in Feb. 1764 but no sittings are listed in 1764; diary of 1763 lost.[5] The pose of the figure and her position in front of a portico on steps carries on the tradition of some of van Dyck's Genoese portraits, such as *Paola Adorna,* Genoa, Palazzo Rosso 1622-27.[6]

Provenance: The picture remained in the family.[7] it was given by Lady Gardner, after her husband's death in 1809, to her only daughter, the Hon. Susannah Cornwall, of Ashcroft House, Wootton-under-Edge, on whose death in 1853 it passed into the possession of the Rev. Alan Gardner Cornwall; exhibited by him National Portrait Exh. 1867, No. 612, and put up for sale Christie's, 16 Nov. 1872, lot 46, bt. in; bought by Bertram Currie in about 1876[8] and passed into possession of Laurence Currie. Acquired by the Felton Bequest on the advice of Randall Davies from A. H. Spink in 1933-4. Engraved R. B. Parkes (1865), 7⅜ in. x 4 in.[9]

References: (1) Algernon Graves and W. V. Cronin, *History of the Works of Sir Joshua Reynolds,* 1899, Vol. I, 342. (2) W. Armstrong, *Sir Joshua Reynolds,* 1909, p. 207. (3) Correspondence Holmes, Davies, No. 7, 1933, N.G. Victoria files. (4) V. Gibbs and H. A. Doubleday, *The Complete Peerage,* 1926. (5) Graves and Cronin, *loc. cit.* (6) E. Schaeffer, *van Dyck,* 1909, p. 175. (7) Source of prov. see note 1. (8) *Catalogue of the Works at Coombe Warren,* p. 35 (Correspondence Ellis Waterhouse, 15 Jan., 1957, N.G. Victoria files). (9) F. O'Donoghue, *Catalogue of Engraved British Portraits, British Museum,* 1910, Vol. II, p. 272. See also: Ellis Waterhouse, *Reynolds,* 1941, p. 89 (engraving only); *Quarterly Bulletin, N.G. Victoria,* 1956, X (3), 2-3.

Illust. 161   3356a/4 **Lady Frances Finch**

canvas, 142.1 x 113.3 cm. Unsigned, undated; inscribed *Frances, Countess of Dartmouth,* lower left; painted 1781-2.

Condition: cleaned prior to purchase by Mr. Valance of Holder's, London; heavy cracking in the background, extensively restored.

Comment: Lady Frances Finch, born London, Grosvenor Square, 9 Feb. 1761, daughter of Heneage Finch, 3rd Earl of Aylesford and Charlotte, daughter of Charles Seymour, Duke of Somerset, died Nov. 1838 at Blackheath. Lady Frances married George Legge, Lord Lewisham who became the 3rd Earl of Dartmouth.

No entries for sittings are recorded in Reynold's notebooks. Graves and Cronin state that she sat for Reynolds as Lady Finch in 1781 and in 1782, The portrait was paid for in March 1782, by "Lord Aylesford for Lady Frances Finch picture".[1]

Provenance: Remained in the Aylesford family: exhibited Grosvenor Gallery 1889, No. 46, as Frances, Countess of Dartmouth lent by the Earl of Aylesford; put up for sale at Christie's, 4 June, 1881, lot 131, by the Earl of Aylesford and withdrawn; sold by Lord Aylesford in 1900 to Agnews; to Herbert Terrell of New York by Agnews in 1901;[2] sold by the grand-daughter of the buyer, Mrs. Herbert L. Terrell van Ingen, New York, to Agnews and Knoedlers, London, in 1955. Acquired from them by the Felton Bequest on the advice of A. J. L. McDonnell in 1956.

References: (1) A. Graves and Cronin, *A History of the Works of Sir Joshua Reynolds,* 1899, Vol. I, pp. 303-4; IV, opp. p. 1536. (2) John Lafargue and August F. Jacacci, *Noteworthy Paintings in American Private Collections,* pp. 413, 412, 405. *Revue de l'Art ancien et moderne,* March 1900, illus. opp. p. 172. See also Ellis Waterhouse, *Reynolds,* 1941, pl. 227 and p. 73. *Quarterly Bulletin, N.G. Victoria,* 1956, X, (3), 1-3. W. Armstrong, *Sir Joshua Reynolds,* 1900, p. 205.

After Reynolds

Illust. 162   540/2 **Miss Offy Palmer**

canvas, 76.5 x 64 cm. Unsigned, undated; painted between 1777 and 1781.

Condition: in excellent condition.

Comment: The sitter is Miss Theophila Palmer, favourite niece of Sir Joshua's. She married Robert Lovell Gwatkin of Plymouth in 1781; died in 1848. The portrait was listed as by Reynolds in the 1948 catalogue. The ascription, based on J. R. Smith's engraving of 1777[1] cannot be maintained. According to Prof. Ellis Waterhouse the engraving was not made from this portrait but from a portrait now in the Gwatkin family, which Reynolds altered considerably in 1781.[2] The Melbourne picture seems to be a copy of the first state of the Gwatkin portrait, made perhaps by Frances Reynolds, younger sister of Sir Joshua,[3] for another member of the Palmer family.

Provenance: Miss Emily Palmer Sale, 4 July, 1874, lot 87 (listed as Mrs. Salkeld), bt. Currie; exhibited Grosvenor Gallery, 1884, No. 17 (owner George Woodhouse Currie), Lord Currie Sale (Phillips Son and Neale) 6 July, 1906, lot 776; bt. Claude Trevalyn; sold to Sir William Bennett, 1906; acquired from Sir William Bennett on the advice of Frank Gibson for the Felton Bequest in 1911.

References: (1) J. Chaloner Smith, *British Mezzotinto Portraits,* Vol. III, 1880, p. 1293, by J. R. Smith, engraver, No. 128. (2) Correspondence Waterhouse-Burke, 15 Jan. 1951, copy on N.G. Victoria files. (3) For the Gwatkin portrait see Ellis Waterhouse, *Reynolds,* 1941, p. 73, size 29⅞ in. x 24½ in. (76cm x 63cm), in Gwatkin coll. (1899); ("a repetition in the Melbourne Gallery"). For comments by Bernard Hall on the acquisition of this picture see articles listed in notes under "Attributed to Hoppner," No. 541/2. See also W. Armstrong, *Sir Joshua Reynolds,* 1900, p. 223.

Sebastiano Ricci   1659-1734

Italian. Born Belluno. Pupil of S. Mazzoni, later of F. Cervelli. About 1682 in Bologna where he trained under Giovanni del Sole, and came under the influence of the work of the Carraccis and Guido Reni. After a period of travel settled in Venice in 1700. 1712-16 in England. Was greatly influenced by the art of Veronese.

Reference: *Th.B.*

Illust. 163   95/5 **The Finding of Moses**

canvas, 235.5 x 308.5 cm. (sight measurements). Unsigned, undated.

Condition: cleaned by the late Sebastian Isepp in 1949; in good condition. The original carved frame is designed in the style of William Kent.

Comment: Pharaoh in an attempt to stem the increase of the Jewish population in Egypt decreed that every male Jewish child should be drowned in the Nile. To save him, Moses' mother placed him in an ark of bullrushes which she put among the flags: "And the daughter of Pharaoh came down to wash herself in the river and her maidens walked along the river's side; and when she saw the ark among the flags, she sent her maid to fetch it". *Exodus* II, 5-10.

The mother of Moses is depicted on the left, wringing the water from her clothes. Pharaoh's daughter stands in the centre of her retinue.

The composition is closely related to the painting of the same subject from the studio of Paolo Veronese, in the Walker Art Gallery, Liverpool.[1] Pharaoh's daughter, clasping the hand of her attendant on the right, the attendant with basket on the left, the mother of Moses and the landscape on the far left in No. 95/5 closely resemble those in the Liverpool picture. A similar dwarf occurs in Veronese's upright version of the theme in the Prado.[2] A halberdier, dwarf and dogs occur in Veronese's oblong version of the theme in the Dresden Gallery in which the child is also held feet forward, as in No. 95/5.[3] Morassi regards the Dresden picture as the main source of inspiration.[3a]

The dog resembles more particularly the one in Veronese's *Feast in the House of Simon.*[4] No. 95/5 appears to be a conscious imitation of the work of Veronese, drawing its motifs from a number of paintings by this artist. When in the Sir William Ingram collection, it bore the label "Veronese"; its attribution to Sebastiano Ricci is due to Mr. J. Byam Shaw and Mr. Francis Watson.[5] Ricci's interest in the work of Veronese is well known.[6] His version of *The Finding of Moses* from the collection of Consul Smith, based on Veronese's Prado picture (see note 2) came to Hampton Court as a Veronese;[7] the attribution recurs on the engraving made from this picture by J. B. Jackson in 1741.[8]

Professor Antonio Morassi believes that No. 95/5 is an exercise in Veronese's style by G. B. Tiepolo,[9] and considers it to have been inspired by Veronese's picture in the Dresden Gallery and to have "evident stylistic links with the copies after Veronese which Tiepolo executed principally in the same period, that is *Christ and the Magdalen in the House of the Pharisee,* now in Dublin, and the *Rape of Europa* now in London".

Provenance: Acquired by Sir William Ingram Bt. (1847-1924) probably at the end of the last century at a country sale; inherited by Sir Bruce Ingram who sold it through Colnaghi's to Francis Stonor in 1949; acquired from P. & D. Colnaghi for the Felton Bequest on the advice of A. J. L. McDonnell in 1958.

126

References: (1) B. Nicolson, *Burl. Mag.,* Vol. XCV, 1953, p. 260, pl. 1; R. Fastnedge, *Liverpool Bulletin,* Vol. III, 1953, No. 1 and 2, p. 21, fig. 1. B. Berenson, *Italian Pictures of the Renaissance, Venetian Schools,* Vol. I, 1957, p. 132 ("in great part autograph, late"). (2) G. Fiocco, *Paolo Veronese,* 1928, p. 201, pl. LXXI (dated about 1575); B. Berenson, *op. cit.,* p. 133, dated 1582; R. Fastnedge, *op. cit.,* fig. 5. (3) Fiocco, *loc. cit.;* Berenson, *op. cit.,* p. 131 ("late"); Fastnedge, *op. cit.,* fig. 2. (3a) A. Morassi, *A Complete Catalogue of the Paintings of G. B. Tiepolo,* London, 1962, p. 23, pl. 14. (4) Fiocco, *op. cit.,* pl. LXIV. (5) Francis Watson, *Arte Veneta,* 1955, p. 260, fig. 293 (as S. & M. Ricci). (6) M. Goering, *Jahrbuch der Preussischen Kunstsammlungen,* Vol. 61, 1940, p. 100 *seq.;* A. Blunt, *Burl. Mag.,* Vol. LXXXVIII, 1946, p. 263 *seq.* (7) Blunt, *op. cit.,* p. 264. (8) An impression is in the Print Room collection. (9) Correspondence Hoff-Morassi 1959, N.G. Victoria files and Morassi, *loc. cit.* See also *Annual Bulletin, N.G. Victoria,* 1959, Vol. I, p. 3; K. E. Maison, *Themes and Variations* 1960, p. 218 note 96 101.

Hyacinthe Rigaud   1659-1743

French. Born Perpignan. Pupil of P. Pezet and Antoine Montpellier, who encouraged him to study van Dyck. 1681 to Paris; was awarded the *Prix de Rome* in 1682 but did not go to Italy, and abandoned history painting for portraiture. With his portrait of *Monsieur* in 1688 he began his career as court portraitist; 1689 portrayed Monsieur's son, the later Regent *Philippe duc d'Orleans.* 1701 created the great state portrait of *Louis XIV* (Louvre) and in the following years portrayed many members of the royal houses of Europe. As can be seen from the detailed entries in his *Livre de Raison,* he often used studio assistants for the execution of backgrounds and accessories; no such assistance is recorded for the picture listed here.

Reference: *Th.B.*

Illust. 164   1205/5 **Monsieur le Bret and his son, Cardin le Bret**

canvas, 219 x 186 cm. Signed and dated *Hyacinthe Rigaud pinxit 1697* on the base of table leg lower left (the H forms a monogram with an F[rançois]).

Condition: excellent; cleaned by A. Vallance, London, prior to purchase.[1]

Comment: Pierre Cardin le Bret (1639/40-1710) held the office of "intendent" in various provinces of France (such as the Limousin in 1680) before becoming First President of the Parlement (High Court in Aix); after his death he was succeeded in this position by his son Cardin le Bret (1675-1734). The sitters occupy two chairs; to the left a carved Louis XIV table; on this a round box which, it has been suggested, may contain a collapsible hat. The identification of the sitters is traditional; the portrait is listed in Rigaud's notebook for the year 1697;[2] the heads were engraved separately in 1706 and 1709 respectively, by J. Coelemans.[3]

The composition is based, as has been suggested by the compiler,[4] on van Dyck's state portrait of *King Charles and Queen Henrietta Maria with Prince Charles and Princess Mary* of 1632 at Buckingham Palace,[5] a copy of which was known to Rigaud.[6]

Provenance: Remained in the possession of the family of the sitters; Comtesse de Courthivon, Château de Bretteville, Normandy; Catalogue Colnaghi, London, April, May 1962, No. 5, pl. V; acquired on the advice of A. J. L. McDonnell under the terms of the Everard Studley Miller Bequest in 1962.

References: (1) A report from A. Vallance of 20 June 1962 is in the Gallery Archives. (2) *Le Livre de Raison du Peintre Hyacinthe Rigaud,* ed. J. Roman, Paris 1919, p. 59. (3) Ursula Hoff, *A New Double Portrait by Rigaud,* in *Annual Bulletin N.G. Victoria,* Vol. V, 1963, p. 14, note 1. (4) *ibid.* p. 11. (5) O. Miller, *The Tudor, Stuart and Early Georgian Pictures in the Collection of Her Majesty the Queen,* London 1963, Vol. I, No. 130, Vol. II, fig. 66. (6) An early copy of the Buckingham Palace portrait (now at Goodwood) was from 1701-1798 in the possession of Phillippe, Duc d'Orléans in the Gallerie du Palais Royal; for its history see Hoff, *op. cit.* note 8. The Goodwood copy shows van Dyck's composition in its original form, it having been enlarged later, by the artist, by c. 12½ in. at the top and 8½ in. on the r. Millar, *op. cit.,* No. 130.

David Roberts   1796-1864

British. Born Stockbridge, Edinburgh. From 1820 worked as a scene painter first for the Royal Theatre, Edinburgh, then for the Drury Lane theatre, later at Covent Garden. During this time formed a lifelong friendship with Clarkson Stanfield *(q.v.).* Foundation member of the Society of British Artists. R.A. 1841. Travelled widely in search of architectural subjects and is famous for views of Egypt, Palestine, Spain and Morocco, lithographed by Louis Haghe.

References: *Th.B.;* T. S. R. Boase, *English Art, 1800-1870,* 1959, p. 51.

Illust. 165   402/1 **Interior of the Church of St. Anne, Bruges**

canvas, 122.3 x 183.5 cm. Signed and dated *David Roberts 1851,* lower right.

Condition: some severe cracking in darker parts.

Provenance: Exhibited by Roberts at R.A., 1851, No. 14; is said to have changed hands once since that date; purchased on advice of Sir George Verdon in 1894,[1] by Langdon, for the N.G. Victoria.

Reference: (1) Correspondence 8 Aug. 1844, LL Book No. 382, State Library of Victoria Archives.

George Romney   1734-1802

British. Born Dalton-in-Furness, Lancashire. 1755 apprenticed to Christoper Steele at Kendal and York. Moved to London in 1762, where alongside Reynolds and Gainsborough he rose to importance as a portrait painter. In Paris in 1764; 1773-5 in Rome and other places in Italy. In 1782 became acquainted with Emma Lyon, later Lady Hamilton, whom he portrayed in mythological and other roles. Contributed to Boydell's Shakespeare Gallery. His subject drawings, some of which are in our Print Room Collection, establish a link with the neo-classicism of Flaxman, Fuseli and Blake. Ceased painting in 1799 on account of a nervous illness and returned to Kendal where he died.

Illust. 166   338/5 **The Leigh Family**

canvas, 185.8 x 202 cm. Unsigned, undated; painted in or before 1768.

Condition: cleaned prior to purchase; in excellent condition.

Comment: The group represents Mr. Jarret Leigh of Wardrobe Court, Great Carter Lane, A Proctor in Doctor's Commons, with his wife and six children.[1] Mr. Leigh was also an amateur painter;[1a] his younger daughter married the painter Wheatly;[2] John Romney gives a detailed description of sketch drawings for this picture in one of his father's sketch books. This sketch book cannot at present be located; another sketch book, however, until recently in the collection of Sir Bruce Ingram and now in the Print Room collection,[3] contains preparatory drawings for the *Leigh Family*.[4] The picture was wittily criticized by David Garrick who saw it on a visit to Romney's studio in 1768.[5] Later authors, for the most part unacquainted with the original, have continued to repeat Garrick's account.[6] An exhaustive analysis of the *Leigh Family* and its relations to the conversation piece and the group portrait was made by Joseph Burke.[7]

Provenance: Seen in Romney's studio by George Cumberland and David Garrick;[8] exhibited at the Free Society of Artists, 1768, No. 180;[9] according to Sothebys Sale Cat. 1958, owned by R. F. Meyrick, Mrs. Charles Eade; Sale Sotheby 10 Dec. 1958, lot 124, bt. Leggatt. Acquired from Leggatt's on the advice of A. J. L. McDonnell for the Felton Bequest in 1959.

References: (1) *The Walpole Society,* 27th Volume, 1938-39, p. 77. John Romney, *Memoirs of George Romney,* 1830, p. 53 *seq.* (1a) Professor Joseph Burke kindly drew my attention to a reference to Leigh in Edward Edwards *Anecdotes of Painters,* London 1808, p. 28; from which we learn that Leigh (here called Jared) painted, for his amusement, landscapes and seaviews, and was an active member of the society for the Encouragement of Arts; he died (in the prime of life) in about 1769. Algernon Graves, *The Society of Artists of Great Britain, 1760-1791, the Free Society of Artists 1761-1783,* London 1907, p. 146 lists exhibits at the Free Society by Jared Leigh from 1761-1767. (2) John Romney, *ibid.,* p. 57, note. (3) I am indebted for knowledge of this sketchbook to Miss Patricia Henderson who has identified eleven drawings in it as sketches for the Leigh family, correspondence Hoff-Henderson, 1959, N.G. Victoria files. (4) For an analysis of the drawings by Joseph Burke, see note 7. (5) R. Cumberland, *Memoirs of His Own Life,* 1806-7, quoted by John Romney, *op. cit.,* p. 56, *note* and more fully by A. B. Chamberlain, *George Romney,* 1910, p. 53. (6) See H. Gamlin, *George Romney,* 1894, p. 64; Lord Ronald Gower, *George Romney,* 1904, pp. 21-22; H. Ward, W. Roberts, *Romney,* 1904, Vol. I, p. 30; Vol. II, p. 93; Randall Davies, *Romney,* 1914, p. 21. (7) Joseph Burke, *Romney's Leigh Family (1768); Link between the Conversation Piece and the Neo-Classical Portrait Group,* Annual Bulletin, N.G. Victoria, Vol. II, 1960, pp. 5-14. (8) John Romney, *op. cit.,* p. 56. (9) *Notes by Horace Walpole, Fourth Earl of Orford, on the Exhibition of the Society of Artists and the Free Society of Artists, 1760-1791, The Walpole Society,* Vol. XXVII, 1939, p. 77; A. Graves, *op. cit.,* p. 218. See also Patricia Milne Henderson, *George Romney* in I Maestri del Colore, 250, pl. II.

Illust. 167   1048/3 **Edmund Law, Bishop of Carlisle**

canvas mounted on panel, 102 x 127.8 cm. Unsigned, undated; painted 1781.

Condition: old varnish removed by Harley Griffiths in 1953, who mounted the canvas on a panel.

Comment: Edmund Law, born at Cartmel, Lancs, in 1703, was educated at St. John's College, Cambridge; Master of Peterhouse, Cambridge, 1756; appointed Bishop of Carlisle in 1769; author of *Considerations of the Theory of Religion,* 1749; *Life of John Locke,* 1777, and other publications; died 1787.[1]

Ward, Roberts quote sittings for this portrait in 1781;[1] other writers give the date as 1783.[2]

An identical version is in the Hall of Peterhouse, Cambridge (size about 126.8 x 127.8 cm);[3] in both the sitter is wearing his robes. Two other portraits by Romney of Dr. Law are mentioned by John Romney[4] and Chamberlain.[5]

Provenance: Painted for Edmund Law's eldest son, Dr. John Law, Bishop of Clonfert;[6] remained in the family of the sitter; purchased by Th. Agnew and Sons from Mrs. Law; acquired by the Felton Bequest on the advice of Frank Rinder in 1920.

References: (1) *D.N.B.* (2) H. Ward, W. Roberts, *Romney,* 1904, Vol. II, p. 91, No. 2; John Romney, *Memoirs of George Romney,* 1830, p. 198, lists the portrait as painted in 1783; A. B. Chamberlain, *Romney,* 1910, p. 135, gives date as 1783. (3) Th. D. Atkinson and J. N. Clark, *Cambridge Described,* 1897, p. 301, and still in situ. The sizes communicated by J. W. Goodison, Fitzwilliam Museum, Cambridge. The portrait hangs too high for close inspection. (4) *op. cit.,* p. 198, lists the portrait for his son, Mr. Edward Law (Lord Ellenborough) under 1786 and refers to two earlier portraits for Sir Thomas Rumbold, painted in 1777 and for Dr. John Law, Bishop of Clonfert in 1783. (5) Chamberlain, *op. cit.,* p. 135, lists "Dr. Law, Bishop of Carlisle, without his robes for his son Mr. Edward Law (Lord Ellenborough) which appears to be the portrait at Peterhouse, Cambridge." The Peterhouse portrait is however a repetition of the Melbourne (Clonfert) one, showing the sitter in his robes. Chamberlain also lists the other two portraits mentioned by John Romney (see note 4); for the Thomas Rumbold portrait see Ward, Roberts, *op. cit.,* p. 91, No. 1, engraved by W. Dickinson. (6) Ward, Roberts, *op. cit.,* p. 91, No. 2.

Salvator Rosa   1615-1673

Italian. Born Naples. Studied with his uncle, Domenico Antonio Greco and his brother-in-law, Francesco Fracanzano. Later with Agnello Falcone. 1635 settled in Rome where he painted landscapes and sea-pieces and also engaged in the activities of actor, poet and musician. In 164? was in Florence, where he set up an Academy of Literature; from 1649 to his death in Rome, where he engaged in history painting. His landscapes were a major influence on the English 18th century Cult of the Picturesque.

References: Th.B.; F. Cumming, R. Wittkower, *Art in Italy 1600-1700,* Detroit Institute of Art, Abrams, New York 1965, p. 139. E. W. Mainwaring, *Italian Landscape in Eighteenth Century England,* London 1925.

Illust. 168   2883/4 **Romantic Landscape with Mercury and Argus**

canvas, 123.8 x 203.4 cm. Signed with monogram *S.R.* on a stone to the left (under Mercury); undated.

Condition: excellent.

Comment: It is told in Ovid's *Metamorphoses,* Book I, v. 568-747, how Zeus, having fallen in love with Io changed her into a white heifer to hide her from jealous Juno. Juno, however, captured the heifer and had her watched by many-eyed Argus. Rosa here depicts Zeus's messenger Mercury lulling Argus to sleep by playing the flute. Mercury will later kill him and release Io.[1] Salerno regards this as a late work by Rosa, of fine quality.[2]

Provenance; Possibly the Argus mentioned in 1824 by Lady Morgan as then in the Aston Bruce collection.[3] It has not been possible to ascertain details of the history of 2883/4 until it was bought by P. & D. Colnaghi from Messrs. Tooth, who had it from a dealer in N.W. England, who claimed to have bought it in the early 1920s from Combermere Abbey; acquired for the Felton Bequest on the advice of A. J. L. McDonnell and Sir Kenneth Clark from P. & D. Colnaghi, 1950-51. R. A. Winter Exhibition of 17th century Paintings, 1950-51, No. 320.[3]

References: (1) Loeb ed. (2) Luigi Salerno, *La Pittura di Salvator Rosa,* Milan, 1963, p. 125, Cat. pl. 46, 47. (3) Michael Levey, *National Gallery of Victoria, Melbourne: Catalogue of European Paintings Before Eighteen Hundred; Melbourne 1961* in *Museums Journal,* Vol. 62, No. 2, pp. 126.

Alexandre Roslin   1718-1793

Swedish-French. Born Malmö. Court painter. Until 1741 worked in the studio of Georg Engelhard Schröder (1684-1750) in Stockholm. Was invited to the Brandenburg court; 1747 in Italy; 1752 in Paris where he portrayed many leading members of the European aristocracy; exhibited at the Salon. Returned to Sweden in 1774; 1775-77 in Leningrad on the invitation of Catherine II. Returned to Paris via Warsaw and Vienna in 1779. Died in Paris in 1793.

Reference: *Th.B.*

Illust. 169   1382/5 **Count Andrey Kyrillovich Razumovsky**

canvas, 63.8 x 52.7 cm. (stretcher size); signed and dated c.r. *Le Chev Roslin 1777* (?) (the last figure seems to read 7 but the portrait must have been made early in 1776).[1]

Comment: The sitter (1752-1836) diplomat, art collector and good amateur violinist, entered the Russian navy and served in an English man-of-war. In 1777 he was transferred into the diplomatic service.[2] Russian ambassador successively at Naples, Venice, Copenhagen, Stockholm; in 1792 and again in 1801 at Vienna. He knew Mozart and was one of the best connoisseurs of Haydn quartets in which he played the second violin. Beethoven dedicated to him the three string quartets *Op. 59* and to him and his brother-in-law Prince Lobkowitz the fifth and sixth symphonies *Op. 67* and *68.*[3] A famous 'galant' he is said to have been banished from the court by the Empress Catherine II on 16 April, 1776, on account of an intrigue which would give the date ante quem for 1382/5.[4]

He wears a blue green coat edged with red and gold braid and buttons, and carries a black hat under his left arm.

Provenance: Razumovsky; Vassiltchikov Kotchoubey (at Dikanka, Poltava) until 1924; in Russian private collection in France.[5] Private collection, Boston; Messrs. Agnew, London. Acquired, Everard Studley Miller Bequest, 1962.

References: (1) Gunnar Lundberg, *Roslin, liv och verk,* Stockholm, III, n.d. (1957 or 8) No. 483, pl. 89 reads date as 77; Müller, Roslin och Ryssland, *Tidskr. f. Konstvet.* XIX, 1936, pp. 115, 121 (gives date as 1776). (2) A. Wheelock Thayer, *The Life of Ludwig van Beethoven,* London 1960, Vol. II, p. 81. (3) Emily Anderson, *The Letters of Beethoven,* London 1961, Vol. I, p. 153, note 2. (4) Daria Olivier, *Burl. Mag.* 1962, Vol. CIV, p. 228, Supplement p. I-III. See also Starye Gody III (July-Sept. 1911) p. 62; Mattison in *Sv. Upplagsbok,* 23, 1935. (5) Lundberg, Roslin portrait in Frankrike *(Tidskr. f. Konstvet,* XIX, (1935) avb. sid. 35, 36, illus. 29, pp. 47, 48). See also: Harley Preston, *Some Recent Acquisitions under the Terms of the Everard Studley Miller Bequest* in *Annual Bulletin, N.G. Victoria,* Vol. V, 1963, p. 21, fig. 18, p. 25.

Illust. 170   E7/1971 **Anastasia Ivanova,** Countess of Hessen-Homburg, Princess Trubetskoij.

canvas, 63.5 x 53 cm (stretcher size). Signed *A. Roslin Le Suédois* on frame of footstool; undated (the companion piece representing Ivan Betskij bears the date 1758[!]); inscribed front lower right *161;* torn Russian label on back of stretcher and a red seal with Russian lettering.

Condition: marked craquelure, but in good condition; relined, cleaned and varnished prior to purchase; wax finish applied by David Lawrence in 1971 on arrival in Melbourne. The portrait of Anastasia hanging on the wall in the companion piece representing Ivan Betskij is differently framed; the antique carved and gilded frame of E7/1971 appears to be original.

Comment: Anastasia Trubetskaia (15. X. 1700 — 7. XII. 1755?), the daughter of Fieldmarshal Ivan Trubetskoi, was much attached to her half-brother, Ivan Ivanovich Betskij (1704-1795). Anastasia first married in 1717, Prince Dimitri Kantimir, Boyar of Walachia and in 1738 the Russian Fieldmarshal Ludwig, Count of Hessen-Homburg (1705-1745) (who never reigned since he pre-deceased his father). She was appointed Lady-in-Waiting to the Empress Elizabeth on 25 November, 1741, and was awarded the Grand Order of St. Catherine the Martyr on 18 December, 1741.[2] This order consists of a white cross in the hands of St. Catherine the Martyr, against a purple background, with lettering DSFR in between the arms of the Cross.[3] The cross is clearly visible in the painting. Lady Dilke transmits the information that the Empress thus rewarded the Countess for her loyal support on the night of the coup d'état of 1741 when Elizabeth assumed the throne.[4] From her marriage with Dimitri Kantimir, Anastasia had a daughter Catherine, married to the prince D. Golitzyne, ambassador in Paris. "A great traveller, famous at European capitals for her beauty and her education, she (Anastasia) lived for long in Paris with her daughter." She died in St. Petersburg on 27 November, 1755, and is buried in the Alexander Newsky monastery in the church of the Annunciation.[5]

After his sister's death Ivan Betskij ordered two paintings from Roslin: her portrait and, as a companionpiece, a portrait of himself; he further commissioned Pajou with a memorial relief and had two medals struck in her honour;[6] Anastasia sits in her salon, at a boulle table, her forearm resting on an open book in which are printed two medallions, perhaps the same which are lying on the table before her and possibly those struck by Betskij in her memory.[7] Also on the table lie what appear to be two gravers and what is possibly a die stamp and a small leather-bound volume. In her hand she holds an unbound book with coloured end papers. Below to the left are a globe, books and a map, all indicative of travel. She sits on a *Louis Quinze* chair; behind her, against the wall is part of an ebony jewel cabinet surmounted by gilt bronze mountings of corded garlands and figures, the whole in the "greek taste".[8]

The Countess sits at an open window through which we look into a cloudy night sky, and on a stormy sea with a sinking ship from which appears to pull away a boat with many oars; there are rocks in the foreground. No information on the meaning of this scene is available.

This portrait of Anastasia or its replica (Lundberg 96 coll. Westerberg) is depicted in the companion portrait (of Betskij, Lundberg 97, 98) hanging on the upper left.[9] Betskij not only has her portrait hanging in his room, but holds Daullé's engraving after it in his hand and has in front of him Pajou's maquette for the marble relief, which he had ordered as a memorial and which shows the Countess in the role of Minerva dedicating the ribbon of the order of St. Catherine "to Friendship on the altar of Immortality". (This relief was in 1932 in the Academy in Leningrad.)[10]

The portraits were painted in Paris where Betskij lived between 1747 and 1762 and where Roslin had arrived in 1752. Betskij's portrait, Lundberg 98 (the companion to E7/1971) is signed *Roslin le Suédois à Paris 1758*. The other version (Westerberg collection, Lundberg 97) is inscribed *Roslin suéd. à Paris 1757*. Since Anastasia died in 1755 her portrait, ordered by her brother as a commemoration, is presumably posthumous, but it is not known to the compiler on what other likeness it was based. The composition closely resembles a portrait by Boucher of Madame de Pompadour known from a soft ground etching by Janinet reproduced in Maurice Fénaille, *F. Boucher,* Paris 1938. Roslin's admiration for and close connection with Boucher can be seen from his correspondence with the attaché to the Swedish Embassy, Count Frederick de Sparre, with whom he was in close touch during the 1750's and to whom he gave detailed accounts of his relations with the French painter.

Engravings: J. Daullé 1761: this engraving was begun in 1757 since it may be seen in Betskij's portrait of that year; but it was the subject of much dispute between Betskij and the engraver and was not finished and signed until 1761.[11]

Other Versions: A replica of E7/1971 was in 1957 in the collection of Sten Westerberg, castle Beatelund, Sweden, Lundberg No. 96. A copy was in 1902 reported to be in possession of I. A. Vsevolozhskij; in 1868 another copy was exhibited in a Moscow exhibition which, in 1902 was in the possession of T. Vlosufiev.[12]

Exh.: Either E7/1971 or its replica (Westerberg coll.) was at the Salon of 1757.

Provenance: Ivan Betskij (1704-1795) (perhaps identical with No. 71 Paris Salon 1757, though see Lundberg's comments No. 95) who probably presented or bequeathed E7/1971 to the Academy of Fine Arts at St. Petersburg, of which he became President in 1962: transferred to the Hermitage, St. Petersburg at some date after 1918; bought in 1936 from the Hermitage by a.-b. Björcks Konsthandel, Stockholm; acquired by the Countess Blanche Bondé, née Dickson, Stockholm;[13] Count Thurée Bonde, sale Sotheby, London Nov. 25, 1970 lot 84; acquired on the advice of Dr. M. Woodall under the terms of the Everard Studley Miller Bequest 1970; arrived 1971.[14]

References: (1) G. W. Lundberg, *Alexandre Roslin*, Malmö, 1957, Vol. III, No. 98. according to the same author E7/1971 carries the date 1757, but this is erroneous. (2) The order is described as *grand ordre imperial de St. Catherine* on the engraving made from the painting of Anastasia by J. Daullé in 1761. See also Chennevières, 'Les Artists Etrangers en France', in *Revue Universelle des Arts,* Paris 1856, p. 410; *Portraits Russes* IV, 1908, No. 26, pl. XXVI. (3) see The *Encyclopedic Dictionary,* gen, editors Andreevskiy, I. E.; Arseniev, K. K. and Petrushevskiy, F. F., St. Petersburg 1894, Vol. 22, p. 568. (4) Lady Dilke, *French Engravers and Draughtsmen of the XVIIIth century,* London 1902, p. 65, note 2; a more elaborate version of the story is told by this author in *French Architects and Sculptors of the XVIIIth century,* London 1900, p. 125. (5) *Portraits Russes, loc. cit.* (see note 2). (6) Carl David Moselius, 'Några bidrag till Roslin-forskningen' in *Svenska Dagbladet,* 21 June 1936, Söndagsbilagan, p. 5. (7) As above. (8) Delignières, *Jean Daullé, Catalogue Raisonné de l'Oeuvre gravé,* Paris, 1873, pp. 2, 3 (the names are mis-spelt in this catalogue). For the jewel case see Svend Eriksen, 'Lalive de Jully's Furniture à la grècque' in *Burl. Mag.* Vol. CIII, 1961, pp. 340-347. I am indebted to Mr. Terry Lane Assistant Curator, Furniture for this reference. (9) G. W. Lundberg, *op. cit.,* Vol. II, pl. 28. (10) U. Thieme, F. Becker, *Allgemeines Lexikon der Bildenden Künstler,* 1932, 'Augustin Pajou' (1730-1809), Mr. Michael Levey kindly brought Pajou's authorship of the relief to my notice. (11) Delignières, *loc. cit.,* for Cochin see Lundberg, I, 148-50. (12) *A comprehensive catalogue of the exhibition of Russian portrait painting for 150 years (1700-1850);* printed by the Society of the Blue Cross, 1902, p. 110. (13) Lundberg, *loc. cit.,* No. 95. (14) I am greatly obliged to V. Lindquist, Stockholm and L. Cartens, Uppsala to have supplied me with the records and their translation used in this entry.

Sir Peter Paul Rubens   1577-1640

Flemish School. Born Siegen, Germany. His family, of Flemish origin, returned to Antwerp in 1589. Pupil of Tobias Verhaecht, Adam van Noort and Otto van Veen. In 1600 Rubens went to Italy where he became court painter to Vincenzo Gonzaga of Mantua. From here he visited Madrid, Genoa, Venice, Milan and Rome. After his return to Antwerp in 1608-9 he was appointed court painter to the Spanish Regents of the Netherlands. He rapidly became the leading master of the baroque style in the north. By 1615 he ran a large workshop, numbering van Dyck among his assistants in 1617; he also trained a group of engravers in the reproduction of his works. He early started his habit of making small oil sketches, to serve as a guide in the execution of large-scale paintings.

Received many commissions for altarpieces for Flemish churches but worked also extensively for foreign patrons. In 1622 in Paris where he began a series of scenes from the life of Marie de Medici for the Luxembourg Palace, finished in 1625; on later stays in Paris, Madrid and London he combined diplomatic activities concerned with peace between the Netherlands and Spain and between Spain and England, with the pursuit of his art. 1628-9 in Madrid he portrayed the King and other members of the Royal Family and copied paintings by Titian in the Royal collection; in London in 1629 he received the commission to decorate the ceiling of Inigo Jones's Banqueting Hall, Whitehall; these paintings were put in place in 1634; in 1636 he began the series for the Torre della Parada for the King of Spain, which was unfinished at his death four years later. He portrayed many of the leading personalities of his day, and painted many religious, historical and mythological scenes and landscapes, as well as making designs for tapestries, book illustrations and triumphal processions.

References: *Th.B.; H. Gerson, E. H. Ter Kuile, Art and Architecture in Belgium, 1600-1800, 1960.*

Illust. 171   315/5 **Louis XIII of France**   (1601-1643)

paper on panel, 42.8 x 32.6 cm. Unsigned, undated; painted 1622.

Condition: though slightly rubbed, in good condition.

Comment: Rubens must have painted this study of the head and shoulders of Louis XIII on his visit to France in 1622 when he was commissioned by Marie de Medici, Regent of France, with the paintings for the Luxembourg Palace.[1] Sculptures, medals, drawings, engravings and paintings of Louis XIII were made about 1622; among these the portrait engraved (in reverse) by Crispen de Passe is outstanding. This engraving, strongly Rubensian in character, though dated 1624, lower centre, appears in both the 1623 and the 1625 edition of Antoine de Pluvinel's *Maneige royal . . . ,* engraved and published by Crispen de Passe, Paris (Bibliothèque Nationale, Paris, Rés. S 151, 152).[2]

Apart from de Passe's engraving which is unrecorded in the Rubens literature, two Louis XIII portraits are described by Rooses. A knee length portrait is in the Norton Simon collection, California, showing the king in royal robes and executed possibly with the help of assistants.[3] Another bust length, in Anhalt Dessau, is considered to be by a Rubens follower.[4] Another autograph study in armour, rather larger and with a sash, is in the Gallery at Halle in East Germany.[5] 315/5 must be regarded as the original sketch or model-study on which all the above mentioned portraits were based.[6] In contrast to the finished portraits quoted above, Louis wears a frilled neckband and a metal collar in our picture, and the lovelock resting so conspicuously on the ruff of the finished portraits is only slightly indicated in the sketch. The irregularity of the features is more marked in the sketch than in the finished versions.

Provenance: In 1955 the portrait was identified as a Rubens while in the possession of A. Harrison Esq., Worcester. Acquired for the Everard Studley Miller Bequest on the advice of A. J. L. McDonnell from T. Agnew and Sons in 1959.

References: (1) M. Rooses, *Rubens*, 1904, Vol. II, p. 367. (2) L. Burchard, letter to Mr. Harrison, 26 July, 1955, copy on N.G. Victoria files; and T. Agnew & Sons, Cat., Recent acquisitions Oct., Nov., 1955, No. 12. I am indebted to Suzanne Lodge for details of the editions of *Maneige royal*. (3) M. Rooses, *L'Oeuvre de Rubens,* Vol. IV, 1890, p. 207, No. 980; G. Glück, *Burl. Mag.,* Vol. LXXVI, 1940, p. 183; Goris and J. Held, *Rubens in America,* 1947, pl. 22. Ella S. Siple, *Burl. Mag.,* 1934, Vol. LXIV, p. 184/5. (4) Rooses, *L'Oeuvre, op. cit.,* p. 207. (5) M. Jaffé, U. Hoff, corr. 5 Feb., 1959, on N.G. Victoria files and Cat. T. Agnew & Sons, *loc. cit.* (6) L. Burchard, *op. cit.,* and M. Jaffé, Cat. Exh. Agnews, 1958, and correspondence, 5 Feb., 1959, on N.G. Victoria files. See also *Annual Bulletin N.G. Victoria,* 1960, Vol. II, p 16. *The Connoisseur,* 1962, Vol. 150, August number, cover illus. and p. 261. U. Hoff, in: *Apollo,* Vol. 79, 1964, p. 454, fig. 9, p. 456.

Illust. 172   1720/4 **Hercules and Antaeus**

panel, 64.6 x 49.5 cm. Unsigned, undated; painted about 1625-30. [1]

Condition: the picture has had to be treated for blistering several times since arrival. [1a] Otherwise in good condition.

Comment: The picture is based on the Greek legend of Hercules fighting against the Lybian giant, Antaeus, in the form in which it is told in the *Imagines* of Philostratus in the 3rd century A.D. "You see them engaged in wrestling, or rather, at the conclusion of their bout, and Hercules at the moment of victory, Hercules . . . at a loss how to deal with Earth (from whom Antaeus drew strength whenever he touched the soil) has caught Antaeus by the middle, just above the waist where the ribs are, and set him upright on his thigh, still gripping his arms about him; then pressing his own forearm against the pit of Antaeus' stomach, now flabby and panting, he squeezes out his breath and slays him by forcing the points of his ribs into his liver. Doubtless you see Antaeus groaning and looking to Earth, who does not help him while Hercules is strong and smiles at his achievement." [2]

Ruben's painting bears no resemblance to the Hercules and Antaeus representations of classical antiquity which show the giant being lifted in the air from the back, not "flabby and panting", but actively trying to free himself from the grip of Hercules. [3] Ruben's painting is related to the early Renaissance rendering of this fight by Antonio Pollaiuolo, and Andrea Mantegna. Pollaiuolo following the mediaeval tradition showed the contestants face to face; [4] Mantegna employed the classical type but showed Antaeus "flabby and groaning". [5]

The representations created by Pollaiuolo and Mantegna inspired a great many renderings of this theme in the 16th and 17th centuries. In an engraving after a painting by Franz Floris of 1554 which Rubens may have known from an engraving by Cornelis Cort, the classical type is used, but Antaeus is cast in the likeness of the late antique statue of the Laocoon. [6] Rubens's sketch of subjects from Hercules legend in the British

Museum[7] reflects his knowledge of Floris's picture. Both in the drawing and in the oil sketch Rubens casts Antaeus in the pose of the (upside down) Laocoon. Antaeus bends over backwards until his head appears upside down, as he vainly looks to Earth for help. The foot of Antaeus is leaving the ground; he is off-balance, white, flabby and groaning in extreme agony. Hercules is strong, contrasting with Antaeus in the vigorous colour of his skin. Rubens seems to combine a fresh reaction to the text of Philostratus with an extensive knowledge of earlier pictorial renderings of this theme.

Provenance: According to Felton correspondence 1946, in 1746 in the collection of J. A. Innes; J. Smith, *Catalogue of Dutch, Flemish and French Painters*, Vol. IX, 1842, Suppl. p. 338, No. 351, lists it as in the collection of the Duke of Rutland, Belvoir Castle, so also *Connoisseur*, Vol. VI, 1903, p. 243, exh. R.A. 1907, No. 65 (owner the Duke of Rutland); repr. E. Dillon, *Rubens*, 1909, p. 236 (as rather by van Dyck); acquired for the Felton Bequest on the advice of A. J. L. McDonnell and Sir Kenneth Clark in 1946-7.

References: (1) Mr. Michael Jaffé suggested the dating which agrees with Held's dating of the B.M. drawing, see note 7. (1a) Arnold Shore, *Quarterly Bulletin N.G. Victoria*, 1953, VII, (1), 2-3. (2) Philostratus, *Imagines*, Book II, 21, Loeb Classical Library, 1931, p. 227. (3) The most important examples: Silver Coin, Tarentum, 4th century B.C. (*Sylloge Nummorum Graecorum*, Vol. III, 1938, No. 306). I am indebted for this reference to the late Mr. Erich Wodak, B.Sc.; marble group in the Pitti Palace (Comte de Clarac, *Musée de Sculpture Antique et Moderne*, 1839/41, *Planches*, Tome V, pl. 802, fig. 2016; S. Reinach, *Répertoire de la Statuaire Grecque et Romaine*, 1897, Vol. I, p. 472, pl. 802). (4) M. Cruttwell, *Antonio Pollaiuolo*, 1907, p. 66 seq.; pp. 81, 82; Kenneth Clark, *The Nude*, 1955, pp. 181-190, pl. 144; medieval representations of the fight often showed the contestants face to face, often Antaeus is represented as a giant; both are clothed. See London, B. M. Stowe 54, *Historia Trojana* late 14th century; B.M. Royal Mss. 17E IV, f. 136r *Ovide Moralisé;* consulted in photographs by courtesy of the photographic section, the Warburg Institute, London. (5) E. Tietze Conrat, *Mantegna*, 1955, pl. 88, Cat. p. 187. A. M. Hind, *Early Italian Engravers*, Vol. V, 1948, p. 25, No. 17, p. 26, No. 19. (6) Wurzbach, *Künstlerlexikon*, Vol. I, 1906, "wall painting in the house of Nickolaas Jongelings." These compositions were engraved by Cornelis Cort and re-engraved by Charles David (about 1600-1636). J. C. J. Bierens de Hann, *Cornelis Cort*, 1948, p. 167, No. 180 and p. 168. (7) A. M. Hind, *Catalogue of Dutch and Flemish Drawings, British Museum*, 1923, Vol. II, No. 23; G. Glück, F. M. Haberditzl, *Die Handzeichnungen von P. P. Rubens*, 1928, No. 145 repr.; Julius S. Held, *Rubens, Selected Drawings*, 1959, Vol. I, pp. 5 (dating) 23, (style) 121, Cat. No. 61, pl. 73. Drawings and oil sketches of the same theme from the Rubens workshop are to be found in the Pierpont Morgan Library, New York, drawing I, 234 c; Aix-en-Provence, Grisaille, 30cm. x 26cm., Nr. 377; Bénézit, *Dictionnaire*, Vol. VIII, 1957, p. 410 (as Rubens); Sale Earl Howe, London, Christie's, Grisaille, 7 Dec. 1933, lot 62 (12 in. x 8 in.). See also *Quarterly Bulletin, N.G. Victoria* 1953, VII, (1) 3; U. Hoff, *The Sources of the Fight of Hercules and Antaeus*, in the *In Honour of Sir Daryl Lindsay, Essays and Studies*, Melbourne, 1964, pp. 67-77.

After Rubens

Illust. 173   138/2 **The Garden of Love**

canvas, 177.8 x 160 cm (sight measurements). Unsigned, undated.

Condition: fair; dark old varnish.

Comment: A number of versions of this theme are known. The best known, given to Rubens himself, is in the Prado;[1] a smaller version with certain alterations is at Waddesden Manor;[2] this version was regarded by Glück

L

as from the studio of the master; White assumes that Rubens worked over the painting afterwards. 138/2 is clearly based on the Waddesden Manor picture. The figure groups correspond exactly; only the little gods of love, interspersed with the figures in the Waddesden Manor picture, have been omitted, and instead of the fountain of Venus and the architecture a landscape background has been introduced. The oblong format of the Waddesden Manor picture has been changed into an upright. For other versions of this theme, see White.[2]

Provenance: Nothing is known of the early history of this painting. Bequeathed by Alfred Felton 1904.

References: (1) G. Glück, in *Jahrbuch d. K. Sammlungen in Wien,* Vol. XXXV, 1920, 49 ff; R. Oldenbourg, A. Rosenberg, *P.P. Rubens,* Berlin, Leipzig, 1928, p. 348. (2) Ch. White, in *Gazette des Beaux Arts,* 6e pér. Vol. 1959, p. 73 f, fig. 7.

Jacob Ruisdael   1628-1682

Dutch School. Born Haarlem. May have been taught by his father, Isaak Jacobsz van Ruisdael, and by his uncle, Salomon Ruysdael *(q.v.).* Settled in Amsterdam in 1657. He seems to have taken a degree of doctor of medicine at Caen in 1676 and in the same year was inscribed on the list of Amsterdam doctors. His early realistic landscapes were painted in the surroundings of Haarlem; since 1650 the composite ideal landscape with waterfalls, dead trees, ruins and castles dominates his work. His most important pupil was Hobbema *(q.v.).*

Reference: *Th.B.*

Illust. 174   1249/3 **The Watermill**

canvas, 65 x 71.3 cm. Signed with monogram *V.R.* on hillside on left; undated; painted about 1653.[1]

Condition: in very good condition; old varnish removed by Harley Griffiths, 1952.

Comment: A drawing of the same view of this mill is in the Teyler Museum in Haarlem.[2] It is there attributed to Hobbema, but the close resemblance to 1249/3 suggests that it is by Ruisdael.[3] Hofstede, on account of two paintings of the same mill by Hobbema in the Rijksmuseum (No. 66, 67) assumed that 1249/3 was painted in 1660-63 when Hobbema and Ruisdael are known to have painted together.[4] Jacob Rosenberg however places the picture in relation to Ruisdael's simple, near-view silhouettes of the early 1650s.[5] For the relation between Ruisdael and Hobbema, see also under Hobbema.

Provenance: In his catalogue of 1835, Smith[6] reports that *The Watermill* was in a collection at Christie's in 1833; it belonged to Henry Galley Knight, from whom Smith purchased it.

According to Hofstede[7] and Smith,[8] *The Watermill* returned to Amsterdam and was sold by Mr. Brondgeest to Mr. van der Hoop. It figured in the auction Jer de Vries, 15 Nov., 1853, lot 100, and was sold to de Vries.[9] According to Christie's Sale Catalogue of 1922 (see below) *The Watermill* was re-imported from Amsterdam in 1854. In the possession of the Hon. Lewis Fry in 1876 (exh. R.A. 1876, No. 80); exh. again in 1902 (R.A. No. 134), (labels on back); Hofstede in 1912 lists *The Watermill* as in possession of the Hon. Lewis Fry, Bristol.[10] Offered at Christie's, 31 March, 1922, lot 106 (Fry coll.), and acquired on the advice of Frank Rinder for the Felton Bequest.

REFERENCES: (1) J. Rosenberg, *Jacob van Ruisdael* 1928, p. 78, No. 98. (2) Reproduced in J. H. J. Mullaert, *Dutch Drawings of the Seventeenth Century*, 1926, pl. 27. (3) Thus G. Broulhiet, *Meindert Hobbema*, 1938, No. 3 repr.; Prof. van Regteren Altena has kindly informed me that he agrees with this attribution. (4) Hofstede, *De Groot Catalogue of Dutch Painters*, Vol. IV, 1912, p. 51, No. 146. (5) Rosenberg, *op. cit.* p. 78. (6) J. Smith, *Catalogue . . . Dutch and Flemish Paintings*, Vol. VI, 1835, p. 142, No. 83. (7) Hofstede, *op. cit.*, p. 58, No. 168. (8) Smith, *op. cit.*, Suppl. 1842, p. 705, No. 73. (9) Hofstede, *op. cit.*, p. 58, No. 168. (10) *ibid.*, p. 51, No. 146. See also: *Masterpieces*, pp. 48, 49 repr.

Russian School   18th Century

Illust. 175   4799/3 (D.A.) **An Icon of Saint Nicolas**

wood panel 35.3 x 31 cm. Inscribed in Russian lettering with names and references to miracles.

Comment: In the centre the half figure of S. Nicolas, with the gospel open at Luke 17; above half figures, to the left, of Christ, to the right, of the Virgin. The portrait of the Saint is surrounded by twelve scenes from his life: from left to right: 1. Birth. 2. Baptism. 3. The boy saint cures a woman of a withered arm. 4. The introduction of the boy saint to the school master. 5. The ordination of the saint as archdeacon. 6. His ordination as archbishop. 7. He appears to the Emperor Constantine. 8. He intercedes for the lives of the imprisoned generals. 9. He saves Demetrias from shipwreck. 10. He restores the young boy Agricola to his parents. 11. He brings dowry money to three maidens too poor to marry. 12. He saves the Patriarch from drowning.

Saint Nicolas of Myra was born at Patara in the 4th century and was bishop at Myra in Lycia (S. Turkey).

W. Culican[1] draws attention to the use of interiors consisting of a stock repertory of arch, pillar, open door and wall pierced by two windows, the use of which is the result of sixteenth century Italian influence in Russian palace architecture; he points out that the use of calligraphic lines to set off the edges of the architecture details as well as some other features are characteristic of the late 17th century style of icon painting in Moscow. The black felt boots of Russian cavalry men worn by the three generals, the loose surcoat are departures from the tradition of byzantine dress and indicate a date between the mid seventeenth and mid eighteenth century. Culican dates the icon "most probably early 18th century".

Provenance: Greek Orthodox Church, Brasso (Kronstadt), Rumania; brought to Australia by Mrs. Michel from whom it was purchased in 1943.

References: (1) W. Culican, *An Icon of Saint Nicolas* in *Annual Bulletin N.G. Victoria,* Vol. VII, 1965, pp. 7-11.

Salomon Ruysdael   ca. 1600-1670

Dutch School. Born Naarden; it is not known who was his master. His landscapes show the influence of Esaias van de Velde and resemble those of Jan van Goyen.

Reference: *Th.B.*

Illust. 176   4729/3 **River Landscape with Boats**

canvas, 105.2 x 111 cm. Unsigned, undated; painted about 1640.

Condition: good. Recent cleaning by Harley Griffiths revealed traces of underdrawing of sails, masts and treetops on the right hand side, ½ in. above the present coastline.

Comment: Stechow suggests that a piece is missing on the left.[1] The picture is relined. The end of the present old canvas, however, cuts right across the face of a man sitting in a barge, on the left hand side.
The warm yellow brown of the foliage, the high vaporous sky suggest a date in the early '40s.[2] The handling of the foliage, consisting of a complicated pattern of irregular dots and textures, is akin to the foliage of the same artist's *Trumpeter* of 1636 (formerly in a private collection, Dortmund).[3]

The boat in the centre carrying the blue, white and red flag, is decorated with the arms of the City of Amsterdam.

Provenance: Lord Castletown from Upper Ossory, sale Christie's, 18 July, 1924, lot 151, bt. P. & D. Colnaghi. Acquired on the advice of Randall Davies for the Felton Bequest from P. & D. Colnaghi in 1933.

References: (1) W. Stechow, *Salomon van Ruysdael,* 1938, p. 118, No. 425. (2) W. Stechow, *Dutch Landscape Painting in the Seventeenth Century,* London 1966, p. 55. (3) U. Hoff, *Apollo,* 1964, Vol. 79, p. 449.

Rachel Ruysch   1664-1750

Dutch School. Born Amsterdam. Pupil of Willem van Aelst. Court painter to the Elector Johann Wilhelm von der Pfalz.

Reference: *Th.B.*

Illust. 177   1417/4 **Flowerpiece**

canvas, 70.5 x 54.5 cm. Signed on table edge to r. *Rachel Ruysch.*

Condition: satisfactory.

Provenance: In memory of Mrs. Norton E. Grimwade, presented by her husband, 1945.

References: *Quarterly Bulletin N.G. Victoria,* 1945, 1, (3) 5; M. H. Grant, *Rachel Ruysch,* 1956, Cat. No. 87, pl. 28.

Guilliam (Willem) de Ryck   1635-1697

Flemish School. Born Antwerp. Painter, etcher, goldsmith. Worked in England in the 1690's. Painted historical pictures, genre scenes and landscapes as well as portraits.

Reference: Ellis Waterhouse, *Painting in Britain, 1530-1790,* 1953, p. 109.

Illust. 178   3008/4 **Jeffrey Amherst Esq.**

canvas, 76.5 x 63 cm. Signed *G. de Ryck pt. l.l.;* inscribed and dated *Jeffery Amherst Esq. of Brooks Place Riverhead d. 1713* l.c.

Condition: good.

Comment: Jeffery Amherst of Riverhead, Kent, barrister-at-law and Bencher of Gray's Inn, member of Parliament for Bletchingley, 1689-90; married 19 July, 1670, to his first wife, Elizabeth, daughter of Henry Yate; and 16 April, 1688, to his second wife, Dorothy Amherst of Pembury. He died in 1713. His grandson, Jeffery, 1st Baron Amherst, 1717-1797, was famous for his share in the capture of Montreal in 1759.

Amherst wears a drape around his shoulders which gives an "antique air" to the portrait. This drape is held in place by a jewelled brooch, inset with what appears to be a cameo head (profile), with a laurel wreath. The border design of the brooch resembles jewellery of the late 16th century.[1]

Another portrait of this sitter in three-quarter length (with same position of head as in Melbourne, signed and with the year 1712) by de Ryck was in the Robinson, Fisher and Harding sale, London, Willis, 20 July, 1937, lot 129, together with a companion portrait of Dorothy Amherst, lot 130, inscribed with the year 1712.

Provenance: The Rt. Hon. The Earl of Amherst (Jeffery John Archer Amherst, M.C., of Aracan, East Indies); Viscount Holmesdale of Holmesdale, Kent; Baron Amherst of Montreal, Kent, Amherst Sale, as above, lot 163. Charles Henschell Esq., New York, who presented it in 1952-3.

Reference: (1) For comparison see Erich Steingräber, *Antique Jewellery,* 1957, fig. 184, an Italian pendant.

Ary Scheffer   1795-1858

Dutch-French School. Born Dordrecht. From 1812 in Paris, as pupil of P. N. Guérin. His early pictures were painted under the influence of Delacroix and Géricault. Became popular for sentimental subject pictures painted in a classical style which he exhibited at the salon in Paris.

Reference: *Th.B.*

Illust. 179   1426/3 **Christ and the Maries**

canvas, 55.2 x 45.6 cm. Signed and dated *Ary Scheffer 1854* l.l.

Condition: satisfactory.

Provenance: William Graham Sale, Christie's, 2 April, 1886, lot 82.[1] Presented by Henry Wagner, 1925, who had bought it at the sale.

Reference: (1) Rinder, Felton Correspondence, 30 Oct., 1924. See *The Times,* 28 Oct., 1924.

Illust. 180   311/1 **Temptation of Christ**

canvas, 75.3 x 55.3 cm. Signed and dated *Ary Schaffer 1854.*

Condition: restored by Mr. Smart, London, prior to shipment.[1]

Comment: This is a small replica of the original in the Louvre. Engraved by François.

Provenance: William Graham Sale, Christie's 2 April, 1886, lot 83. Purchased 1886 on the advice of A. T. Thomson.

Reference: (1) State Library Archives, 86/245, description of condition.

William Clarkson Stanfield   1793-1867

British School. Born Sunderland. In 1818, after a period of service in the navy became a scene painter, and also painted marines and landscapes. Worked together with David Roberts (*q.v.*) in Edinburgh and in London at the Drury Lane theatre, but abandoned scene painting when his marines became famous. R.A. 1835.

References: *Th.B.;* T. S. R. Boase, *English Art, 1800-1870,* 1959, p. 126.

Illust. 181   4514/3 **St. Michael's Mount, Cornwall**

canvas, 152.4 x 243.2 cm.

Condition: in good condition.

Comment: The picture ensured Stanfield's election as an Associate of the Royal Academy in 1832.[1]

Provenance: Exhibited by the artist at the R.A. 1830, No. 284, purchased by J. A. Hartley at Christie's and presented by him in 1931.[2]

References: (1) Bryan's *Dictionary of Painters and Engravers,* 1895. (2) Correspondence N.G. Victoria, 31/384.

Illust. 182   312b/1 **The Morning After Trafalgar**

canvas, 64.6 x 106.4 cm. Painted 1863.

Condition: badly damaged, 1967.

Comment: On the back is the following description in Stanfield's writing: "the situation of H.M.S. 'Defence' and her prize 'Il St. Ildefonso' on the morning following the battle of Trafalgar. Cadiz and Rota in the distance with many of the captured ships ashore on the coast between Cadiz and Cape Trafalgar C. Stanfield R.A."

Provenance: Exhibited R.A. 1863, No. 123 (owner the artist); 1870 No. 213 (owner James Price). Purchased from the Melbourne Exhibition 1888, by the Trustees.

Reference: Correspondence H. Goodhir Sir George Verdon, 554, 1888, State Library of Victoria Archives.

James Stark   1794-1895

British School. Born Norwich. Boyhood friend of John Berney Crome and pupil of John ("Old") Crome (*q.v.*). 1812 member of the Norwich Society of Artists. 1814 went to London, became a friend of William Collins. 1817 pupil at the Royal Academy. 1818-30 in Norwich, where he painted the surrounding rural scenery. 1830-40 in London. 1840-50 in Windsor from where he returned to remain in London until the end of his life.

Reference: H. M. Cundall, *The Norwich School,* The Studio, 1920.

Attributed to Stark

Illust. 183   2334/4 **Landscape with a Donkey**

canvas, 37.1 x 31.8 cm. Unsigned, undated.

Condition: satisfactory.

Comment: Formerly listed as Landscape with Horse.

Provenance: Bequeathed by Walter Cobbold Cain, 1950.

Jan Steen   1626-1679

Dutch School. Born Leyden. Said to have been a pupil of Nicolaus Knüpfer at Utrecht, Adriaen van Ostade at Haarlem and finally of Jan van Goyen at The Hague. 1648 member of the Guild of S. Luke at Leyden. 1649 lived at The Hague. With the help of his father leased a brewery at Delft in 1654. In 1656 he lived in Warmond, and settled in Haarlem in 1661. Back in Leyden in 1670 where he kept an inn. The stories by Houbraken and Weyermann about his disorderly way of life are untrue. His genre subjects carry on a tradition which began with the moralising peasant scenes of Pieter Bruegel, the Elder and Adriaen Brouwer. Many of his pictures were inspired by the stage.

References: *Th.B.; C.N.G.*

Illust. 184   1248/3 **Interior**

panel, 55.3 x 42.8 cm. Signed *J. Steen* l.l.; undated; painted probably early 1660s.

Condition: cradled prior to being sent to Australia. Rinder reported a small damage on the forehead of the woman which was attended to at the London National Gallery. Dull varnish. An old photograph of 1248/3, preserved in the Netherland Institute for Art History at the Hague, shows a drawing of an owl on the wall above the old man on the right. The owl in Dutch popular language is a symbol of stupidity because it sees nothing in broad daylight.[1]

Provenance: Possibly from the Tendall Sale, The Hague, 1809, lot 564;[2] William Wells of Redleaf, 1833, sold 1848, Christie, 12 May, lot 86, bt. Duke of Cleveland; Raby Castle, Yorkshire, inherited by Lord Barnard from whom it was acquired for the Felton Bequest on the advice of Frank Rinder in 1922.

References: (1) U. Hoff, *Apollo* 1964, Vol. 79, p. 450, fig. 3. (2) J. Smith, *Catalogue . . . Dutch and Flemish Paintings* 1833, Vol. IV, p. 54, No. 161; T. van Weestrheene, *Jan Steen, Etudes sur l'Art en Hollande,* 1856, p. 126, No. 119; Hofstede de Groot, *Catalogue of Dutch Painters,* Vol. I, 1907, No. 579; E. Trautschold, in Thieme Becker's *Künsterlexikon,* Vol. 31, 1937, p. 512.

Leopold von Stoll   Active 1828-1869

Dutch School. No biographical detail available. According to Wurzbach, of Dutch origin; about 1828 in Cracow and Warsaw; was employed from 1830-1834 at Botanical Gardens at St. Petersburg (Leningrad); from 1834-1869 in Vienna.

Reference: A. v. Wurzbach, *Niederländisches Künstlerlexikon,* 1906.

Illust. 185   3282/4 **Flower Piece**

canvas, 95.3 x 73.8 cm. Signed and dated *L. v. Stoll, 1837* l.c.

Condition: satisfactory.

Provenance: Collection F. Schwitzer, Vienna (a collection of Biedermeier work); Dr. G. Papp from whom it was purchased in Melbourne in 1956 on the advice of Eric Westbrook.

Bernardo Strozzi   1581-1644

Italian School. Born Genoa. Entered the Order of the Capuchins in 1598, but left the monastery to support his mother and spent the rest of his life as a painter. Was affected by the work of Rubens who stayed in Genoa in 1607. From 1630 he lived in Venice where he based his style on that of the Caravaggisti and of the Venetian School.

Reference: *Th.B*

School of Strozzi

Illust. 186   219/4 **S. Lawrence Distributing the Treasures of the Church to the Poor**

canvas, 112 x 152.5 cm. Unsigned, undated.

Condition: satisfactory; several small repaints.

Comment: S. Lawrence was one of the seven deacons at Rome during the pontificate of Sixtus II and suffered martyrdom under Emperor Valerian. According to S. Ambrose and Prudentius, on being asked by the Prefect of Rome to deliver up the treasures of the Church he assembled the poor among whom he had distributed the ecclesiastical possessions and presented them to the Prefect saying "these are the treasures of the Church." He was punished by being burnt to death on a gridiron.

The painting, formerly attributed to Ribera, was assigned to the School of Strozzi by Prof. Martin Soria.[1] A painting by Strozzi of the same theme is in the St. Louis City Art Museum;[2] another with composition reversed, in the Royal Palace, Genoa (Alinari, 30225); similar profile heads occur in the *Calling of S. Matthew* by Strozzi in the Worcester Art Museum[3] or in *S. John and the High Priests* in Vienna, Kunsthist. Museum (Invent. 256); a similar silver urn occurs in Strozzi's *Prophet Eliah and the Widow of Sarepto,* also in Vienna (Invent. 258); the Melbourne picture, tightly and smoothly painted, does not reveal Strozzi's characteristic open brush work.

Provenance: Acquired on the advice of Randall Davies for the Felton Bequest from T. S. Teague, London, in 1934.

References: (1) Correspondence Soria-Hoff, 17 May, 1954, N.G. Victoria files. (2) B. C. Heyl, *Worcester Art Museum Annual,* Vol. V, 1946, p. 41, fig. 8; *St. Louis City Art Museum Bulletin,* 1944, Vol. 29, p. 11-12, p. 16 n. Denis Mahon, *Apollo,* Vol. LXXXII, 1965, p. 380, fig. 3. (3) *Art Through Fifty Centuries,* Worcester Art Museum, 1948, fig. 78.

George Stubbs   1724-1806

British School. Born Liverpool. After some early endeavours in engraving and portrait painting went to York where he studied anatomy. In 1754 he went to Rome and to Morocco. Returned to Liverpool and after two years settled on a farm in Lincolnshire where he prepared his *Anatomy of the Horse,* published with his own engravings in London in 1766. Stubbs had been resident in London since 1760. In 1773 he became President of the Society of Artists; 1781, A.R.A. Painted many sporting pictures and worked on a book of the comparative anatomy of Man, Tiger and Fowl.

Reference: P. & L. Murray, *A Dictionary of Art and Artists,* 1959.

Illust. 187   1270/3 **A Horse**

canvas, 71 x 81.5 cm. Unsigned, undated; probably an early work.

Condition: not re-lined; satisfactory.

Provenance: Presented by Colonel Whitwell, 1923.

Illust. 188   2052/4 **A Lion Attacking a Horse**

canvas, 69 x 100.8 cm. Unsigned, undated.

Condition: cleaned prior to purchase; marked craquelure, but in good condition.

Comment: The theme of a horse attacked by a lion pre-occupied Stubbs for over thirty years from 1760 onwards. He treated the theme in three different episodes, in the third of which the lion crouches on the horse's back and bites its flank, as here. Of this episode Basil Taylor lists six oil paintings, one enamel painting and one mezzotint, and assumes the life-size group with light-brown horse now in the collection of Mr. and Mrs. Mellon to be the earliest. The companion piece to this, the lion attacking a stag, is also in the Mellon collection. These may have been completed by 1763, and are followed by the Melbourne version, dated by Taylor 1765.[1] The enamel now No. T1192 in the Tate Gallery London, is signed and dated 1769.

The composition appears to the compiler to be a cross of two classical types. A. As Taylor indicates, the Roman copy of a Pergamon original in the Palazzo dei Conservatori shows a lion burying his two claws and teeth in the flank of a broken-down horse.[2] Stubbs was in Italy in 1750 and could have seen the Roman group then on the Capitol, which enjoyed a special fame in England. Jonathan Richardson the Elder described the Capitoline group in 1722[3] and referred to a replica of this group in Florence as 'finer than that famous one in the Capital.'[4] Professor Joseph Burke has referred me to a replica of the Palazzo dei Conservatori group which is at Rousham.[5a] A version formerly at Incehall now in the Liverpool City Museum, probably an eighteenth century marble, based on the Conservatori group, shows the horse's head turned towards its attacker. This motif would there appear to be inspired by Adamo Ghisi's leonardesque motif of the horse biting the mane of the lion (B. 107).[5b] In Stubbs's picture the head is turned even more sharply into a full profile view.

B. Some details of Stubbs's group may owe their origin to a classical representation of a stag attacked by a dog, as it appears in a group now in the Vatican; here the stag stands upright, turning his head towards the dog on its back and raising its right foreleg; the dog crouches, burying its teeth and one claw in the stag's side, in a manner closer to 2052/4 than the lion of the classical horse and lion group. The theme of the stag (attacked by a lion) formed the companion piece to Stubbs's first version of *Lion and Horse* as mentioned above.[6]

A story connecting the paintings of the lion and horse theme with an alleged visit by Stubbs to North Africa appears to be apocryphal.[7]
Géricault painted a copy after the engraving of one of the versions by Benjamin Green.[8]

Provenance: The Hon. Esme Smythe, Ashton Court, Somerset. According to an old label on the back, exh. Bristol Art Gallery, 1908, No. 60 (owner Lady Smythe). Acquired for the Felton Bequest on the advice of A. J. L. McDonnell and Sir Kenneth Clark from Rowland, Browse and Delbanco in 1949.

References: (1) Basil Taylor, *George Stubbs, The Lion and Horse Theme* in *Burl. Mag.*, 1965, Vol. CVII, pp. 81 ff. (2) *ibid.* fig. 39. (3) Professor Joseph Burke has kindly drawn my attention to the following passages in Jonathan Richardson the Elder, assisted by his son, *An Account of some of the Statutes, Bas-reliefs, Drawings and Pictures in Italy,* ed. by Mr. Richardson, London, 1722, p. 114. (4) *ibid.,* p. 59. (5a) A small illustration may be found in

Oswald Sirén, *China and the Gardens of Europe of the Eighteenth Century,* 1950, pl. 17.
The horse bends its head back as in the Incehall group. (5b) Taylor, *op. cit.,* p. 86.
According to Bartsch, the Ghisi engraving was derived from a painting by Giulio Romano,
fig. 42. (6) Photo Alinari Pe I No. 6491. I am indebted to Dr. Suzanne Lodge for this
comparison. (7) Taylor, *op. cit.,* 82 f. (8) Benjamin Green's mezzotint, a copy of which is
in the Print Room collection, N.G. Victoria, was "done from an Original Picture in the
Collection of Luke Scrafton, Esq., 1769." B. Taylor, *The Listener,* 11 Dec. 1952, p. 979,
repr (Géricault). See also: Basil Taylor, *The Prints of George Stubbs,* The Paul Mellon
Foundation for British Art, London 1969, pp. 14, 28, No. 4.
Exh.: la peinture, romantique anglaise et les preraphaelites Petit Palais,
Jan.-April 1972 (organized by the British Council, Le Ministère de Affaires
Etrangers, Le Ministère des Affaires Culturelles et la Ville de Paris), No. 262

David Teniers II   1610-1690

Flemish School. Born Antwerp; son and pupil of the painter David Teniers
I. Became master in Antwerp in 1632-3. Married Anna, daughter of Jan
Brueghel *(q.v.).* In 1651 settled in Brussels where he became court
painter and curator of the famous art collection of Archduke Leopold
Wilhelm and continued in this position under Don Juan d'Austria. Took
a leading part in the promotion of an Art Academy in Antwerp which
opened in 1665. Best known for his peasant pictures in which he
developed the style of Brouwer into an original manner of his own. Copied
many of the pictures in the collection of Archduke Leopold Wilhelm; 244
of these copies were engraved in the *Theatrum Pictorum,* 1660, a copy
of which is in the Print Room collection.

Reference: *Th.B.*

Illust. 189   1051/3 **The Gazette**

panel, 45 x 65.6 cm.
Signed *D. Teniers f.,* lower right.

Condition: satisfactory.

Other Versions: A poor copy of this was in the Ahlmeyer sale, Cologne,
23 March, 1909, lot 185.

Condition: cleaned prior to purchase; in excellent condition.

Provenance: Engraved by Joseph or Ch. Nicolas Varin (1740-1800) or (1745-1805) and
again by Jean Pelletier (b. 1736) probably while in the collection of the Duke of Orléans (as
David Teniers I); according to Waagen[1] and Buchanan[2] sold in England in 1792; according
to Smith[3] in 1798; bt. Sir Philip Stephens; Sale Christie's, 17 May, 1810, lot 95; sale Lord
Viscount Ranelagh, dec. (Fulham), Christie, 22 June, 1821, lot 88 (bought in according to
Smith); Sale Lord Viscount Ranelagh, Christie's, 16 May, 1829, lot 19; coll. William Cririe,
Manchester, 1831 (according to Smith); at one time property of Mr. G. E. C. Clayton,
Ppenarell Llandbedrog, N. Wales (label on back). Acquired on the advice of Frank Rinder
for the Felton Bequest in 1920.[4]

References: (1) G. F. Waagen, *Kunstwerke und Künstler* in England, 1837, Vol. I, p. 519,
No. 6 (under Galerie Orléans), ditto in English ed. 1854, Vol. II, p. 503, No. 6.
(2) W. Buchanan, *Memoirs of Painting,* Vol. I, 1824, pp. 17-18, 159-164, 189, No. 6.
(3) J. Smith, *Catalogue Dutch, Flemish Painters,* 1831, Vol. III, p. 355, No. 358. (4) Rinder
corr. 27.1.1920.

Illust. 190   2050/4 **The Skittle Players**

canvas, 98.4 x 206.6 cm. Unsigned, undated.

Condition: cleaned prior to purchase; in excellent condition.

Provenance: Exhibited R.A. 1886, No. 91 (owner Miss Cooper); *ibid.,* 1910, No. 79 (owner R. J. Cooper); when acquired for the Felton Bequest on the advice of A. J. L. McDonnell and Sir Kenneth Clark, in 1949, from T. Agnew and Sons, the picture was the property of the Trustees of the late Brigadier-General R. J. Cooper.

Reference: Listed in the *Burl. Mag.,* Vol. XCIII, 1951, p. 145.

Gerard Terborch   1617-1681

Dutch School. Born Zwolle. Trained by his father, Gerard Terborch the Elder and by Pieter Molyn in Haarlem.
In 1635-6 he was in England. In 1637-40 he is stated to have been in Rome, Naples and Spain. In 1645-8 in Münster where he painted the group portrait of *The Oath of the Treaty of Münster* in the London N.G. and is said to have entered the services of the Spanish delegate, the Count de Peneranda. In 1654 he married in Deventer where he settled for the rest of his life. His early work consisted of genre scenes in the manner of Hendrik Pot, Dirk Hals, etc. In the fifties he developed the elegant conversation pieces and the small scale full length portrait figures of which the picture listed below is an example.

Reference: S. J. Gudlaugsson, *Gerard Ter Borch,* 1959.

Illust. 191   1542/4 **Lady with a Fan**

canvas, 67.2 x 51.4 cm. Signed GTB (monogram)
lower right, undated; painted 1660, furniture slightly later, workshop addition.

Comment: The companion piece of a man is at the William Rockhill Nelson Gallery of Art, at Kansas City.[1]

Copy: According to Gudlaugsson copies of No. 1542/4 and the Kansas City picture are in the Museum of Leipzig, formerly in the Speck van Sternberg collection, Lützschena,[2] made before the addition of the furniture.

Provenance: Poss. Sale J.v.d.Bergh, Amsterdam, 15.7.1833, No. 242; Martin Rikoff, 1903; Sold 4.12.1907, No. 22 in Paris; bt. Kleinberger, Paris. M. Bromberg, Hamburg (1913); Dr. Grunden, Hamburg; Wildenstein, London, 1945; acquired by the National Gallery of Victoria, Melbourne.[3]

Exh.: Guildhall, London, 1903, No. 178.

References: (1) S. J. Gudlaugsson, *Katalog der Gemälde Gerard Ter Borchs sowie biographisches Material,* The Hague, 1960, p. 179, No. 177. (2) *ibid.* and Hofstede de Groot, *Catalogue of Dutch Painters,* 1913, Vol. V, No. 393 and 311. (3) The Provenance is given according to Gudlaugsson, No. 178. See also, Quarterly Bulletin, N.G. Victoria, 1948, Vol. III (1), 1, detail.

Giovanni Battista Tiepolo   1696-1770

Italian School. Born Corte di San Domenico. Pupil of G. Lazzarini; studied the work of G. B. Piazzetta and Sebastino Ricci *(q.v.)* and had a marked preference for the work of Veronese *(q.v.)*. Lived in Venice but carried out commissions in many of the North Italian cities. For instance, the famous decorations in the Villa Valmarana date from 1757. In 1743 formed a friendship with Count Algarotti who gave him commissions on behalf of King Augustus of Saxony 1751-3 in Würzburg where he decorated the staircase ceiling and the Kaisersaal in the palace of the Prince-Bishop. 1756 first President of the new Academy of Painting and Sculpture in Venice. In 1762 went to Madrid in the service of King Charles III and remained there until his death. Tiepolo is the great master of the Rococo style in Italy.

Reference: Antonio Morassi, *G. B. Tiepolo,* 1955.

Illust. 192   103/4 **The Banquet of Cleopatra**

canvas 248.2 x 357.8 cm. Unsigned, undated; painted 1743-4.

Condition: the painting was cleaned in 1955 by H. A. Buttery, London, whose comments have been referred to by Francis J. Watson[1] and Michael Levey;[2] in perfect condition but for a thin vertical strip running the length of the canvas (through the salver with fruit) which is due to folding. There are also some major re-paints to the left of the fruit salver, the wine vessels and along the edges of the canvas.

Comment: The story represented is drawn from Pliny, *Naturalis Historia,* Book IX, Ch. LVIII: in speaking of pearls Pliny related that the two largest in history were owned by Cleopatra, Queen of Egypt; she poured contempt on the banquets of Anthony (Roman Consul in Egypt) and made a wager that she would spend 10,000,000 sesterces on a single banquet. When the banquet was in progress "she ordered the second course. In accordance with previous instructions the servants placed in front of her only a single vessel containing vinegar, the strong rough quality of which can melt pearls. She was at the moment wearing in her ears that remarkable and truly unique work of nature . . . she took one earring off and dropped the pearl in the vinegar, and when it was melted, swallowed it." Pliny stressed the tension of the scene, the curiosity of Anthony and the restraining action of Lucius Plancus who was umpiring the wager and prevented the destruction of the second pearl. Told by Pliny disapprovingly as an instance of utmost luxury, the story is understood by Tiepolo as the height of splendid extravagance.

The Melbourne *Banquet,* which at one time was thought to be largely studio work,[3] is completely autograph with the exception of the architecture which was, like other decorative architecture in Tiepolo's work, probably carried out by Girolamo Mengozzi-Colonna.[4]

In what appears to be a draft letter of about 1744 to Count Brühl, (King August III's minister in Dresden)[5] Francesco Algarotti,[6] the King's buyer in Venice, related that he had acquired a modello for the large banquet and that this modello was engraved by Pietro Monaco under the title *The Banquet of Nabal* so that it could be published in Monaco's book of sacred pictures. It is held by many that this modello is the small banquet now in the Musée Cognacq Jay in Paris.[7] Algarotti stated that Tiepolo improved the composition in the large painting, and praised the erudition shown in the sculptural decorations. The documents relating to the commission of the large *Banquet* which Algarotti acquired for King August III make it probable that the picture was begun not later than 1743 and certain that it was finished by February 1744[8] (see under provenance).

The colonnaded backdrop is used again in *Maecenas*[8a] presenting the Arts to Augustus painted c. 1745.

Drawings: A drawing in Florence of Cleopatra must be preparatory to the modello in the Musée Cognacq Jay, since the Queen is holding the pearl in her right and not yet in her left hand as in Melbourne. Two further drawings of Cleopatra and servants and several of Anthony and Plancus precede the Melbourne version, as do drawings of a fruit dish (at Trieste).[9]

Copies: The so-called Stroganoff drawing, held by Roger Fry[10] to be preparatory to the Cognacq Jay modello, is a monochrome oil copy of the Monaco engraving; it has been rejected by Michael Levey and is not referred to by other authors.[11] A copy thought by Sack to be of the Melbourne Banquet in the Gothic House at Worlitz, Germany, is a repetition of the Cognacq Jay picture.[12]

Other Versions and Companion Pieces: The Melbourne Banquet and its modello precede the other versions of the same theme, that is: the Alexander modello[13] and the Yussupov Banquet (1747),[14] the Stockholm University modello[15] and the fresco in the Palazzo Labia (1745-1750);[16] other versions in existence appear to be studio work.[17] A contemporary copy from the Melbourne picture of the head of Cleopatra is in the collection of the Earl of Roseberry.[17a]

All these banquet scenes have companion pieces representing the Meeting of Anthony and Cleopatra.[18] The Melbourne Banquet is the only one which does not have such a companion piece. George Knox suggests that two drawings in the Victoria and Albert Museum of a Roman Officer leading a lady by the hand show that Tiepolo was contemplating a Meeting of Anthony and Cleopatra at the same time at which he created the Melbourne Banquet.[19]

Iconography: The theme is rarely represented in the earlier history of painting. It occurs in Dutch art of the 17th century (Jan Steen)[20] but more relevantly to our picture in the work of Sebastiano Mazzoni, of about 1683 in the Smithsonian Institution, Washington.[21] Mazzoni, a Florentine who worked in Venice, was a pupil of Bernardo Strozzi and influenced

150

Sebastiano Ricci. It is possible that Tiepolo knew Mazzoni's Banquet, which reflects Veronese's *Banquet in the House of Levi*,[22] and resembles the Alexander and Yussupov versions by Tiepolo. It has been pointed out that a renewed interest in themes from classical antiquity in Venetian eighteenth century painting and particularly in the work of G. B. Tiepolo may have been due to Francesco Algarotti.[23] In his letter to Mariette[24] of 1751 Algarotti praised the sculptures of Isis and Serapis and the Sphinx in the Melbourne Banquet in which "Tiepolo shows the erudition of a Raphael or a Poussin." The figure of Serapis is after a statue in the Maffei collection which Tiepolo had drawn for one of the plates of *Verona Illustrata*.[25] Algarotti rightly recognized that the layout of the architecture, the bizarre costumes, are reminiscent of Veronese.[26]

Roger Fry pointed to the changes in composition which occurred between the Cognacq Jay and the Melbourne versions,[26a] the early version being more strongly built on counter-diagonals and recession; the Melbourne version arresting recession and stressing horizontal lines. The incident of the pearl has gained in dramatic effect in the Melbourne picture; instead of holding the pearl low down in her right hand (Cognacq Jay), Cleopatra holds it high up in her left in Melbourne, just above the glass of vinegar, thus fixing an exact moment in time. The heads of the turbaned man at the back and the bearded standing figure recall the fantasy heads of Orientals which Tiepolo used also in his etched *Capricci* (1743).[26b] A ceiling painting by Francesco Fontebasso of the *Banquet of Cleopatra* reveals the influence of the Melbourne Banquet as well as that of the other versions.[27]

Provenance: Algarotti refers in two letters to the Melbourne Banquet as having "been begun for another and ceded to me by Tiepolo."[28] The "other", so Levey[2] and Haskell[5] assume, may have been Consul Smith, since he was the second owner of the modello which Algarotti may have given to him in compensation for the loss of the big picture. On February 10, 1744, Algarotti paid for a frame for the picture and on March 5 he paid Tiepolo 300 sequins for the picture itself.[29] It was despatched to Dresden in the same month. The Banquet did not remain long in Dresden, it seems; it does not figure in Guarienti's inventories of the King's picture gallery in Dresden, drawn up in 1750 and 1754,[30] but appears at the sale of 22 May, 1765, lot 54, at Amsterdam, at which paintings from August III's hunting castle Hubertusburg were sold.[31] It was bought by Yver for Catherine II of Russia.[32] Sack states that under Emperor Paul it was used as ceiling decoration in the Michel palace in St. Petersburg.[33] In 1891 it figured in the catalogue of the Hermitage. It was offered for sale in England in 1932 and acquired for the Felton Bequest on the advice of Randall Davies in that year; arrived 1933.

Exhibitions: Prior to shipment to Australia the picture was exhibited at the Imperial Institute Buildings, at the City of Manchester Art Gallery and at the London N.G. Room IX, June-August, 1932. In 1954-5 it was shown at the R.A. Winter Exhibition, No. 51, and at the London National Gallery from Oct., 1956, to Aug., 1957, in Room XX.

References: (1) Francis Watson, *The Connoisseur,* Vol. CXXXVI, 1955, p. 214. (2) Michael Levey, *Arte Veneta,* 1955, p. 199 *et seq.* (3) Roger Fry, *Burl. Mag.,* Vol. LXIII, 1933, p. 131 *seq.* (4) M. Levey, *Painting in Eighteenth Century Venice,* 1959, p. 184, fig. 91. (5) F. Haskell, *Burl. Mag.,* Vol. C, 1958, pp. 212, 213. (6) For biogr. see O. E. Schmidt, *Minister Graf Brühl und Karl Heinrich von Heinecken, Briefe . . .* (1733-1763) Berlin, 1921, Ch. III, 5, p. 257 *seq.* (7) The small banquet, in 1904 in the possession of the Princes Mathilde, now in the Musée Cognacq Jay, is regarded as identical with the modello owned by Algarotti and Consul Smith and as an original by Tiepolo by Sack, *Giambattista and Domenico Tiepolo,* 1910,

fig. 82, p. 214, No. 467; Fry, *op. cit.*, p. 132, pl. II; George Knox, *Catalogue of the Tiepolo Drawings in the Victoria and Albert Museum*, 1960, p. 18; the same, *The Connoisseur*, Vol. CXXXV, 1955, p. 37-38 and Morassi (see note 18). Watson, *op. cit.* (see note 1), p. 214, regards the small banquet as close to the Melbourne Banquet but later; F. Haskell (see note 5) as possibly a copy of the original modello. (8) H. Posse, *Jahrbuch der Preussischen Kunstsammlungen*, Vol. LII, 1931, Beiheft, pp. 22, 27, 64-5, *et seq.* (letter 22). (8a) P. Descargues, *The Hermitage*, London 1961, p. 109. (9) Knox, *Catalogue V. and A.* (see note 7), p. 18: (i) *Cleopatra receives the glass of vinegar*, Fondazione Horne, Florence; (ii) *Cleopatra*, V. and A., No. 71; (iii) *Anthony and a Man*, V. and A., No. 72; (iv) *Anthony and a Man*, V. and A., No. 73; (v) *Study of Anthony with Helmet*, Morgan Library, New York; (vii) *Studies of Fruit Dish*, Trieste, Vigni 57-9. (10) Fry, *op. cit*, (see note 0), p. 132 *et seq.* (11) G. Stroganoff Catalogue; Vol. II, 1911, pl. 20, see Levey, *Arte Veneta*, 1955, p. 202, and Morassi. (12) E. Sack, *op. cit.* (see note 7), p. 95; a photograph made available by the Institut für Denkmalpflege, Halle (Saale), is on the files of the N.G. Victoria. (13) R.A. Cat. 1954/5, No. 513, and previous literature; present owner National Gallery, London.
(14) Described by Waagen in 1864 in St. Petersburg, Yussupov collection (quoted by Sack); not seen by Sack, *op. cit.* (see note 7), p. 208, No. 428; re-discovered by Grabar, *Iskustvo*, March, April, 1947, p. 63, who reads date as 1747; reproduced by M. Chamot, *Burl. Mag.*, 1959, Vol. CI, p. 47, fig. 7; the picture and its companion piece hang now at Arkhangelskoye, formerly the country-house of the Yussupov family. (15) O. Siren, *Dessins et Tableaux de la Renaissance Italienne dans les Collections de Suède*, 1902, opp. p. 112 repr.; p. 111-12; A. Morassi, *Tiepolo*, 1955, p. 24, fig. 32. (16) Sack, *op. cit.* (see note 7), p. 124, fig. 114; Morassi was the first to attack the date 1757 given by previous writers, A. Morassi, *Tiepolo*, 1943, p. 28; and *Tiepolo*, 1955. As Watson, *op. cit.* (see note 1) and Levey, *Painting in Eighteenth Century Venice*, 1959, p. 184, have pointed out, a date *ante quem* is given by Reynolds's sketch of the *Meeting of Anthony and Cleopatra* at the Palazzo Labia (B.M. Print Room, Reynolds, *Notes and Sketches in Italy*, a9, p. 201), which was made in 1752. Tiepolo in 1752 was in Würzburg, and must have finished the frescoes in the summer and autumn of 1750. (16a) Morassi, *op. cit.*, II, p. 20. (17) Sack, *op. cit.* (see note 7), p. 211, No. 454, fig. 116 (Amiens version and related works), p. 163, fig. 150, No. 122 (Museo Civico version); M. Levey, *Arte Veneta*, 1955, p. 202 (Zugno's picture in Ca Rezzonico). (18) A. Morassi, *Tiepolo*, 1955, figs. 30-33, pls. 46, 47; the same, *Tiepolo's Banquet of Cleopatra*, in *In Honour of Daryl Lindsay, Essays and Studies*, Melbourne, 1964, pp. 100-109. (19) G. Knox, *Catalogue, V. & A.* (see note 7), p. 19, pls. 69, 70.
(20) Hofstede de Groot, *Dutch Painters*, Vol. I, 1908, Nos. 85, 86, p. 31. (21) G. Knox, *Connoisseur*, Vol. CXXXV, 1955, p. 38; *The Art Quarterly*, 1954, p. 102 repr. (22) P. H. Osmond, *Paolo Veronese*, 1927, pl. 44. (23) Haskell, *Burl. Mag.*, Vol. C, 1958, p. 213.
(24) Sack, *op. cit.* (see note 7), p. 95; see also the draft-letter to Brühl, Haskell (see note 5); Fry, *op. cit.*, p. 131. (25) G. Knox, *The Connoisseur*, Vol. CXXXV, 1955, p. 37. The figure of Isis is also drawn from a classical statue in Italy; Haskell, *Burl. Mag.*, Vol. C, 1958, p. 213. (26) Several resemblances to Veronese can be found: a high priest in Veronese's *Disputation of the Doctors* (Fiocco, *Veronese*, 1928, pl. X), (Prado) resembles Mark Anthony in the *Banquet of Cleopatra;* a balustrade architecture in the background, enlivened by small figures, occurs in Veronese's *Family of Darius* (Fiocco, pl. LII); here we also find women's costumes resembling that worn by Cleopatra; a boy with curly hair and high collar similar to those in the Banquet occurs in Veronese's *Supper of San Gregorio Magno* (Fiocco, pl. LXIII); Veronese's *Supper in the House of Levi* resembles in the centre the banquet in the Palazzo Labia; Veronese's *Christ and the Centurion* has background architecture with niches and sculpture, comparable in general effect to the same motifs in Melbourne (Fiocco, pl. LXXXV). (26a) *Burl. Mag.*, LXIII, 1933, p. 132. (26b) R. Pallucchini, *Gli Incisori del Settecento*, 1941, p. 75, gives date as "1743 or earlier". (27) R. Palluchini, *Arte Veneta*, 1957, p. 165. (28) F. Haskell, *Burl. Mag.*, Vol. C, 1958, p. 212, 213, and H. Posse, *op. cit.* (see note 8), p. 65 (letter 22). (29) Posse, *ibid.*, p. 28, note 1, note des Depence 12f and p. 65, note I. (30) *Inventar Guarienti delli quadri, che Sono nel Cabinetto di Sua Maesta, May 1750* and *Inventarium von der Königlichen Bilder Galerie zu Dresden, gefertiget Mens: July & August 1754*. Mrs. A. Mayer Meintschel has kindly consulted these inventories for me. The assumption made in the Tiepolo literature from Molmenti and Sack onwards that the Melbourne Banquet had been taken over by Count Brühl is erroneous.

The error seems to have arisen in the catalogue of the Hermitage of 1891, Vol. I, where the name Brühl is attached to the Banquet (No. 317) and not to the painting of *Maecenas presenting the Liberal Arts to Augustus* (No. 318) which had indeed been commissioned by Brühl from Tiepolo; see Posse, *op. cit.* (see note 8), p. 49, letter 9, and *Burl. Mag.,* Vol. LXIII, 1933, p. 234. (31) Quoted in translation by Posse (excerpt only), *ibid.,* p. 23, note 1; the original text was made available to me by Dr. Gudlaugsson from the Rijksbureau voor Kunsthistorische Documentatie in The Hague: *Catalogus van een Koninglijke Verzameling van zeer uitmuntende en kostbare schilderijen, gekommen uit Saksen . . . Al de welke verkocht zal wordn op Woensdag den 22e Mei 1765 ten huize van Arnoldus Dankmeijer, Kasteleijn in Oude-Zijds Heerenlogement tot Amsterdam, door de Makelaar Hendrik de Winter, No, 54, Gio Batta Tiepolo, Venetian. De Maaltijd van Cleopatra en Marcus Antonius, hoog 07 duim, breed 141 duim, *The copy of this catalogue held by the Dresden Gallery had on the title page the following contemporary inscription. "Dieses sind die Schildereyen aus der Hubertusburger Gallerie, Ausschuss der Dresdner Gallerie" (quoted by Posse, *ibid.).* This catalogue was destroyed during the 1939-45 war. (32) F. Lugt, *Répertoire des Catalogues de Ventes,* 1600-1825, (1938), No. 1462. (33) Sack, *op. cit.* (see note 7), p. 96. See also *Quarterly Bulletin N.G. Victoria* 1957, XI (1), 1-3. For the most recent authoritative account, see A. Morassi, *Complete Catalogue of the Paintings of G. B. Tiepolo,* London, 1962, p. 23.

Jacopo Tintoretto (Jacopo Robusti)   1518-1594

Italian School. Born Venice. Is said to have studied with Titian, and may have worked under Bonifazio or Paris Bordone. Made drawings from statues of classical antiquity and by Michelangelo. Worked for the Venetian state and from 1564 for the Confraternity of San Rocco of which he became a member in 1565. The main work of his early period, the *Miracle of S. Mark,* shows the dramatic foreshortening, the sharply diagonal composition which reflect the influences of Michelangelo's late frescoes. In their rhythmic organisation, their pronounced effects of light and dark, their denial of natural, three-dimensional space, the decorations for the Scuola of San Rocco of the 60s are leading examples of the mannerist style.

Reference: H. Tietze, *Tintoretto,* 1948.

Illust. 193   3677/3 **Doge Pietro Loredano**

canvas, 109.5 x 93 cm. Unsigned, undated; painted between 1567-70.

Condition: examined by Holder, London, in 1927; reported to be "in very good condition: the one or two slight damages in unimportant places, which have been suitably treated, not being worthy of mention. It was re-lined many years ago, and recently the old varnish has been removed".

Comment: The sitter is identified by comparison with an engraving by Nicolo Nelli, 1568, inscribed with the name Petrus Lauredano.[1] From 1559 onwards Tintoretto held the office of the Senseria for the Hall of the Great Council in the Palazzo Ducale which entitled him to paint the portraits of the Doges. Loredano was presumably painted during his tenure of office as Doge 1567-70. Tintoretto also painted a votive

M

picture of the Doge before the Virgin for the Sala dei Pregati, in the Palazzo Ducale. Both paintings were destroyed in the fire which ravaged the Ducal Palace in 1577. The existence of several other portraits of Doge Loredano is attested by 17th century writers;[2] of the remaining variants of the portrait 3677/3 is regarded by Bercken as the best.[3] Another (seated) in the Budapest Museum is described by Bercken as not by Tintoretto.[4] Another in the Ross Delafield Collection, New York, is described by Bercken as a replica of the Melbourne version.[5] Another version, head and shoulders only, close to the Ross Delafield version, was in the Beurdeley Sale, G. Petit, Paris, 6, 7 May, 1920, lot 197.[6] The portrait was exhibited at the London National Gallery from Oct. 15, 1927-Jan. 16, 1928.

Provenance: Prince Lichnowsky, Castle of Kuchelna, Czechoslovakia, said to have been in the family for over a century, bt. by Messrs. Knoedler, London, on the continent from an agent of the Prince. Acquired for the Felton Bequest on the advice of Frank Rinder in 1927.

References: (1) G. Lorenzetti, *Dedalo,* Vol. VI, 1925-6, p. 310, *seq.* repr., p. 314. (2) *ibid., et seq.,* and F. Philipp, *Quarterly Bulletin, N.G. Victoria,* 1957, Vol. XI (2), 2-4. (3) E. v.d. Bercken, *Jacopo Tintoretto,* 1942, p. 115, No. 217, pl. 336; 3677/3 was first published by T. Borenius, in *Apollo,* Vol. VI, 1927, p. 217; it is referred to by Bercken in the list of works of Tintoretto, *Thieme Becker's Künstlerlexikon,* Vol. XXXIII, 1939, p. 194; and B. Berenson, *Italian Pictures of the Renaissance,* Venetian School, Vol. I, 1957, p. 175. (4) Bercken, *op. cit.,* No. 55, and p. 106. (5) *ibid.,* p. 118, No. 255; for other references to the Ross Delafield picture see: Lorenzetti, *Dedalo,* Vol. VI, 1925/6, p. 310, *seq.,* repr.; B. Berenson, *Pitture Italiane del Rinascimento,* Milan, 1936, p. 483; H. Tietze, *Tintoretto,* 1948, pl. 154. (6) Photograph with notes, Witt Library, Courtauld Institute, London.

Titian (Tiziano Vecellio)   Active before 1511, died 1576

Italian School. Born Pieve de Cadore. The date of his birth cannot be documented with certainty. According to Dolce first taught by Zuccati, mosaicists; then by Gentile and Giovanni Bellini and later by Giorgione. Worked in the service of the Venetian Republic and later for the families of the D'Este, the Gonzaga, the Farnese, the Della Rovere, Francis I of France, Charles V Emperor of Germany, Philip II of Spain. During a long development Titian passed from the High Renaissance manner of his early work to affinities with Mannerism and anticipations of the Baroque. He opposed the Florentine emphasis on contour and drawing with a style based on colour and tone. The work listed below belongs to the end of his middle period.

Reference: *Th.B.*

Illust. 194   1334/3 **Bust of a Franciscan Friar with a Book**

canvas, 84.5 x 74.3 cm. Unsigned, undated; painted about 1550.[1]

Condition: excellent.

Comment: Seen by D. v. Hadeln;[1] known from a photograph only to Tietze; an old copy, attributed to Moroni (37 in. x 29½ in.), was bought by E. J. Moore at Christies in 1921 (previous owner Th. Agnew & Sons).[2]

Provenance: Purchased by Th. Agnew and Sons from Prof. Publio Podio (restorer), in Italy;[3] acquired from them on the advice of Frank Rinder for the Felton Bequest in 1924. Exhibited at the London National Gallery, Jan. 17-June 19, 1925.

References: (1) Oskar Fischel, *Tizian* (Klass. d. Kunst, 5th ed.)? 1924, No. 219, dated the picture in the 1560s; D. v. Hadeln, *Burl. Mag.*; 1924, Vol. XLV, p. 179 and H. Tietze, *Titian*, 1937, p. 208, gave the date of about 1550. (2) Rinder correspondence Felton letter 25, 3 Nov., 1927. (3) Correspondence Colin Agnew to U. Hoff, 1959, N.G. Victoria files. Other references: B. Berenson, *Pitture Italiane del Rinascimento*, Milan, 1936, p. 492; the same, *Italian Pictures of the Renaissance*, Venetian School, 1957, Vol. I, p. 188. (4) Rinder corr. 1 11 1923, 16.11.1900, 0,1.1924, 6 3,1925. (5) *ibid.*, 20.3.1924.

Francesco Trevisani   1656-1746

Italian School. Born Capodistria. Pupil of A. Zanchi and Joseph Heinz the Younger in Venice. About 1678 went to Rome where he studied the works of Carraccis and Correggio. Among his patrons were the Elector of Cologne, Lothar Franz of Schönborn (Pommersfelden), as well as Pope Clement XI and many Italian members of the nobility. Specialised in Cabinet pictures and intimate religious paintings for private devotion, in a style which is a classicist interpretation of the baroque.

Reference: *Th.B.*

Illust. 195   3209/4 **Joseph being sold by his Brothers**

canvas, 112 x 156.7 cm. Signed *F.T.* on box hanging on camel on left; undated.

Condition: excellent.

Comment: Jacob's sons hated their younger brother, Joseph, and threw him into a pit; "then there passed by Midianite merchantmen; and they drew and lifted up Joseph out of the pit and sold Joseph to the Ishmaelites for twenty pieces of silver; and they brought Joseph into Egypt". Gen. ch. XXXVII, v. 28.

Provenance: Recorded in the collection of the Duke of Westminster, Grosvenor House, in *Catalogue of the Pictures at Grosvenor House, London, with etchings by John Young*, 1821, No. 94 repr.; Jameson, *Companion to the most celebrated Private Galleries of Art in London*, 1844, the Grosvenor Gallery, p. 262, No. 81; not referred to in the 1913 catalogue of Grosvenor House. Acquired on the advice of A. J. L. McDonnell for the Felton Bequest in 1954/5. See also: *Quarterly Bulletin, N.G. Victoria*, 1955, IX (3), 4.

Allessandro Turchi   1578-1649

Italian School. Born Verona. Pupil of Felice Brusasorci, later influenced by Venetian painters and Saraceni, and especially by the school of the Carraccis. The influence of the work of Guido Reni, Annibale Carracci and of Michelangelo da Caravaggio may be found in his work. From 1604 belonged to the Goldsmiths' Guild in Rome; 1619 member of the Roman Academy of S. Luke; from 1638 member of the Congregazione dei Virtuosi. Painter of religious subjects on canvas, black marble, slate and copper.

References: *Th.B.;* N. Pevsner, O. Grautoff, *Barockmalerei in den Romanischen Ländern* (Handbuch für Kunstwissenschaft) 1928, pp. 140, 174, fig. 132.

Illust. 196   3077/4 **Charity**

canvas, 206 x 101.6 cm. Unsigned, undated.

Condition: Satisfactory; cleaned prior to purchase.

Comment: Previously attributed to Lodovico Carracci;[1] re-attribution by Dr. H. Voss,[2] who calls it a "Characteristic and outstanding work by Alessandro Turchi." It depicts an allegorical figure of Charity, based on a type created by Jacopo della Quercia in the fifteenth century.[3] The woman suckles one child (love of one's neighbour) while another child, holding her hand, carries a burning torch (love of God). For comparison see Crispin van der Passe, *Charity,* engraving, in which the child walking at Charity's right side carries a flaming heart (Nagler 92).

Provenance: Old label on back Leger and Son, "1853, Turchi"; listed by G. F. Waagen, *Treasures of Art in Great Britain, Suppl.* 1857, p. 362, as in the possession of the Earl of Radnor, Longford Castle (Carracci); exh. R.A. 1873, No. 156 (Carracci), (owner the Earl of Radnor); (see Smith, Mss. Catalogue 1829 (kindly brought to my attention by Frank Simpson); Art Journal, 1897, p. 145; *Radnor Catalogue,* 1909, Vol. I, pp. 74-5, No. 102); acquired by the Felton Bequest on the advice of Daryl Lindsay and A. J. L. McDonnell 1953-4.

References: (1) Waagen and R.A. 1873, *loc. cit.* (2) Dr. H. Voss, Certificate, copy on N.G. Victoria files. (3) Freyhan, *Journal of the Warburg and Courtauld Institutes,* 1948. See also *Real-Lexikon zur Deutschen Kunstgeschichte* 1952 (Caritas); C. Ripa, *Iconologia,* ed. 1630 (Carita). See also: *Quarterly Bulletin, N.G. Victoria,* 1954, VIII, (4) 5.

Joseph Mallord William Turner   1775-1851

British School. Born London. Worked with Thomas Girtin at Dr. Monro's house, mainly in watercolours. Exhibited his first oil paintings at the R.A. in 1796-7 which showed study of the Dutch landscape painters. Richard Wilson *(q.v.)* and after 1800, Claude *(q.v.)* were emulated by him. Between 1807 and 1819 he published a series of mezzotints called the *Liber Studiorum* which is a visual demonstration of his theory of landscape art (a set is in the Print Room Collection). He went on many painting tours in England and on the Continent during which he collected subjects for his paintings and for series of views, compiled for engraving. Southern sunlight and colour in Italy in 1819 left a deep impression. His later pictures became increasingly concerned with the depiction of light. The N.G. Victoria owns the watercolours *Linlithgow Castle* (1801); *Okehampton Castle* (1826); *Red Rigi (*1842) as well as the oils listed below.

Reference: A. J. Finberg, *The Life of Turner,* 1939, revised 1961.

Illust. 197   313/1 **Dunstanborough Castle, Sunrise after a Squally Night**

canvas, 92.2 x 123.2 cm. Unsigned, undated, painted 1798.

Condition: old varnish removed by Harley Griffiths in 1953. Excellent

Comment: Dunstanborough Castle in Northumberland, was built about 1315 and was owned originally by Prince Edward, Duke of Lancaster. It became a ruin in the wars of York and Lancaster in 1463. Turner made a tour in 1797 to record ruined abbeys and castles in the north of England. Two drawings in the *North of England Subjects* (1796-7) are preparatory to No. 313/1: (i) drawing in pencil, white chalk and wash, about 10⅜ in. x 13 in., probably done from nature;[1] (ii) a watercolour elaboration of (i), 7 10/16 in. x 17⅞ in. Both drawings and the painting show the advances made by Turner in those years under the stimulus of the work of Richard Wilson;[3] his handling of wash and watercolour becomes freer and richer, and he conceives his subject in an expressive and romantic rather than in a purely topographical vein. The foreground rocks which contrast so vividly with the castle do not belong to the site (photograph of Dunstanborough Castle from the south on N.G. Victoria Condition: old varnish removed by Harley Griffiths in 1953. In excellent of 1798 Turner printed a stanza from James Thomson's *The Seasons* (1744) which dwells on the horror of storm-swept sea breaking on rocks at night and the relief felt at the first feeble gleam of a new day.

The drawing in the *North of England Sketchbook* of 1797, usually described as the nature study for No. 313/1, is taken from a point further to the left.[4] It was used by Turner in 1808 for an elaborate wash drawing[5] preceding the etching *Liber Studiorum* No. 14.[6] Though the inscription on this print ("the picture in the possession of W. Penn Esq.") suggests that it reproduces No. 313/1, it is in fact an independent creation.[7]

Another version of Dunstanborough Castle, known as the Milliken picture now at Dunedin, New Zealand, made about 1798-9 is based on a very broad, faint wash study in the *North of England Subjects;*[8] in both the tendency seen in the earlier versions to enlarge the foreground rocks and reduce the size of the castle has been carried to greater lengths.

Provenance: Exhibited by Turner at the R.A. 1798, No. 322; the *Liber Studiorum* mezzotint, No. 14, 1808, refers to the owner of the picture: W. Penn (of Stokes Poges); M. T. Birchall, who exhibited the picture at the Manchester Art Treasures Exhibition in 1857, No. 198, and London International Exhibition 1862, No. 350; John Heugh Esq., exh. R.A. 1873, No. 16, and sold the picture at Christie's, Holmwood collection, John Heugh, 24 April, 1874, lot 184, bought Mayne; Winter Exhibition, *A Century of British Art, 1737-1837,* Grosvenor Gallery 1888, No. 69, lent by the Duke of Westminster; the Centennial International Exhibition, Melbourne, 1888, owner the Duke of Westminster, and acquired by the Gallery through presentation.[9]

References: (1) A. J. Finberg, *A Complete Inventory of the Drawings of the Turner Bequest,* Vol. I, 1909, p. 79, XXXVI, S. (2) Finberg, *Inventory,* Vol. I, p. 67, XXXIII. (3) W. Armstrong, *Turner,* 1902, p. 47. (4) Finberg, *Inventory,* p. 71, XXXIV, No. 45. (5) Finberg, *Inventory,* p. 317, Q; the same, *The History of Turner's Liber Studiorum,* 1924, pp. 53-5. (6) Finberg, *Liber,* No. 14. (7) Finberg, *The Life of J. M. W. Turner,* 1939, p. 48. (8) Finberg, *Inventory,* Vol. I, XXXVI, T. and W. Armstrong, *op. cit.,* p. 215 repr.; Finberg, *Life, loc. cit.* (P. A. Tomory, *Old Master Paintings, New Zealand,* Exh. Auckland City Art Gallery, 1959, No. 14). (9) C. F. Bell, *A List of Works Contributed to Public Exhibitions by J. M. W. Turner,* 1901, p. 72, No. 86. See also J. Rothenstein, M. Butlin, *Turner,* London, 1964, pp. 9 f, pl. 9.

Illust. 198   981/3 **Walton Bridges**

canvas, 91.2 x 122.2 cm. Unsigned, undated, painted in 1806.

Condition: cleaned by Harley Griffiths in 1952; old varnish removed. In excellent condition.

Comment: Turner made two paintings of Walton Bridges, both of which may have been exhibited at Turner's own Gallery in 1806.[1] One was bought by John Leicester and was later owned by Lady Wantage.[2] It shows the bridges with the low arches on the right hand side and cattle in the left foreground; the other was bought by the Earl of Essex and is now our No. 981/3.[3] Among the preparatory drawings in the British Museum only one is related to our No. 981/3, in the *Hesperides (2) Sketchbook,* 1805-7,[4] a pencil line study of the composition, showing slight differences in the figure group but already diagonal rays in the sky.

Provenance: Finberg[1] assumes that the picture was exhibited in 1806 in Turner's own gallery in Harley Street; it was bought by the Earl of Essex,[5] who exhibited it at the Royal Academy in 1878, No. 131, and sold it in 1893 to Th. Agnew and Sons;[6] bought by James Orrock who showed it at the Winter exhibition, New Gallery, 1899-1900, No. 189, and sold it in 1904; it was bought by Sir Joseph Beecham who exhibited it at the International Fine Arts Exh., British Section, Rome, 1911, No. 98; sold in 1917;[7] acquired for the Felton Bequest by Frank Rinder in 1919-20.

References: (1) A. J. Finberg, *The Life of J. M. W. Turner,* 1939, p. 125. (2) W. Armstrong, *Turner,* Vol. II, 1902, p. 236. (3) Finberg, *Life, op. cit.,* p. 125, 467, No. 101. (4) A. J. Finberg, *Inventory,* 1909, XCIV, 5a. (5) Finberg, *Life, op. cit.,* p. 125. (6) Armstrong, *loc. cit.* (7) Rinder Corr. 19.11.1919, 20.1.1920.

Perino del Vaga (Pietro Buonaccorsi)   1501-1547

Italian. Born Florence. Pupil of Andrea de' Ceri, and Ridolfo Ghirlandaio. Assistant of il Vaga whose name he adopted. According to Vasari studied Michelangelo's and Raphael's works and the "grottesque" of antiquity in Rome. Worked in the Vatican with Giulio Romano and Francesco Penni probably 1517-18, and participated in the decorations of the Loggie under Raphael. 1523 returned to Florence to escape the pest in Rome; returned there in 1525. 1528 in Genoa where he painted extensive decorations in the Palazzo d'Oria; 1539 again in Rome; the decorations of the Castle S. Angelo date from this period. Died 1547 in Rome.

Reference: *Th.B.*

Illust. 199   1666/5 **The Holy Family**

panel, 100.8 x 47.2 cm. Painted c. 1539; unsigned, undated.

Condition: cleaned and restored prior to purchase by Mr. Deliss, London; cradled in England some eighty years ago. In excellent condition, except for some damage to the Virgin's hand and knee, well restored. The design has been pricked through a cartoon to the ground. Pricking marks and some of the underlying drawing can be seen.[1] Frame near contemporary.

Comment: The identification is supported by Mr. Philip Pouncey who dates the picture to about 1539 on stylistic grounds to the period after the artist returned from Genoa to Rome. The changing pinks and greens, reds, yellows and pale blues are typical of the middle years of the Cinquecento.[2]

A version of this Holy Family is in the Spada Gallery in Rome; in this S. Anne is also introduced; Philip Pouncey attributes this version to Niccolo Cercignani; the Spada picture has long been thought to be a copy of a Perino del Vaga, which was lost.[3]

Provenance: Nothing is known of the origins and history of this painting. Acquired by the Felton Bequest in 1966 on the advice of M. Woodall from the Hazlitt Gallery, London.

References: (1) M. Woodall, Felton letter No. 15, 2.4.66, archives N.G. Victoria. (2) *Burl. Mag.,* Vol. CVII, 1965, following p. 654, appendix, pl. XV. (3) F. Zeri, *Catalogue Spada Gallery,* Rome, No. 172, panel, 40⅛ in. x 28⅜ in.

Paolo Caliari, called Veronese   ca. 1528-1588

Italian School. Born Verona; pupil of Antonio Badile; in Venice probably in 1553, where he painted altarpieces, ceilings and wall decorations, chiefly influenced by Titian, but using the complicated poses and daring perspective effects of the mannerist style. He specialised in decorative pageantry; the profane details, dogs, German soldiers, buffoons and dwarfs which he introduced into his religious pictures caused his appearance before a tribunal of the Inquisition in 1573. His brother. Benedetto, and his sons, Carlo and Gabriel, collaborated with him and carried on in his studio under Giacomo Contarini after his death.

References: *Th.B.;* E. Holt, *Literary Sources of Art History,* 1947, pp. 247-8.

Illust. 200 1707/4   **Nobleman between Active and Contemplative Life**

canvas, 134 x 204.5 cm. Unsigned, undated.

Condition: unfinished; there is evidence of some alterations in the figure of Venus, whose right leg should take her weight rather than the left as it does at present. The unfinished sky shows underpainting in a strong blue-green, which also underlies the platform on the right, the balustrade and the figure of the nobleman. The group of falconers, the dogs, horse and architecture on the right are all unfinished.

Comment: Berenson did not list the picture in 1894[1] or in 1897;[2] in 1936 he listed it under Veronese, Paolo, later work;[3] Borenius called it School of Veronese and compared it to late workshop paintings;[4] the abridged catalogue of the Cook collection said "no longer regarded as a mere School picture";[5] the N.G. Victoria Catalogue of 1948 carried it as Veronese; Berenson in 1957 listed it as an early work by Veronese;[6] this was attacked by E. Tietze Conrat who rejected the attribution to Veronese himself and called it "later than Paolo".[7]

Berenson in 1936 called the picture *Tentazione del filosofo.* The *Masterpieces* stated that the female figures are allegories of active and contemplative life;[8] Erika Tietze Conrat, comparing the picture with representations of the Choice of Hercules and the Judgment of Paris, stressed the fact that the nobleman is making a choice;[9] according to her, the female figures in the picture are, from left to right; Minerva, Juno, Venus; these goddesses who appear in the Judgment of Paris, had been allegorically interpreted by Fulgentius in the 5th century A.D. as Vita Contemplativa, Vita Activa, and Luxuria.[10] The solid square block on which rests the foot of Minerva, and against which the sleeping cupid who covers his "shame" presses his feet, is the emblem of stability ("squareness").[10a]

No. 1707/4 is close in type or representation to a Choice of Hercules, who is traditionally shown flanked by vice and virtue; it is close in meaning to an allegorized Judgment of Paris, because there are three allegorical figures, not only two.[11] Fulgentius' allegorical interpretations of the Greek gods were best known in the Renaissance through Boccaccio's *Genealogia Deorum.*[12]

Provenance: From the collection of Sir Herbert Cook, Doughty House, Richmond, Surrey, England. The earliest reference to it occurs in the Doughty House catalogue of 1913.[13] Acquired for the Felton Bequest by Sir Kenneth Clark in 1947.

References: (1) B. Berenson, *Venetian Painters,* 1894 (1st edition). (2) The same, 1897 (3rd edition). (3) The same, *Pitture Italiane del Rinascimento,* Milan, 1936, p. 365. (4) T. Borenius, *A Catalogue of the Pictures at Doughty House,* 1913, Vol. I, p. 197, No. 174 repr. (5) M. W. Brockwell, *Abridged Catalogue of the Pictures at Doughty House,* 1932, p. 69, No. 174 (as "an allegory"). (6) B. Berenson, *Italian Pictures of the Renaissance, Venetian School,* 1957, Vol. I, p. 133, Vol. II, pl. 1043. (7) E. Tietze Conrat, *Art Bulletin,* Vol. XL, 1958, p. 347; book review. (8) *Masterpieces,* pp. 24, 25 repr. (9) E. Tietze Conrat, *Arte Veneta,* 1953, p. 98, fig. 87, and note 2. (10) F. P. Fulgentius, *Mythographorum Latinorum,* liber II, pp. 65-72, in T. Munckerus, *Mythographi Latini.* (10a) Valeriano, *Hieroglyphica,* fol. 290, r, quoted by Edgar Wind, *Pagan Mysteries in the Renaissance,* London, 1967, p. 102 and note 16. (11) E. Panofsky, *Hercules am Scheidewege,* 1930, p. 59 *seq.* (12) Boccaccio, *Genealogia Deorum,* 1472. See also: *Quarterly Bulletin, N.G. Victoria* 1947, II (4), 2. (13) See note (4). For further variations on this theme see Arthur Henkel and Albrecht Schöne, *Emblemata, Handbuch zur Sinnbild Kunst des XVI-XVIII Jahrhunderts,* Stuttgart, 1967, p. 1054.

Antonio Vivarini   Active 1440(?)—1476-80

Italian School. Signed Antonio da Murano. Worked in Venice and Padua. Collaborated with his brother-in-law, Giovanni d'Alemagna. Influenced by Gentile da Fabriano, Pisanello and later by Mantegna and Giovanni Bellini.

Reference: *Th.B.*

School of Antonio Vivarini

Illust. 200   1827/4 **The Garden of Love**

panel, 153 x 241.3 cm. Unsigned, undated; painted about 1465-70.

Condition: apart from several small re-paints in good condition.

Comment: One of a series of four panels: (i) 1827/4. (ii) a corresponding panel with a similar enclosure, a young man holding a dish with plants, a lady gazing at an object held in both hands (photograph Cooper 117792). (iii) a similar enclosure, no figures. (iv) a lady and a unicorn (not related in format).[1] This series was discovered in 1939; no. (iv) only had been published previously.[2]

The content of 1827/4 is related to the Garden of Love representations such as those on maternity plaques in the Figdor and Liechtenstein collections but more charged with symbolism. We see an enclosed garden, to the left a lady carrying an ermine. The youth next to her points to the figure on the fountain, while looking at the spectator; the lady to the right of him appears to be drawing water from the fountain with a syringe; on the right side a youth holding his hat before his face; the lady behind him seems to be about to blindfold him. On top of the fountain a classically dressed female figure, lifting one hand to heaven and carrying a dish of plants in the other; she is standing on a ball flanked by two eagles.

Several features of the painting point to the symbolism of Chastity. The ermine,[4] the enclosed garden;[5] the figure on the fountain is dressed like Chastity in a Florentine engraving (c. 1470-90);[6] she holds a dish with plants like the figure of Chastity in the Venetian woodcut of 1488;[7] Chastity has the emblem of a ball in the cassone panel attributed to Matteo di Giovanni;[8] the same figure, on a ball with eagles, appears again in Antonio Vivarini's *Martyrdom of S. Lucy* in Bergamo.[9] S. Lucy was martyred for her vow of Chastity. The unicorn which formed part of the series, is, like the ermine, a symbol of Chastity. Yet such explanation of the figure on the fountain is problematical and the figures to the right of the fountain remain unexplained.

The picture was listed in the 1948 catalogue as "School of Pisanello". As King pointed out,[10] the panels resemble stylistically those in the Walters Art Gallery in Baltimore, depicting the Legend of Paris and Helen. Ragghianti,[11] apparently not familiar with King's article, published 1827/K4 as "of the same series and by the same hand" as the Baltimore panels; these panels however contain full figures with ground before them; 1827/4 and one related panel (iii) have half figures; Ragghianti called 1827/4 "fragmentary", yet it is of almost identical size with the Baltimore panels and it seems reasonable to assume with King that the half figures of 1827/4 and the other panel were meant to be cut across by the cornice of the wainscoting covering the lower half of the wall which they decorated.[12]

Berenson[13] and King attribute both the Baltimore series and the series belonging to 1827/4 to the studio of Antonio Vivarini, dating them about 1465-70. Van Marle did not feel sure that the Baltimore panels were executed in Venice.[14] Ragghianti suggests the attribution of all the panels in question to Benedetto Bembo, who worked in Bergamo.

E. Berti-Toesca had attributed the *Lady with the Unicorn* to the Lombard School.[15] While the presence of certain Paduan characteristics in the style of the panels must be admitted,[16] the recent tendency has been to assemble most of the comparable panels under the School of Antonio Vivarini. In addition to the similarity between the figure at the fountain in 1827/4 and the *Martyrdom of S. Lucy* in Bergamo noted above we may refer to the presence of a comparable fountain in a panel in Stuttgart described in a recent catalogue as the *Victory of Christianity over Paganism,* called Venetian and dated about 1400 (surely too early!).[17] Michael Levey describes 1827/4 as more probably North Italian.[18] Laura Marussigh proposes to attribute this and the Walters Art Gallery series to Dario da Treviso, called Dario da Pordenone.[19]

Provenance: From the collection of Mrs. S. M. Crossley, Burton Pynsent, Curry Rivel, Somerset, auctioned by Wooley and Wallis, 22-24 March, 1939, lot 475, illust. (cat. not seen). Purchased by the Felton Bequest from Tomas Harris, Spanish Art Gallery, in 1947/8, on the advice of Sir Kenneth Clark.

References: (1) E. S. King, *The Journal of the Walters Art Gallery,* 1939, p. 67, note 15; No. (iii), then in the possession of Tomas Harris, has been described as badly damaged. The whereabouts of No. (ii) could not be elicited, photographs of No. (ii) and (iv) are in the Gallery Archives. (2) By E. Berti-Toesca, *Dedalo,* Vol. XII, 1932, p. 958, repr. (3) R. van Marle, *Iconographie de l'art profane, Allegories et Symboles,* 1932, pp. 428, 429, figs. 456, 457. (4) L. Réau, *Iconographie de l'Art Chrétien,* 1955, Vol. I, p. 104/5: "symbole de la pureté". (5) *ibid.,* Vol. II, p. 80, refers to the Immaculate Virgin: "l'Immaculée est un Jardin clos (Hortus conclusus)". (6) A. M. Hind, *Early Italian Engraving,* Vol. II, 1938, B.II, 2, 1. (7) van Marle, *Iconographie, op. cit.,* p. 133, fig. 130. (8) van Marle, *Iconographie, op. cit.,* p. 132, fig. 152. (9) A. Morassi, *La Galleria dell Accademia Carrara di Bergamo,* Rome, 1934, p. 78, repr. B. Berenson, *Italian Pictures of the Renaissance,* Venetian School, 1957, Vol. I, p. 197 (no. 179). (10) See note 1. (11) C. L. Ragghianti, *La Critica d'Arte,* Vol. VIII, p. 298, note 29. (12) On the location of the picture, King, *op. cit.,* pp. 67/68, note 15 (3), quotes an earlier cycle of frescoes, in the Palazzo Davanzati, Florence, in which the figures are half covered by the wainscoting. (13) B. Berenson, *op. cit.,* p. 198, pl. 90, and King, *op. cit.,* p. 67, note 5. (14) R. van Marle, *Italian Schools of Painting,* Vol. XVIII, 1935, p. 43. (15) See note 2. (16) Ragghianti, *loc. cit.,* and King, *loc. cit.,* compare certain figures to the cavalier on the Tarocchi cards dated before 1468. (Hind, *loc. cit.,* and allied engravings). (17) Catalogue Stuttgart Gallery, 1957, p. 309, *loc. cit.* See also *Quarterly Bulletin, N.G. Victoria,* 1948, III (2), 3. (18) Michael Levey, review of the 1961 edition of this catalogue, in *Museums Journal,* Vol. 62, No. 2, pp. 124-6. (19) Corr. Marussigh, Hoff, 27.12.68, see also Luigi Coletti, in *Pittura veneto dell Quattrocento,* Novara, 1953, pl. 84 and list of plates p. XC, p. XLIV.

Hendrick Cornelisz van der Vliet   1611-12—1675

Dutch School. Born Delft. Pupil of his uncle, Willem Van Der Vliet, and of M. J. Miereveld. Specialised in church interiors.

Reference: *Th.B.*

Illust. 201   4716/3 **Interior of a Church**

canvas, 110.8 x 128.7 cm. Signed and dated *1662.*

Condition: satisfactory.

Comment: Vliet's architectural interiors usually represent one of the two main churches in Delft.

Provenance: Exhibited Royal Academy, 1907, No. 72 (owner Lord Huntingfield). The picture was in the sale of the Huntingfield Estate, Christie's, 25 June, 1915, lot 129, bt. Grimm; for the Dutch ancestors of Lord Huntingfield see Cuyp, No. 4664/3, provenance. The picture was offered to Randall Davies by Mrs. Dudley Blois (a cousin of Lord Huntingfield); it was acquired for the Felton Bequest in 1932/3.

Abraham de Vries   ca. 1590—ca. 1650

Dutch School. Born Rotterdam. Active in Amsterdam from 1628-1640. 1644 member of the Guild at The Hague; Vries was a capable portraitist who was celebrated in two poems by the poet Jan de Vos, and referred to in letters by Peiresc and Puteanus.

Reference: A. von Wurzbach, *Niederländisches Künstlerlexikon,* 1910.

Illust. 202   1218/3 **Portrait of a Dutch Gentleman**

panel, cradled, 74.3 x 59.7 cm (in painted oval). Signed and dated *fecit Hage A. de Vries, anno 1647.*

Condition: good.

Provenance: Presented in memory of the Hon. William Cain, by his family, under the terms of the will, in 1921.

References: Felton Correspondence, 24.2.1921.

James Ward   1769-1859

British School. Born London. Trained as an engraver under J. R. Smith. Later specialized in animal painting in which he showed the successive influence of Sawrey Gilpin, Morland *(q.v.)* and Rubens *(q.v.).*

Reference: *Th.B.*

Illust. 203   133/2 **Sheep**

panel, 21.5 x 30.2 cm. Signed *Ward* l.l.; undated.

Condition: excellent.

Provenance: Acquired in 1903 from N. Lynch sale, Melbourne, on the advice of Bernard Hall.[1]

Reference: (1) State Library of Victoria Archives, 03/1430.

Jean Antoine Watteau   1685-1721

French School. Born Valenciennes. Pupil of Gillot, theatrical scene painter in Paris, in 1704-5 and of Claude-Audran in 1707-8. His style grew out of his acquaintance with the work of Rubens, Teniers, Veronese, and he became the creator of the "fêtes galantes", which remained unequalled in their wistful poetry.

After Watteau

Illust. 204   496/2 **Jealousy (Les Jaloux)**

panel, 34.1 x 44.8 cm. Unsigned, undated; original painted in 1712.

Condition: old varnish.

Comment: The original (now lost) was painted about 1712; it was one of the pictures with which the artist successfully passed the first stage of admission to the Academy, on July 30, 1712. According to M. Edmond de Goncourt, the original was last heard of in 1786. Several replicas or copies are known.[1] An engraving by Scotin, after the original, is in the Print Room.

Reference: *Th.B.*

Provenance: From the collection of the Prince de Waagram. Acquired on the advice of Frank Gibson for the Felton Bequest in 1910.

References: (1) H. Adhémar and R. Huyghe, *Watteau,* 1950, p. 208, Cat. No. 64, pl. 31.

Richard Wilson   1713-1782

British School. Born Penegos, Montgomeryshire. In 1729 became a pupil of the portrait painter Thomas Wright in London. From 1747-1750 practised as a portrait painter, but also painted landscapes as early as 1746. In 1750 he went to Venice and arrived in Rome in 1752. Encouraged by the advice, perhaps, of Zuccarelli and C. J. Vernet, he devoted himself entirely to landscape painting. He worked in the Campagna and here developed his classical style based on Claude *(q.v.),* Gaspar Poussin *(q.v.)* and Cuyp *(q.v.).* He continued to paint Italian motifs after his return to England about 1756; from the English and Welsh scene he chose motifs which "fell into the classical mould" yet his tones are true to the native scene. Was a foundation member of the Royal Academy which later, when his work had fallen into public disfavour, appointed him librarian (1776). In 1781 he retired to Colomendy where he died.

References: W. G. Constable, *Richard Wilson,* 1953; Ellis Waterhouse, *Painting in Britain, 1530-1790,* London 1953.

Illust. 205   623/5 **Captain Michael Everitt, R.N.**

canvas, 127.5 x 101.8 cm. Signed *R. Wilson f.* on the anchor; undated; painted probably 1747-8.

Condition: cleaned prior to purchase; in excellent condition.

Comment: Michael Everitt was born in 1717 and died 13 Sept., 1776 at Fareham, County of Southampton. [1] He became Lieutenant in the Royal Navy on 15 June, 1744, and Captain 23 Dec., 1747. In 1756 Everitt was appointed Captain to Rear Admiral West, second in command under Admiral John Byng and thus took part in the engagement between the English and the French Fleets at Port Mahon, Majorca; [2] in his despatch of 25 May, 1756, Byng commented on West's and Everitt's gallantry in the engagement. [3] Everitt was recalled at the end of the year to give evidence at Byng's trial and was soon afterwards appointed to another ship.
The portrait which closely resembles that of Admiral Thomas Smith of 1746 [4] may have been painted on the occasion of Everitt's appointment as Captain in 1747. Though an old label written in 1844 describes the sitter as "Charles Everitt father of Admiral Calmady", it appears from documents that Admiral Calmady's name was "Charles" and that his father was called "Michael". [5] (Charles, son of Captain Michael Everitt, adopted the name of Calmady upon marriage.)

Provenance: The label on the back, signed Emily Calmady 1844, shows that the portrait was still in the possession of descendants of Michael Everitt in that year. Admiral Calmady died in 1807; in 1836 his son, Charles Briggs Calmady, of Langden Hall, Devonshire, was described as his heir. [6] Nothing is known about the further history of the painting which was acquired in 1959-60 under the terms of the Everard Studley Miller Bequest on the advice of A. J. L. McDonnell and U. Hoff, from Montagu Bernard, London.

References: (1) Will of Captain Michael Everitt, PCC 420 "Bellas", dated 12 March, 1776. Proved 16 Oct. 1776. (2) John Charnock, *Biographia Navalia,* 1794-8, Vol. VI, pp. 41, 42, and verbal information received from M. S. Robinson, National Maritime Museum, Greenwich. (3) Charnock, *op. cit.,* Vol. IV, p. 150. (4) W. G. Constable, *Richard Wilson,* 1953, pl. 2a, Cat. p. 151. (5) Burke's *Landed Gentry* 1837 (Calmady), and Will of Captain Michael Everitt (see note 1). See also: W. G. Constable, *Burl. Mag.,* Vol. CIV, 1962, pp. 142-5, fig. 15. (6) Burke's *Landed Gentry* 1837. Repr. *Annual Bulletin, N.G. Victoria,* 1960, Vol. II, 18.

Illust. 206   2055/4 Llyn Peris and Dolbadarn Castle

canvas. 85.5 x 131.4 cm. Unsigned, undated; painted 1760-63.

Condition: excellent; cleaned prior to purchase.

Comment: Painted at the time of Holt Bridge of 1762 in which the influence of Claude's style on Wilson's work is joined by that of Zuccarelli who was in London when Wilson returned from Italy in 1757-8. [1]
Pennant says that Dolbadarn Castle seems to have been built to defend the pass into the interior of Snowdonia and that it was used as a state prison. [2] Wilson took certain liberties with the topography of the place. [3]
This and other versions are listed by W. G. Constable. [4] The composition was used again by Wilson in 1763-7 for the background of his *Diana and Callisto,* originally made for Ince Hall. [5]

Provenance: From a pencilled note on the back, Anon. Sale Christie, 15 July, 1899, lot 67, as *Italian Riverscene, and Castle;* bt. Tooth; Pierpont Morgan, New York; Mrs. Herbert Satterlee, New York (the former owner's daughter); Herbert L. Satterlee, New York, sold Park Bernet, 22 April, 1948, lot 21, as *Pozzuoli from across the Bay of Baiae;* bt. Weitzner, New York, 1948; with Tooths, London; acquired by the Felton Bequest on the advice of A. J. L. McDonnell and Sir Kenneth Clark, 1948-9, from Tooths.

References: (1) W. G. Constable, *Richard Wilson,* 1953, p. 88-9. (2) Quoted from Constable, *op. cit.,* p. 176. (3) P. J. Barlow, *The Connoisseur,* Vol. CXXXIX, 1957, p. 85, No. 11. (4) *op. cit.,* 176-7. (5) *ibid.,* p. 89/90.

School of Wilson

Illust. 207   750/2 **Lake Avernus I**

canvas, 40 x 50.8 cm. Unsigned, undated; original painted 1764.

Condition: good.

Comment: Listed in 1948 catalogue as *Ancient Ruins and Men.* Copy of the picture in the F. S. Clarke Collection,[1] 16½ in. x 20½ in. *Lake Avernus,* 1764. Our picture slightly cut.

Provenance: Presented by John Connell, 1914.

Reference: (1) W. G. Constable, *Richard Wilson,* 1953, pl. 69a.

After Wilson

Illust. 208   480/2 **River View (On The Arno) I**

canvas, 47.5 x 62.6 cm. Unsigned, undated; original dated 1764.

Condition: some old retouches in hillside.

Comment: The picture is close in detail to the one in the possession of John Wyndham, Petworth,[1] which carries the above title on the authority of Th. Hastings;[2] 480/2 was previously known as *Lake Nemi.* Constable describes 480/2, only known to him from a photograph, as "doubtfully by Wilson".

Provenance: An old, partly torn label on the back reads: "Lent by . . . ither, Esq., Perdiswell Park, Worcestershire." Acquired for the Felton Bequest in 1909 by Frank Gibson from Shepherd Bros., London.

References: (1) W. G. Constable, *Richard Wilson,* 1953, p. 213, pl. 100a repr. (2) Constable, *ibid.;* and p. 3. Th. Hastings, *Etchings from the Work of Richard Wilson, with some Memoirs of his Life,* 1825, Introductory Remarks, 11, repr. opp.

Attributed to Wilson

Illust. 209   1939/4 **St. David's, Pembrokeshire**

canvas, 112 x 142 cm. A signature, *R.G.* appears on lower left under the varnish.

Condition: old, yellow varnish.

Comment: According to Constable the identification of the place is unsatisfactory, the picture "very doubtfully by Wilson."[1]

Provenance: Purchased by F. J. Nettlefold from Messrs. Spink, London, after 1927.[2] Presented by F. J. Nettlefold in 1948.

References: (1) W. G. Constable, *Richard Wilson,* 1953, p. 236, pl. 140b. (2) Grundy and Roe, *Catalogue of the Collection of F. J. Nettlefold,* 1938, Vol. IV, p. 166, repr. in colour.

Follower of Wilson

Illust. 210   144/2 **Landscape With Italian Buildings And A Shepherd**
panel, 39 x 29.7 cm. Unsigned, undated.

Condition: good.

Comment: Not related to any known composition by Wilson.

Provenance: Bequeathed by Alfred Felton 1904.

Philips Wouwerman(s)   1019-1668

Dutch School. Born Haarlem. May have been a pupil of his father, Paulus
Joosten Wouwerman(s) (d. 1642). According to Cornelis de Bie, *Het Gulden
Cabinet, 1661,* studied under Franz Hals. Became a member of the Guild in
Haarlem in 1640 and was one of the officers of this Guild in 1645.
Specialised in landscapes with horses, battles, camps and hunts, and often
used a white horse as the focal point of his compositions.

Reference: *C.N.G.*

Illust. 211   4730/3 **Landscape With Dogs And Horse**

panel, 50.5 x 44.2 cm. Signed with initials *Ph.* (monog.) *W.,* lower right
painted probably in the 1640s.

Condition: satisfactory.

Comment: Dr. Gerson writes "An early picture in the tradition of Isaac van
Ostade and Paulus Potter, also with the early monogram". [1]

Provenance: Exhibited by Roger William Wilbraham, Delamere House, Cheshire,
R.A. 1892, No. 96; acquired from Colnaghi's on the advice of Randall Davies for the Felton
Bequest in 1933.

References: (1) Correspondence Hoff-Gerson 1958, N.G. Victoria files; Hofstede de
Groot, Catalogue, *Dutch Painters,* Vol. II, 1909, No. 428, p. 378.

Johann Zoffany (or Zauffelij)   1734-5—1810

German-British School. Born Frankfurt on Main. His father came from
Bohemia; since 1748 resident in Regensburg. Pupil of Martin Speer in
Regensburg; went twice to Rome. After some work in Germany went to
London about 1761, where he worked as drapery painter to the portraitist
Benjamin Wilson. Through Wilson he met Garrick in whose house he lived
in 1762. Zoffany's painting of Garrick in *The Farmer's Return* established his
fame as a painter of theatrical conversation pieces. Made several journeys
on the continent. From 1783-9 went to India where he painted portraits.

References: *Th.B.; C.N.G.*

Illust. 212   4614/3 **Caritas Romana (Roman Charity)**

canvas, 76.3 x 63.5 cm. Signed *J. Zoffany inv.* centre, under male figure.

Condition: Randall Davies reported in 1931 that the picture had been relined, probably on account of an injury to the canvas which is just discernible on close scrutiny; he reported that "about a square inch on the left hand side had apparently been re-painted."

Comment: The subject is based on the story of Cimon and Pero told by Valerius Maximus as an example of filial piety. Cimon had been thrown into prison when already an old man. His daughter Pero nourished him "like an infant" and thus saved his life.[1] The title *Caritas Romana* probably stems from the time of the humanists.[2] The picture was seen in 1931 by Basil Long, Victoria and Albert Museum, and Herbert Hughes Stanton.

Provenance: According to Randall Davies presumably identical with the picture mentioned in the Sale Catalogue of Pictures belonging to Robert Hamilton Esq., of Bloomfield House, Norwood, Surrey, Sale Ed. Foster, 15 March, 1832, as follows: "Back Drawing Room 190, Zoffany, Roman Charity". Found by R. Davies in a small dealer's shop in Yarmouth, and acquired by him for the Felton Bequest in 1931-2.

References: (1) Valerius Maximus, *De Dictis Factisque Memorabilibus,* V, 4. (2) E. W. Braun, in Schmitt, *Real-Lexikon zur Deutschen Kungstgeschichte,* Vol. III, 1954, p. 355.

Illust. 213   1728/5 **Elizabeth Farren As 'Hermione' In 'A Winter's Tale'**

canvas, 245 x 167 cm. Unsigned, undated; painted c. 1780.

Condition: very good.

Comment: Elizabeth Farren (1759(?)-1829), actress, was the daughter of a surgeon from Cork. She played in juvenile parts at Bath at an early age and made a career on the stage in the provinces before appearing in London at the Haymarket in June 1777 as Miss Hardcastle. She later played at Drury Lane and occasionally at Convent Garden and was hailed by the critics as a worthy successor to Mrs. Abingdon who left Drury Lane in 1782. In 1797 she left the stage and married Edward, twelfth Earl of Derby.[1] Hazlitt speaks of 'Miss Farren, with her fine-lady airs and graces, with that elegant turn of her head and motion of her fan and tripping of her tongue.'[2] Walpole regarded her as the most perfect actress he had ever seen.[3] A portrait of her by Sir Thomas Lawrence, now in the Metropolitan Museum, New York, shows her as an elegant lady of leisure in a landscape.[4] Zoffany here portrayed her in one of her favourite roles as Hermione, wife of Leontes, King of Sicilia, in Shakespeare's *A Winter's Tale*. The painter has chosen the famous *dénouement* of the last act. Leontes believed her dead as a result of his jealous ill-treatment. After years of concealment she re-emerges, posing as a statue which dramatically 'comes to life'.[5] Chaloner Smith assumed that the artist had painted her from life, in the position she assumed on the stage;[6] her pose (in reverse) is however remarkably like that of *Mrs. Abingdon as Comic Muse* by Reynolds.[7] For the question whether such poses were invented by the artist or by the actress model, see Edgar Wind.[7a] Miss Farren stands against a sarcophagus on which there is a medallion with a male and female genius clasping hands; Professor Boase kindly pointed out that on Fisher's engraving of the portrait it is clearly seen that the cupids below are turning down their torches and he suspects that the whole sarcophagus motif is meant to be the tomb of Leontes' dead love. (Letter to Dr. M. Woodall 9.1.67.) Engraved in mezzotint by E. Fisher, publ. 1781.[8]

Provenance: Archibald Seton of Touch to whom 1728/5 is said to have been given by the sitter; remained at Touch.[9] Sir James Seton Stuart; the Rt. Hon. Viscount Kemsley, O.B.E., sale Sotheby's, 24th March, 1961, lot 41, illust. (bt. in); acquired from Agnews, London, on the advice of Dr. Mary Woodall under the terms of the Everard Studley Miller Bequest 1966/7.

References: (1) *D.N.B.* 1908. (2) W. Hazlitt, *Criticism and Dramatic Essays,* London, 1851, p. 49. (3) *D.N.B.* (4) K. Garlick, *Sir Thomas Lawrence,* London, 1954, pl. 3. (5) Shakespeare, *A Winter's Tale,* Act V, Sc. III, 98-103. (6) J. Chaloner Smith, *British Mezzotinto Portraits,* London, 1883, II, p. 492, No. 17. (7) Ellis K. Waterhouse, *Reynolds,* London, 1941, pl. 100. (7a) Edgar Wind, *Humanitatsidee und Heroisiertes Portrait in der Englischen Kultur des 18. Jahrhunderts* in *Vorträge der Bibliothek Warburg, England und die Antike,* 1930/31, Leipzig, Berlin 1932, p. 224. (8) J. Chaloner Smith, *op. cit.,* p. 492, No. 17. L. A. Hall, *Catalogue of Dramatic Portraits, in the Theatre Collection of Harvard College Library,* Cambridge, Mass., Vol. I, 1930, p. 359, No. 21. (9) Lady Victoria Manners, J. C. Williamson, *John Zoffany,* London, 1920, pp. 148 f, repr.

N

Antoine Louis Barye   1796-1875

French. Born Paris, the son of a goldsmith. Pupil of metal engraver Fourier; studied painting under Gros and sculpture under Bosios at the Ecole des Beaux Arts from 1818. Won the Rome prize in 1820. As a painter Barye drew inspiration from Gros, Géricault and Delacroix. He drew animals at the Jardin des Plantes and attended lectures in the anatomy theatre. His romantically conceived fighting animals and beasts of prey are carried out with exacting naturalism and fine craftsmanship.

References: F. Novotny, *Painting and Sculpture in Europe, 1780 to 1880,* Pelican *History of Art,* London 1960, p. 226; Lee Johnson, *Delacroix, Barye and the Tower Menagerie, an English Influence on French Romantic Animal Pictures,* in *The Burlington Magazine,* CVI, 1964, 416-419.

Illust. 1   236/2 (ptg.) **Panther and Gazelle**

bronze statuette, H. 33.6 cm. inscribed *BARYE* 1. at back.

Condition: excellent.

Exh.: bronze groups of the same title were exhibited at the Salon 1834 (no. 1973); exposition universelle (1855, no. 63).

Provenance: Acquired on the advice of Bernard Hall under the terms of the Felton Bequest in 1905.

References: Stanislas Lami, *Dictionnaire des Sculpteurs de l'Ecole Française au dix-neuvième siècle,* 1914, Vol. I, pp. 75, 80. *Catalogue, N.G. Victoria,* 1948, p. 250.

Illust. 2   237/2 (ptg.) **Lion and Boar**

bronze group

Comment: Listed in 1948 catalogue; cannot be located 1971.

Exh.: Exposition Universelles, 1855, unnumbered.

Reference: Lami *loc. cit.,* p. 84.

Provenance: Acquired on the advice of Bernard Hall from under the terms of the Felton Bequest in 1905.

Illust. 3   2845/3 (D.A.) **Walking Lion**

bronze statuette, H. 5.2 cm. signed *BARYE* from left; undated.

Comment: According to information received on acquisition from Frank Rinder, this work was personally worked on by Barye. According to Lami it was first cast in silver for a M. de Lagrange whose horse 'Daughter of the Air' had won the grand prix de Paris. Later cast in bronze for commerce. A silver model is in the Walters Art Gallery, Baltimore.

Exh.: Exposition Universelle, de 1855, no. 53.

Provenance: Duc de Nemours who had it direct from the arist. Rinder advised that the duc de Nemours was the brother of the duc d'Aumale, one of Barye's chief admirers. Acquired under the terms of the Felton Bequest on the advice of Frank Rinder from D. Croal Thomson in 1927. Letter June 2, 1927.

Reference: Lami, *loc. cit.* pp. 78, 80. *Catalogue, Nat. Gal. Victoria,* 1948, p. 249.

Illust. — 2846/3 (D.A.) **Walking Tiger**

bronze statuette, H. 5.2 cm. undated, exh. 1855

Condition: excellent.

Comment: This piece forms a pair with No. 2845/3, but exists in bronze only.

Exh.: Exposition Universelle de 1855, No. 54.

Provenance: Duc de Nemours who had it directly from the artist. (See under 2845/3.)
Acquired under the terms of the Felton Bequest on the advice of Frank Rinder from D. Croal Thomson in 1927.

Illust. 4 3556/3 (D.A.) **Lion Attacking a Horse**

bronze group, H. 6.8 cm. Signed *BARYE* on base, undated;
plastermodel exh. 1833.

Condition: perfect.

Comment: If this is the group a cast of which once belonged to the duc de Luynes the latter was exhibited at the Salon in 1834 (No. 1972) a sketch is in the museum of Montpellier, plastermodel was exhibited at the Salon of 1833 (No. 3295).¹ Barnard Hall advised that it was 'hand-finished' by Barye.

Provenance: Acquired under the terms of the Felton Bequest on the advice of Bernard Hall in 1934 from Barbizon House, London.

Reference: Lami, *loc. cit.,* p. 73. See also *Catalogue Nat. Gal. Victoria,* 1946, p. 249.

Antonio Begarelli late 15th century — 1565

Italian. Born Modena; nothing is known about his training. He is referred to in Lancellotti's *Cronaca Modenese* and in Vasari's *Lives.* He continued the tradition of large scale terracotta sculpture established in Modena by Guido Mazzoni (d. 1518 in Modena). Many of his works are in the churches in Modena. The group of the *Deposition,* the sketchmodel for which is listed here, was finished and in *situ* in 1521; this group has been described as Begarelli's most popular, his largest and boldest work, which must have occupied him over several years. The composition is related to engravings by Marc Antonio Raimondi, whose prints frequently inspired Begarelli.

Reference: *Th.B.*

Illust. 5 E.21. 1971 **The Virgin Attended by Three Holy Women**

terracotta on wooden base (18th century), H. 42.5 cm. incl. base
W. 71 cm. Unsigned, undated; modelled c. 1530.

Condition: good.

Comment: This is a sketch model for the central group in the altarpiece of the *Deposition of Christ* (now in the church of S. Francesco in Modena), which was completed in August 1531 for the Franciscan Church of Santa Cecilia in Modena. Another sketch model for this group, less evolved and presumably earlier, is in the Victoria and Albert Museum, London.[1]

Provenance: Ogetti Collection, Florence; private collection, London. Acquired under the terms of the Felton Bequest from Heim Gallery, London on the advice of Dr. M. Woodall and Mr. Terence Hodgkinson, Victoria and Albert Museum, in Nov. 1971; arrived Dec. 1971.

References: John Pope Hennessy, *Catalogue of Italian Sculpture in the Victoria and Albert Museum,* Vol. II, No. 529, p. 501-502.

Bartolommeo Bellano   c. 1434-c. 1496

Italian. Date and place of birth uncertain. Worked as sculptor and architect in Padua; was influenced by the work of Donatello, and is known to have spent a considerable period in Florence. From there he went in 1466 to Rome and Perugia. 1469 again in Padua; later also worked in Venice and Constantinople. Worked in bronze and marble the most prominent sculptor of the Paduan school in its early Renaissance phase.

attributed to Bellano

Illust. 6   1276/4 (D.A.) **Lamentation of Christ**
stone relief, H. 91.5 cm. Unsigned, undated.
Condition: fair.
Comment: A closely related composition occurs in a painting by Carlo Crivelli of 1476 which is in the Metropolitan Museum, New York.[1] Philipp compares 1276/4 with Bellano's *Entombment* in the Victoria and Albert Museum, London (Nr 314-1878), and with a bronze relief attributed to Donatello in the same collection (No. 8552-1863) but notes the lesser quality of the work here.[2] The very close similarity to the Crivelli painting is unusual for Bellano.

Provenance: Origin unknown; presented by Thomas Harris, London, 1952.
References: (1) Pietro Zampetti, *Carlo Crivelli,* Milan, 1961, fig. 75. Gordon Thomson first drew our attention to the relation between this picture and 1276/4. The *Lamentation* was part of the Demidoff polyptich. (2) *Catalogue, N.G. Victoria,* Appendix II, 1954, p. 52; F. Philipp, *Q. Bulletin, N.G. Victoria,* Vol. VIII, No. 2, 1954, repr.

Gian Lorenzo Bernini   1598-1680

Italian. Born at Naples, the son of a sculptor who removed to Rome in 1605, where Gian Lorenzo continued to live until his death. His early sculptures are indebted to Michelangelo and the Mannerists, but he soon developed a new concept of the animated figure seen from one view point and sharing the space of the spectator. Some of Bernini's most famous works are the *Barberini Fountain* (1642-43), the *Ecstasy of St. Teresa* (1645-52) in the commissioned in 1656 and the *Tomb of Pope Alexander VII,* in St. Peter's (1671-78), all in Rome.

Reference: R. Wittkower, *Gian Lorenzo Bernini,* London 1966.
Illust. 7   E.2 1970 **The Countess Matilda of Tuscany**
gilt bronze statuette on contemporary black marble base, H. 40.5 cm.
Inscribed on base: *MATHILDI GRATI ANIMI ERGO URBANUS VIII POSUIT.*

Condition: repairs on neck (fracture on neck in centre fold at back, under right arm) gilt tarnished; inside has modern gesso filling; various holes, under gold of garment, near key, near top of key; other holes have been filled.

Comment: Mathilda, Marchioness of Tuscany (1046-1115) is connected with the triumph of the Papacy over the German Emperor; her hereditary fief of Canossa was the scene of the celebrated penance in 1077 of Henry IV before Pope Gregory VII. Her ashes had been resting in the Benedictine monastery at Mantua. Pope Urban VIII (reigned 1623-44) had them secretly transported to Rome and commissioned Bernini in 1633 to erect a tomb for her in St. Peters (finished 1637). Bernini, probably following the Pope's wishes, interpreted Mathilda as a personification of the Papacy, holding the keys of St. Peter in her left hand, supporting the papal tiara with her left arm, while wielding the baton of temporal power in her extended right. Five casts from Bernini's terracotta model for the over-life size marble figure in St. Peters are known; they belong to 1. The Principe Giuliano Barberini 2. North Carolina Museum of Art, Raleigh 3. Max Falk, New York 4. Cyril Humphris, London 5. E 1. 1970.

Provenance: Prince Altieri, Rome; Prince Ruspoli, Rome; private collection, Paris. Acquired from Heim Galleries, London, on the advice of Dr. M. Woodall and Professor Rudolf Wittkower, under the terms of the Felton Bequest 1969. Arrived 1970.

References: Rudolf Wittkower, 'Two Bernini Bronzes in the National Gallery', *Art Bulletin of Victoria,* 1970-71, pp. 11-13, figs. 16-21.

Illust. 8   E. 1. 1970 **Cardinal Richelieu**

bronze bust, H. 71.4 cm. Unsigned, undated.

Condition: excellent.

Comment: Armand Jean du Plessis de Richelieu (1585-1642), French statesman became chief minister to Louis XIII and the chief consolidator of centralized power in France. He achieved internal power through crushing the protestants and weakening the nobility; externally he maintained the supremacy of France against the Habsburgs by supporting Gustav Adolph of Sweden. Richelieu lived in Imperial state; Jacques Lemericer built the Palais Royal for him; he extended patronage to Corneille, and created the French Academie in 1635, commissioned Lemercier to re-build the Sorbonne and commissioned the leading painters of his time, Simon Vouet, Philippe de Champaigne and Nicolas Poussin.

Cast from a preparatory terracotta model, made prior to the marble bust of the sitter, now in the Louvre. A terracotta model of the Cardinal is mentioned in the inventory of Bernini's house taken in 1706 (Franschetti, p. 432). A bronze of the Cardinal by Bernini's hand in Paris is mentioned by Baldinucci, in *Vita del Cav. Bernini,* Florence, 1682. Baldinucci states (p. 89 f) that Richelieu begged Cardinal Antonio Barberini to approach Bernini to make his portrait. Wittkower quotes the sources which confirm

173

that Bernini made a marble bust, now in the Louvre. Bernini must have made the model from the triple portrait of the Cardinal by Philippe de Champaigne which according to an old Italian inscription on the back was made for the sculptor Mochi to work from.

Provence: Humphris, London; acquired on the advice of Dr. M. Woodall and Professor Rudolph Wittkower under the terms of the Everard Studley Miller Bequest in 1969; arrived 1970.

References: (1) For this and the following information see R. Wittkower, *Gian Lorenzo Bernini, The Sculptor of the Roman Baroque,* London 1966, No. 42; the same 'Two Bronzes by Bernini in the National Gallery', in *Art Bulletin of Victoria,* 1970/71, pp. 13-18, figs. 26-28. See also *Burl. Mag.,* Vol. CXII, 1970, pl. XXX, reproducing a bronze variant, made posthumously from Bernini's marble bust of Cardinal Richelieu in the Louvre, by Antoine Coisevox.

British   15th Century

Illust. 9   1301/3 (D.A.) **St. John the Baptist**

alabaster relief, H. 75.1 mm.

Comment: The saint is wearing a robe and camelskin with hoofs and skull still attached. Faint traces of blue on the robe, of red on the lining and of gilding on the lamb's flag remain. White, red-centred flowers decorate the background. Probably part of a retable; panels like the one here often occurred on either side of a retable, flanking a series of narrative relief; but such panels often also stood by themselves.[1]

The art of alabaster carving developed in the 14th and 15th centuries notably in Nottingham, Lincoln and York. A considerable export trade in statues and reliefs for church use developed.[2]

Exh.: *British Primitives,* Royal Academy, London 1923, No. 131[3] Victoria and Albert Museum, London, 12 July 1923, top of staircase leading to Room 62.

Provenance: Said to have come from a collection in France; acquired under the terms of the Felton Bequest by Frank Rinder in 1923 from the widow of Grosvenor Thomas (art dealer).[4]

References: (1) Cl. F. Pitmann, 'Reflections on Nottingham Alabaster Carvings', *The Connoisseur,* May 1954, p. 217 seq. (2) E. S. Prior and A. Gardner, *An Account of Medieval Figure Sculpture in England, Cambridge,* 1922. (3) *British Primitives,* Exhibition Catalogue, Royal Academy, London, 1923, No. 131, pl. LX. (4) Rinder corr. 31.5.23, 7.6.23, 14.6.23.

British   16th Century

Illust. 10   569A/4 (D.A.) **Young Man in Armour**

marble bust, H. 21½ in.   26¾ in. w. Pedestal.

Condition: satisfactory, minor chips around back of shoulders.

Comment: The decoration of the armour consists of plant motifs; the head is turned slightly towards the left shoulder.

Provenance: Purchased 1947.[1]

Reference: (1) *Catalogue Nat. Gal. Victoria,* 1948, p. 253.

Illust. 11   569B/4 (D.A.) **Bearded Man in Armour**

marble bust, 58.4 cm.

Condition: satisfactory, minor chips around back of shoulders.

Comment: The head is turned slightly towards the left shoulder; the armour is decorated with grotesques.

Provenance: Cannot be traced. Purchased 1947.[1]

Reference: (1) Catalogue Nat. Gal. Victoria, 1948, p. 253.

Benedetto Di Giovanni Buglioni   1461-1521

Italian. Born Florence; a worthy follower of Andrea della Robbia. Mainly worked in glazed terracotta.

Reference: *Th.B.*

Illust. 12   1394/5 (D.A.) **Madonna and Child**

Glazed terracotta relief, 77.5 x 35.6 cm. Unsigned, undated; 54.6 cm, (without base).

Condition: chipped in many places: the base does not belong.

Comment: The base was added after 1938; the relief was placed in a frame on arrival in Melbourne. A similar relief by Buglioni is in the Museo Nazionale in Florence.[1] The figures have a distinct resemblance to a terracotta *Virgin with a Laughing Child* of about 1465 by Antonio Rossellino (1427-1479), in the Victoria and Albert Museum, London.[2]

Provenance: Stephano Bardini Collection, Florence, Catalogue No. 513, pl. 22; Bardini sale Christie, 29 May 1902, lot 547 as Andrea della Robbia (size 22 in. x 14½ in.), remained unsold; Mortimer Schiff collection, New York, 1908-38; sale Schiff collection, Christie, 23 June, 1938, lot 133 as Benedetto and Santi Buglioni, 21 in. x 13 in. buyer's name illeg.; acquired under the terms of the Felton Bequest on the advice of A. J. L. McDonnell from Messrs. Partridge, London, 1953; arrived 1954.[3]

References: (1) A. Marquand, *Benedetto and Santi Buglioni,* Princeton, 1921, p. 109, fig. 83, No. 122. (2) James Mollison, *Renaissance Art,* National Gallery Booklets, Oxford University Press, 1968, fig. 12, p. 26. (3) *Catalogue Nat. Gal. Victoria,* Appendix 11, 1954, p. 52-3.

Sir Francis Legatt Chantrey   1781-1841

British. Born at Norton near Sheffield. Was apprenticed to a Sheffield Carver in 1797. Arrived in London in 1802 where he became acquainted with the sculptor Nollekens who helped him to obtain portrait commissions. In 1812 he received the first of a number of large-scale commissions for tombs, public monuments and full length statues of prominent men for public places. His statue of Canning stands in Westminster Yard. Canning's tomb, by Chantrey is in Westminster Abbey. In 1830 he became sculptor to the Court and was knighted in 1835. Together with Flaxman the most noted English exponent of neo-classicism. He left a considerable fortune, which after the death of his wife came to the Royal Academy as the Chantrey Bequest for the "Encouragement of British Art in Painting and Sculpture only".

Reference: *Th.B.;* R. S. R. Boase, *English Art 1800-1870,* Oxford History of English Art, Oxford, 1959, pp. 139-142.

Illust. 13   4428/3[1] **Sir Joseph Banks 1818**

marble bust H. 53.7 cm. Signed *Chantrey sculptor 1818* at end of right hand shoulder inscribed *Sir J. Banks Bart.* on back.
Condition: nostril broken and repaired; scratches on right shoulder; damages at back above inscription; left shoulder bevelled off at back; underneath, a piece has been cut out measuring length 7¾ in.; height 2 in.; depth 2¼ in. at back and 4½ in. (towards the front of the bust). This may have been done later to allow the bust to be fitted into a particular setting.

Comment: Sir Joseph Banks (1743-1820) became a Fellow of the Royal Society in 1767 and its President in 1778. Inherited wealth enabled him to be a patron and personal bent inclined him towards the natural sciences. In 1766 he made his first scientific expedition into Newfoundland and Labrador from where brought back the nucleus of his great Herbarium. In 1768 he and his suite joined Captain Cook on the Endeavour which had been fully equipped for a scientific expedition into the South Seas. Banks thus participated in the discovery of Australia and he played an important part in the development of the settlement of New South Wales.[2] The bust, herm-shaped and undraped, is based on the plaster model in the Ashmolean Museum, Oxford.[3] Chantrey's bust of Banks occurs in several versions, all herm-shaped, either undraped like the Roman republican busts, or draped. For comment on the classical influence see under *Rysbrack.* A replica of 4428/3 is at Petworth, ordered from Banks by Lord Egremont 'for his gallery at Petworth in 1837' (Chantrey Ledger). In addition there are two draped busts also based on the undraped Ashmolean model: 1. ordered by William Henderson of the British Museum in 1814 and apparently not delivered to him; exhibited at the R.A. in 1818, and in 1819 presented by Chantrey to the Royal Society, where it still is. 2. In the possession of the Linnean Society, recorded in the Chantrey ledger as ordered in 1882 and so inscribed on the back.[4]

Unlike his youthful portraits these busts show Banks with his natural hair cut short as in the painting in the National Portrait Gallery, London (dated 1778).

Provenance: A bust of Banks was ordered in 1818 by Mr. G. Watson Taylor, completed in 1820, and delivered; but does not appear in the Watson Taylor sale and was probably disposed of at some other time. Dr. Whinney suggests that this may have been identical with No. 4428/3.[5] Local sale, Bristol, 1938, bt. Bristol Art Gallery which ceded it to Sir Sydney Cockerell for acquisition under the terms of the Felton Bequest in January 1939.[6]

References: (1) Decorative Arts Stock Book No. 3. (2) H. C. Cameron, *Sir Joseph Banks,* Sydney, 1966. (3) Lane Poole No. 8. (4) I am indebted to Mr. Nicholas Draffin for having ascertained for me the whereabouts of the versions of this bust and to have got in touch with Dr. Margaret Whinney on this question. Letter 5 VI 71, Chantrey ledger p. 41. (5) I am indebted to Dr. Whinney for making her unpublished information available to us. (6) Felton Corr. Cockerell, Jan. 13, 1930.

Illust. 14   1540/5 (D.A.) **George Canning**

marble bust h. 21 in. (53.3 cm.) inscribed on back of bust: *The Gift of Sir Francis Chantrey to John Backhouse 1828.*

Condition: good.

Comment: The sitter (1770-1827) was a noted Tory statesman. He was Under-Secretary for Foreign Affairs under Pitt from 1796 to 1799 and treasurer for the Navy after Pitt's return in 1806, Foreign minister from 1807-9. He planned the capture of the Danish fleet by Lord Cathcard which constituted an important British victory during the Napoleonic wars. Returned to Ministry of Foreign Office in 1822; an office he retained until his death. Canning's political tenets included the maintenance of Royal Prerogatives, the repeal of the Roman Catholic disabilities and the achievement of a balance between oligarchic and democratic extremes. He had few rivals in literary eloquence and was a life long friend of Sir Walter Scott.[1]

The sitter is shown looking towards his r. shoulder; in allusion to the classical past he is dressed in a toga, with bare neck, the shaped bust rests on a pedestal. The bust here is posthumous; it is a replica of the marble bust in the National Portrait Gallery No. 282 signed F. Chantrey 1821, (h. 27½ in.). This in turn is based on a model at the Ashmolean Museum, Oxford, where the drapery is treated rather differently.[2] An earlier bust of Canning dated 1819 is in the National Museum of Wales, Cardiff.

A further version with a differently treated head is in the Palace of Westminster; a full length standing monument independently conceived is in Westminster Abbey. Other busts recorded are 1820 for Mr. Bolton of Liverpool, for Mr. Ellis, finished 1822; 1826 Chatsworth.[3]
A drawing from the front (probably made with a camera lucida) in the National Portrait Gallery 316A cannot be specifically connected with No. 1540/5.[4]

Provenance: Collection of John Backhouse, England; acquired under the terms of the Felton Bequest on the advice of Dr. M. Woodall from Heim Gallery London in 1968.

References: (1) D.N.B. (2) Mr. Nicholas Draffin kindly checked photographs against the London and Oxford busts. (3) For these see R. Gunnis, *Dictionary of British Sculpture, 1660-1851,* London n.d. (4) Information received from Mr. Draffin.

Flemish, Antwerp, 16th Century

Illust. 31 . 3660/3 (D.A.) **Retable of the Passion**

carved centre, polychrome 208 cm. x 100.3 cm. Unsigned, undated.
Comment: For painted wings see p. 61.

Provenance: A church in Tongres, Belgium; in the collection of Count van der Straeten-Ponthoz; acquired on the advice of Sir Sydney Cockerell under the terms of the Felton Bequest 1937.

French Early 15th Century

Illust. 30   518/4 (D.A.) **St. Barbara**

oak statue, H. 107.4 cm. Unsigned, undated, dateable about 1420.

Condition: cracking due to ageing wood; some slippage due to checks across grains; requires minor restoration. Faint evidence of polychrome. Comment: The story of the saint occurs in the Golden Legend: Afraid that St. Barbara might be taken from him in marriage, her father shut her in a high tower. Here she read and meditated and at the secret request a disciple of Origen of Alexandria converted her to Christianity. At her command three windows were built in her prison, symbolizing the Trinity. When her father discovered her conversion he had her tortured and beheaded; immediately afterwards he himself perished in a violent tempest. The saint is shown holding a book and has as an attribute the tower with three windows on the right. She is dressed in the fashion of the gothic period; the elegant statue is a good example of the courtly style of 'International Gothic'. It may have originated in northern France.

Provenance: From the Brummer collection, New York; acquired under the terms of the Felton Bequest on the advice of Sir Daryl Lindsay 1946.

References: *Catalogue N.G. Victoria*, 1948, p. 255; U. Hoff, M. Plant, *Painting, Drawing, Sculpture, National Gallery of Victoria*, Melbourne, 1968, pp. 34, 35, illust.

German Early 16th Century

Illust. 15/16   4791, 4792/3 (D.A.) **St. John and Mary**

lindenwood, polychromed, H. 133 cm. Unsigned, undated.

Condition: evidence of polychrome; light plaster over wood finish. General deterioration of wood progressively worn from the hands down. Evidence of inactive insect infection. Condition delicate. Numerous small breakages; St. John has lost all toes of both feet.

Comment: The two statues originally flanking a crucifix stood on an outside wall of the church at Karlstadt am Main near Würzburg. They were protected by iron baldacchins.[1] Lübbecke compared the figures with early works by Backofen (d. 1519) such as the Crucifixion Group in Wimpfen i. Th.[2] Schädler believes that the figures are made by an artist under the influence of Backofen and compares them to the Crucifixion groups of Haltenheim (1508-10), Hessenthal (1519) and Mainz, St. Ignaz.[3]

Provenance: In 1916 in the collection of Albert Ullmann, Frankfurt a/Main, Germany; brought to Australia in the 1930s by Mrs. Ullman; acquired under the terms of the Felton Bequest in 1941 from Mrs. A. Ullman (Ullm) Melbourne.

References: (1) Old photographs in Gallery archives. (2) Friedrich Lübbecke, 'Die Sammlung Ullmann su Frankfurt a.M. I, I, Die Mittelalterliche Plastik', in *Der Cicerone*, VIII, Oct. 1916, pp. 387; fig. 5. (3) This information was kindly made available by Dr. Alfred Schädler, Bayerisches National Museum, Munich; corr. Hoff-Schädler, 11.11.70. P. Kautzsch, *Hans Backofen und seine Schule*, Leipzig, 1911, pls. II, 4, III, 6, IV, 7. See also *Quarterly Bulletin, N.G. Victoria*, VI, 1.2.1952, *Catalogue N.G. Victoria*, 1948, p. 249; O. Schmitt, G. Swarzenski, *Meisterwerke der Bildhauerkunst in Frankfurter Privatbesitz, I. Deutsche und französische Plastik des Mittelalters*, Frankfurt am Main, 1921, Nos. 33, 34.

German 17th Century

Illust. 17   4105/3 (D.A.) **Pieta**

wood relief, polychrome, H. 48 cm.

Condition: sound; numerous paint losses; fingers of Virgin's hand broken off, clumsily replaced.

Comment: The hood and mantle of the Virgin are blue, dress red; the fleshtones of Christ are pale, the wounds red. Base dark green. The raised hand probably held a kerchief. Probably Bavarian or Suabian, of the middle of the 17th century. The group is a variation on a type of about 1600, to be compared with an engraving by Jan Sadler after a lost *Pieta* by Hubert Gerhard[1] but 4105/3 introduces an archaising, gothicing trait by setting the figure of Christ upright as in *Pietas* of the 14th century.[2]

Provenance: Bequeathed by Howard Spensley 1939; previous history unknown.

References: (1) Pelzer in *Kunst und Kunsthandwerk*, Vol. XXI, Vienna, 1918, p. 124, fig. 16. (2) Information kindly made available by Dr. Alfred Schädler, Bayerisches Nationalmuseum, Munich (corr. Hoff Schädler, 30.12.70). See also *Catalogue N.G. Victoria*, 1948, p. 256; *Quarterly Bulletin, N.G. Victoria*, VIII, 3, 2, 1954, repr.

German Franconian 15th Century

Illust. 18   4790/3 (D.A.) **Mary, St. John and St. Mary Magdalene**

limewood group polychromed, H. 124.8 cm.

179

Condition: remains of red in garment of St. John, blue in mantle of the Virgin, grey in mantle of Mary with olive green reverse, over a red dress; remains of red border in mantle of Virgin. Brown border with red stripe on mantle of Mary. Dark green base. Dark brown hair of St. John; brown hair of the Maries. Evidence of past infection by borers; parts of surface very brittle. Light plaster over wood. Fingers of Mary's hand partly missing. Condition delicate.

Comment: While in the Ullmann collection, the group was described as Nürmberg school, of the late 15th century.[1] In the Catalogue National Gallery of Victoria, 1948, it was described as Suabian. Dr Schädler suggests that it is Franconian, 1480-90, and points to the expressive faces and dry linear pattern of the folds.[2]

Provenance: In 1916 documented as being in the Albert Ullman collection in Frankfurt am Main, Germany,[3] brought to Australia in the 1930s; acquired under the terms of the Felton Bequest from Mrs. A. Ullmann (Ullin) Melbourne in 1941.[4]

References: (1) Friedich Lübbecke, 'Die Sammlung Ullman zu Frankfurt a/M I, Die Mittelalterliche Plastik', in *Der Cicerone,* VIII, Oct. 1916, pp. 398, 399, fig. 21. (2) Dr. Alfred Schädler, Bayerisches National museum (corr. Schädler Hoff, 11.11.70). (3) See note (1). (4) *Quarterly Bulletin,* N.G. Victoria, I, 1.2.1945, repr.

Jean Antoine Houdon   1741-1828

French. Born Versailles; pupil of Pigalle and Lemoyne at the Academie royale, later at the Ecole royales des Elèves protégés in 1761. 1764 to Rome where he was influenced by Bernini, as well as by sculpture of classical antiquity. Returned to Paris 1769; elected member of the *academie* with his marble of Morpheus now in the Louvre. His marble statue of Diana 1780 executed for the Duke of Saxe/Coburg Gotha, later acquired by Katherine II of Russia and now in the Gulbenkian collection Lisbon, is perhaps the best known of his figurative works. His portraits contain many of the greatest men of his time. In addition to the Voltaire cited below there is a seated Voltaire of 1781 in the Comédie Française and several other busts in either contemporary dress or Roman toga or 'en nudité héroique'. In 1785 Houdon was called to U.S. to carry out a statue of Washington for the State Parliament of Virginia.

References: *Th.B.*

Illust. 19   4427/3 **Voltaire**

Bronze bust, H. 13¼ in. Inscribed Houdon 1778 on r. shoulder.

Condition: excellent.

Comment: François Marie Arouet, later called Voltaire 1694-1778, philosopher, historian and man of letters was twice imprisoned in the Bastille. After his second imprisonment he spent three years in England

(1726-9). After this until 1749 he stayed at the country seat of Madame de Chatelet and 1749 paid a visit to Frederick II of Prussia. He generally made his home at Ferney but returned to Paris on the eve of his death in 1778; he was brought to Houdon's studio where the scultor was able to observe him; Houdon worked however from the deathmask which he took after May 30, 1778. The existing portraits are, like No. 4427/3, posthumous.[1] As in the case of Rousseau, the various busts were available with or without a wig, in French costume or antique, according to the wishes of the patrons.

Other versions see Réau, II, p. 357 and III, 16, Réau quotes two bronzes as being particularly fine, one in the Louvre, the other in the collection of Mrs. Astor, New York.

Provenance: Lord Kinnaird, Rossie Priory; acquired from Messrs. P. & D. Colnaghi London in 1939 under the terms of the Felton Bequest, on the advice of Sir Sydney Cockerell and Miss Longhurst of the Victoria and Albert Museum.

References: 1. L. Réau, *Houdon, sa vie et son oeuvre*, Paris, 1964, II, pp. 355 *seq;* III, 44 No. 202. See also G. Giacometti *Houdon*, n.d. I, p. 184; S. Lami, *Dictionnaire des Sculpteurs de l'école française au dix-huitième siècle*. Paris, Vol. I, 1910, p. 259; U. Hoff, M. Plant, *Painting, Drawing, Sculpture, Nat. Gal. Victoria*, Melbourne 1968. pp. 90-91, illus.

Illust. 20   E5/1972   **Jean Jacques Rousseau 1712-1778**

plasterbust, H. 38.7 cm. H. with pedestal 45.7 cm. Signed on r. shoulder houdon f. 1778 and bears on the hollowed-out reverse a red wax seal with the inscription Academ. Royale de Peinture et Scult. Houdon Sc.[1]

Condition: undamaged but for slight surface scratches.

Comment: Jean Jacques Rousseau, French philosopher was born in Geneva in 1712. He early became a friend of Diderot and a contributor to the *Encéclopedie;* in 1749 the Academy of Dijon awarded him a prize for his essay Discours sur les arts et les sciences in which he developed his theory of the superiority of the primitive man over the civilized man. The Contract Social (1762) endeavours to base all government on the consent of the governed. Emil, de l'éducation advocates natural methods of education much at variance with those of formal education of his time; the book anticipates features of the advanced educational theory of the 20th century.

Rousseau's unorthodox ideas forced him into exile; in 1765 he accepted asylum in England offered him by David Hume. The Confessions (1781) were written in Derbyshire. One of the most influential thinkers in European history, Rousseau played a decisive part in the new cult of sensibility, in the belief in beauty and innocence of nature, the nature mysticism of the period and his writings influenced all the great major writers of the 19th century.

All Houdon's portraits of Rousseau are posthumous. Rousseau died at Ermenonville on July 3, 1778, and Houdon immediately went there to take a death mask[2] on which he based his terracotta model. No. ES/1972 was taken from this terracotta in Houdon's own studio and retouched by the artist himself.[3] It is slightly tinted. Various busts were made by Houdon, showing Rousseau either in contemporary dress and wig, or with bare head and Roman toga or, as above, en nudité héroique in the manner of the undraped Republican busts of Rome. A marble bust of the type of No. ES/1972 is in St. Jean at Angers.

Exh:. Exposition du Centénaire de Houdon, Gallery Buvelot, Paris, 1928.

Provenance: Atelier Houdon; inscribed on old base; 'provident du Cabinet de M. le Marquis de Flamarens'; Madame la Marquis de Caussade No. 63; Madame André Cammoin, No. 71; acquired from Cyril Humphris, London, on the advice of Dr. M. Woodall and Mr. Terence Hodgkinson, under the terms of the Everard Studley Miller Bequest, 1971. Arrived 1972.

References: (1) Louis Réau, Houdon, sa vie et son oevre, 1964, II, p. 481. (2) Rousseau's death mask is now in the Musée Jean Jacques Rousseau in Geneva, F. C. Green, Jean Jacques Rousseau, Cambridge 1955, p. 358. (3) Réau, loc. cit., II p. 475, 476; 360; III, 41, No. 184, pl. LXXXIX, XC, XCI. (4) G. Giamcometti, la vie et l'oeuvre de Houdon, Paris, n.d., I, p. 184.

Italian Flemish   16th Century

Illust. 21   1662/4 (D.A.) **Dancing Children**

bronze group, circular, diam. approx. 83.2 cm. H. 50.1 cm.
Condition: excellent; black patina.

Comment: A circular arrangement is most unusual; no comparable piece is known.

Provenance: Lord Ashburnham. Acquired under the terms of the Felton Bequest on the advice of A. J. L. McDonnell in 1956.

References: U. Hoff, 'A. J. L. McDonnell as Adviser to the Felton Bequest' in Bulletin, N.G. Victoria, Vol. VI, 1964, p. 5, fig (detail).

Italian, Venetian, 16th Century

Illust. 32   704/4 (D.A.) **Anthony and Cleopatra**

marble relief, 33.7 cm. x 38.1 cm. Unsigned, undated.

Provenance: Sir Herbert Cook, Doughty House, Richmond; acquired under the terms of the Felton Bequest 1948.

References: Burlington Fine Arts Club, Exhibition of Italian Sculpture, Catalogue, No. 34, pl. XX.; L. Planiscig, Venezianische Bildhauer, p. 270, ill. 280.

Jean Baptiste Pigalle   1714-1785

French. Born Paris; pupil of J. B. Lemoyne; 1736-39 in Rome where he made copies from classical antique sculptures. 1741 returned to Paris. 1744 member, 1752 professor, 1777 rector, 1785 chancellor of the academie. Pigalle was the most popular of the French sculptors of the Louis XVI period.

Reference: Th.B.

Illust. 22   1509 (D.A.) **Georges Gougenot**

marble bust, 53 cm., on period pedestal; inscribed on back, inside, incised in the marble: J. B. Pigalle fecit 1748/Georges Gougenot, Ecuyer, Seigneur de Croissy et de L'isle &c. Tuteur des Prince de Condé. né le 28 Dec. 1674 Mort le 10 Juin 1748.

Condition: excellent.

Comment; The sitter (1674-1748) was seigneur de Croissy-sur-Seine et de l'Isle-sur-Arnon on Berry; he was the tutor to the Princes of Condé and Secretary Councillor to the King, to the Royal House and Crown of France. He wears a wig, a coat with fur revers, which opens on a waistcoat bordered with lace and a large neckcloth knotted around the neck. He was 74 years of age when his son Louis Gougenot commissioned this bust from Pigalle and he died the same year. [1]

Provenance: In the family Gougenot de Croissy. Baron de Soucy. Sale Paris, Galerie Charpentier, Dec. 14, 1937, No. D and at Hotel Drouot in 1941 (bought in by the heirs). Family de Soucy and heirs until 1966. Acquired on the advice of Dr. M. Woodall and Terence Hodgkinson of the Victoria and Albert Museum from Heim, London, under the terms of the Everard Studley Miller Bequest in Nov. 1966. Arrived October 1967.

Exhibition: l'art français sous Louis XIV et sous Louis XV, Hotel de Chimay, Paris, 1888, No. 89 bis.

References: (1) L. Réau, *J. B. Pigalle,* Paris, 1950, No. 53, pp. 167-168, pl. 40, p. 112 and previous literature.

John Michael Rysbrack   1694-1770

Flemish-British. One of a group of Flemish sculptors who settled in England following the peace of Utrecht.

Born at Antwerp as the son of the landscape painter Pieter R. Between 1706-12 studied under the sculptor Michael van der Voort; became Master of the Guild of St. Luke at Antwerp in 1714. According to Vertue came to England in 1720, where he worked at first under the architect James Gibbs (1682-1754); between 1720 and 40 he became the leading sculptor, cultivating the attentuated baroque of the Duquenoy school, but sometimes also revealing the growing enthusiasm of his period for the antique. In the 1740s his success was impaired by the vogue for the more brilliant work of Roubiliac, but he continued to receive commissions, particularly for monuments. Returned to Antwerp shortly before his death.

Reference: Margaret Whinney, *Sculpture in Britain 1530-1830* Pelican History of Art, London 1964.

Illust. 23   1508/5 (D.A.) **Sir Peter Paul Rubens**

terracotta bust, with added bronze 'patina', H. 60.5 cm. Signed and dated on reverse, inside; Mich. Rysbrack 1743.

183

Condition: very good; bronze patina dates from the 18th century.

Comment: For biography of sitter see p. 134. This posthumous bust has some resemblance to plate No. 62 from van Dyck's Iconography, engraved by Paul Pontius;[1] which shows the painter with long curly hair and beard, in a jacket with lace collar, wearing the chain of honour. The mantle of the engraving has been replaced in the bust by the kind of drapery conventionally in use in this kind of work. The model for Pontius' engraving is not known. Rysbrack, who made the bust at the same time at which he carried out three statuettes, of Rubens, van Dyck and Duquesnoy[2] may have been familiar with some of Rubens self portraits, such as the one now at Vienna, in which Rubens has his hand on the handle of his sword as in Rysbrack's statuette. In these statuettes, which Vertue states were made 'with much study', Rysbrack attempted to rival the statue of Shakespeare for which Scheemakers had gained considerable praise in 1740. Like the latter Rysbrack here exploited the picturesque effects of 17th century costume.

Other versions: A marble version of the Rubens bust, unsigned and undated, is at Hagley Hall, in the collection of Viscount Cobham.[3] Such a marble bust had been listed by Vertue.[4]

Provenance: Collection of the artist; Rysbrack sale, London, April 20th, 1965, lot 44; Lady Theodore Guest; Lady Charlotte Schreiber; Count Guy de Pelet Inwood, Templecombe, Somerset, a Collection of English lead Garden Statuary, Sale Christie 29.6.1961, lot 117, bt. Marcusen;[5] private collection, London; acquired from Heim, London, in 1966 on the advice of Dr. M. Woodall under the terms of the Everard Studley Miller Bequest; arrived 1967.

References: (1) Marie Mauquoy Hendrickx, *L'Iconographie d'Antoine van Dyck,* Brussels, 1956, No. 62 illust. (2) Margaret Whinney, *Sculpture in Britain, 1530-1830,* Pelican History of Art, London 1964, p. 116. (3) F. J. B. Watson, 'A Bust of Fiammingo by Rysbrack Re-discovered' in: *Burl. Mag.,* Vol. CV, 1963, p. 441, pl. 26. (4) Vertue Notebooks, III, p. 132, *Walpole Society,* XXII, 1933-4. (5) Information kindly supplied by J. P. Harthon and B. Galbraith, Victoria and Albert Museum Library, London.

Scheemakers (Scheemaekers) Peter II   1691-1781

Flemish-British. Born Antwerp, son of Peter Scheemaekers I, 1640-1713, an Antwerp sculptor, under whom Peter II studied. Spent four years in Copenhagen with J. C. Sturmberg, then was in Rome and London. c. 1733 took part (unsuccessfully) in the competition for the Statue of William III. From 1728 to 1730 back in Rome. Between 1735 and 1770 again in Rome. Between 1735 and 1770 in London, where he competed with Roubiliac and Rysbrack *(q.v.).* Since 1770 back in Antwerp. His most successful work was the statue of Shakespeare in Westminster Abbey. Among his sculptures are the busts of the Hon. Laurence Shirley, his wife and four of their children formerly at Staunton Hall. Three of these are listed below.

Reference: *Th.B.*

Illust. 24   129/5 (D.A.) **A Member of the Shirley Family: Middle aged Man in Roman Toga**

marble bust, H. 61.6 cm., shaped bust on contemporary marble pedestal (measurements without pedestal).
From a series carved before 1745 (according to an old inventory) for Staunton Harrold, Leics., the seat of the Shirley Family. The bust is probably Laurence Shirley (1720-1760) 4th son of Sir Robert Shirley, 1st Earl Ferrers, Laurence, who became 4th Earl Ferrers murdered his Steward in a fit of rage and was hanged at Tyburn in 1700

Provenance: Purchased from Frank Partridge & Sons, London, Jan. 1960 on the advice of A. J. L. McDonnell.

Illust. 25   130/5 (D.A.) **A Member of the Shirley Family: Young Man in Roman Toga with head turned towards his right shoulder**

marble bust, H. 59.1 cm., shaped bust on contemporary marble pedestal.

Condition: excellent.

Comment: See under 120/5 (D.A.). One of the five sons of Laurence Shirley. He has a ship carved on his breastplate.

As under 129/5.

Illust. 26   131/5 (D.A.) **A Member of the Shirley Family: Young Man in Roman Toga and armour with head turned towards his left shoulder**

marble bust, H. 59 cm.

Condition: excellent.

Comment: see under 129/5 above.

Spanish Catalan   14th Century

Illust. 27   1262/4 (D.A.) **St. Catherine c. 1350**

limestone statue, H. 118.5 cm. Unsigned, undated.

Condition: good, remains of blue and green colouring on dress, yellow on hair, gold on wheel and palm can be discerned. Head re-worked.

Comment: The figure carries the wheel, the emblem of her martyrdom and the palm, the emblem of spiritual victory. Probably circle of Bertomeu Robió.

Provenance: Presented by Tomas Harris, 1952. Earlier history unknown.

References: *Quarterly Bulletin, N.G. Victoria,* VII, 1.5.1953 repr. *Catalogue N.G. Victoria,* Appendix II, 1954, p. 53.

o

Spanish   16th Century

Illust. 28   1338/4 (D.A.) **Virgin Enthroned with the infant Christ**
limestone, H. 123.2 cm. Unsigned, undated, made early 16th century.

Condition: satisfactory; remains of flesh colour on the legs of the Child Christ and on the hands of the Virgin. Remnants of red in the folds of the Virgin's dress and on her lips; traces of blue-grey-green on her mantle. Remains of gold appear in the hair of the Child Christ, on the band around the hem of the Virgin's mantle and on her crown. Green remains on the stem of the flower and traces of red, blue and gold on the throne.

Provenance: Early history unkonwn; purchased in 1953 on the advice of Sir Daryl Lindsay and A. J. L. McDonnell from Tomas Harris, London.

Michael Zuern, the Younger   active 1679—after 1686 school of

Austrian; came from a well known woodcarver family orginally stemming from Überlingen at Lake Constance in Suabia. Known to have worked in Olmütz in Czechoslovakia between 1679-1681 and later in Gmünden in Austria, his main work being the high altar at Kremsmünster (1682-86).

Reference: *Th.B.*

Illust. 29   1495/5 (D.A.) **Madonna and Child**

lime wood (silver ground, overpainted with tempera), H. 84.6 cm.

Condition: arm of child broken at shoulder, otherwise in good condition.

Comment: The motif of the Madonna holding a flower or fruit for the attention of the Christ Child is current on the art of the gothic period. A famous example is the engraving of Veit Stoss where the Virgin holds an apple. [1]

Provenance: Previous history unknown. Sold at Christie's, May 1965, by Charles Worel, London; acquired on the advice of Dr. M. Woodall and John Beckwith under the terms of the Felton Bequest 1966.

References: (1) C. Zigrosser, *The Book of Fine Prints,* New York, 1958, illust. 125, *Annual Bulletin N.G. Victoria,* VIII, 1966-7, fig. 25. U. Hoff, M. Plant, *National Gallery of Victoria, Painting, Drawings, Sculpture,* Melbourne, 1968, pp. 76, 77 repr.

INDEX OF TITLES

188

189

Illustrations

1. Amiconi
Portrait Group

2. After Barocci
Portrait of a Young Girl

3. Barret
View of Windermere Lake

4. School of F. Bassano
The Mocking of Christ

5. J. Bassano
Portrait of an Old Man

6. Batoni
Gaetano Sforza-Cesarini

7. Batoni
Sir Samson Gideon and his Tutor

8. Beechey
Portrait of A Lady

9. Begeyn
Landscape with Cattle

10. Bellotto
Ruins of the Forum, Rome

11. Berckheyde
The Town Hall, Amsterdam

13. Bourdon
The Adoration of The Magi

12. After Boulanger
Bacchus and Satyrs

P

14. British, XVI Century
Portrait of a Lady in Rich Attire

15. British, XVI Century
Earl of Leicester

16. British, 18th Century
Acting Lieutenant Thomas Wallis

17. British, early 18th Century
A Gentleman with Long, Dark Wig

18. British, early 18th Century
Portrait of A Lady

19. British, middle 18th Century
A Gentleman with Grey Wig

British, 18th Century
  Gentleman in Black Coat

21A. British, 18th Century
  Drake Brockman Conversation Piece

British, 18th Century
Drake Brockman Conversation Piece

22. After Brown
  Marquess Townshend

23. Studio of Brueghel
Calvary

24. Byzantine
Christ as The Lord of All

25. Byzantine
SS. Basil, Chrysostom and Gregory with
a Kneeling Donor

204

26. Byzantine
Triptych

27. Byzantine-Italian
Nativity

28. Byzantine-Russian
Nativity

29. Calvert
Souvenir of Claude

30. Calvert
The Soul Crossing The Styx

31. Studio of Canaletto
Grand Canal and Rialto Bridge from the East

Candid
The Lamentation over The Dead Christ

33. Carloni
Hercules Led by Knowledge

207

34. Carracci
The Holy Family

35. Attr. to Castello
Susannah and the Elders

36. Cavallino
The Virgin Annunciate

37. Claude
River Landscape with Tiburtine Temple at Tivoli

38. After Claude
Landscape with Piping Shepherd and a Flight to Egypt

209

39. Cola dall'Amatrice
The Finding of the True Cross

40. Constable
Naworth Castle, Cumberland

41. Constable
Keswick Lake

42. Constable
"The Quarters"

43. Constable
Sunset

44. Constable
Clouds

45. Constable
Hampstead Heath

46. Constable
West End Fields

212

47. Constable
Boat Passing a Lock

48. Corot
The Quay of the Schiavoni

49. Corot
The Bent Tree (Morning)

50. Corot
Landscape

51. Corot
Sketch at Scheveningen

52. Corot
The Model, Nude Study

53. Cotes
Flower Painter

54. Cotman
Hay Barges

215

56. Crome
Woodland Path

55. Cranach
Philip Melanchthon

57. Cuyp
Landscape with Cattle

58. van Dael
Flowerpiece

59. School of David
  Head of a Man

60. Davis
  Equestrian Group

61. Delacroix
The Confession of the Giaour

Q

62. Dorner
The Hard Landlady

63. Drouais
Madame Sophie De France

64. Duparc
Old Lady

65. Dutch, 17th Century
Interior with Soldiers

66. Dutch, 18th Century
Death and the Fortune Teller

67. Dutch or Flemish
Reading a Letter

68. van Dyck
Philip, Earl of Pembroke

69. van Dyck
Countess of Southampton

70. School of van Dyck
Mary Lucas

71. After van Dyck
Cornelius van der Geest

72. After van Dyck
The Marriage of St. Catherine

73. Etty
Nude Woman Asleep

74. Etty
Dorothea Bathing

75. After van Eyck
The Madonna and the Child

221

76. Ferneley
Squire George Osbaldeston

77. Flemish, about 1500
The Multiplication of the Loaves and Fishes

79A. Flemish, about 1500
The Raising of Lazarus

78A. Flemish, about 1500
The Marriage of Cana

78B. Flemish, about 1500
Rest on the Flight to Egypt

79B. Flemish, about 1500
S. Peter

80. Flemish, 16th Century
The Descent from the Cross

81. Flemish School, 16th Century
S. Jerome

82, 83. Flemish, Antwerp, 16th Century
Carved Retable of the Passion of Christ
The Wings

84. Fontana
Holy Family with S. Jerome

85. French (?), 18th Century
Gentleman in Green Coat

86. Gainsborough
Duchess of Grafton

87. Gainsborough
An Officer of the 4th Regiment of Foot

88. Gainsborough
A View at the Mouth of the Thames

89. Gainsborough
Speaker Cornwall

90. de Gelder
King Ahasuerus Condemning Haman

92. Giordano
S. Sebastian

91. Géricault
The Entombment

94. El Greco
A Cardinal

93. Attr. to Goya
A Lady

227

95. Guardi
Gates of Venice

96. Guardi
The Lock at Dolo on the Brenta

97. Haydon
Marcus Curtius

98. de Heem
Still Life with Fruit

99. van Heemskerk
Family Group in a Landscape

100. Herring
Horses and Pigs

101. Herring
Cleveland Bays

102. Highmore
Samuel Booth

103. Highmore
Self Portrait

104. Highmore
Anthony Highmore

105. Highmore
Portrait of a Young Girl

106. Highmore
Pamela Fainting

107. Highmore
Pamela Preparing to Go Home

108. Highmore
Pamela Greets Her Father

109. Highmore
Pamela and Lady Davers

110. Hobbema
The Old Oak

111. de Hondecoeter
The Poultry Yard

112. Hoppner
Portrait of a Lady

113. Attr. to Hoppner
"Perdita" (?)

R

114. Attr. to Jackson
Sir David Wilkie

115. Italian, 15th Century
Madonna and Child

116. Italian, 15th Century
St. George Slaying the Dragon

117. Italian, 15th Century
The Adoration of the Magi

118. Italian, 15th Century
Profile Portrait of A Lady

119. Italian, 16th Century
A Youth

120. Italian, 17th Century
A Man's Head

121. Italian, 18th Century
Luigi Boccherini

122. School of Jordaens
The Satyr and the Peasant

123. Kalf
Still Life

124. Kneller
Sir Thomas Aston

125. de Largillière
Frederick August of Saxony

126. Lawrence
Robert Hobart

127. After Lawrence
The Duke of Wellington

129. Lee
Ben Lawers

128. Lawrence
George IV of England

130. Lee
River, Mill and Farm

31. Linnell
Wheat

2. Marmion
The Virgin and Child

133. Marshall
Lord Jersey's Middleton

239

134. Memling
The Man of Sorrows

135. Mor
A Lady

136. Morland
The Farmyard

137. Murillo
The Immaculate Conception

240

138. Myiens
Sir John Ashburnham

130. Nasmyth
River and Trees

140. Owen
Rachel, Lady Beaumont

141. Palmezzano
The Baptism of Christ

241

142. Veneziano
The Crucifixion

143. Perronneau
Petrus Woortman

144. School of Pesellino
Madonna and Child with Three Angels

145. Pittoni
The Miracle of the Loaves and Fishes

146. Follower of G. Poussin
Landscape with Christ and Mary Magdalene

147. Poussin
The Crossing of the Red Sea

243

148. Preti
Sophonisba receiving the Poison

149. Raeburn
Admiral Robert Deans

150. Raeburn
James Wardrop

152. Ramsay
The Countess of Cavan

151. Raeburn
John Guthrie of Carbeth

53. Ramsay
Earl Temple

154. Rembrandt
The Two Philosophers

162. After Reynolds
Miss Offy Palmer

164. Rigaud
Monsieur le Bret and His Son

163. Ricci
The Finding of Moses

248

165. Roberts
Interior of the Church of St Anne, Bruges

166. Romney
The Leigh Family

S

169. Roslin
Count Razumovsky

167. Romney
Edmund Law, Bishop of Carlisle

168. Rosa
Romantic Landscape

170. Roslin
Anastasia Ivanova

171. Rubens
Louis XIII of France

172. Rubens
Hercules and Antaeus

173. After Rubens
The Garden of Love

174. Ruisdael
The Watermill

252

175. Russian School, 18th Century
An Icon of Saint Nicolas

176. Ruysdael
River Landscape with Boats

177. Ruysch
Flowerpiece

178. de Ryck
Jeffrey Amherst Esq.

179. Scheffer
Christ and the Maries

254

180. Scheffer
Temptation of Christ

181. Stanfield
St. Michael's Mount, Cornwall

255

182. Stanfield
The Morning After Trafalgar

183. Attr. to Stark
Landscape with a Donkey

184. Steen
Interior

185. von Stoll
Flowerpiece

187. Stubbs
A Horse

186. School of Strozzi
S. Lawrence Distributing Treasures

257

188. Stubbs
A Lion Attacking a Horse

189. Teniers
The Gazette

190. Teniers
The Skittle Players

191. Terborch
Lady with a Fan

193. Tintoretto
Doge Pietro Loredano

192. Tiepolo
The Banquet of Cleopatra

194. Titian
Franciscan Friar with Book

196. Turchi
Charity

195. Trevisani
Joseph being Sold by His Brothers

197. Turner
Dunstanborough Castle

198. Turner
Walton Bridges

261

199. del Vaga
The Holy Family

200. Veronese
Nobleman between Active and Contemplative Life

1. **School of Vivarini**
   The Garden of Love

. **van der Vliet**
   Interior of a Church

203. **de Vries**
   A Dutch Gentleman

263

204. Ward
Sheep

205. After Watteau
Jealousy

206. Wilson
Captain Michael Everitt, R.N.

264

207. Wilson
Llyn Peris and Dolbadarn Castle

208. School of Wilson
Lake Avernus I

209. After Wilson
River View (on the Arno) I

T

210. Attr. to Wilson
St. David's Pembrokeshire

211. Follower of Wilson
Landscape with Italian Buildings

212. Wouwerman(s)
Landscape with Dogs and Horse

213. Zoffany
Caritas Romana (Roman Charity)

214. Zoffany
Elizabeth Farren

2. Barye
Lion and Boar

1. Barye
Panther and Gazelle

3. Barye
Walking Lion

4. Barye
Lion Attacking a Horse

5. Begarelli
The Virgin Attended by Three Holy Women

6. Bellano
Lamentation of Christ

7. Bernini
The Countess Matilda of Tuscany

8. Bernini
Cardinal Richelieu

9. British, 15th Century
St. John The Baptist

10. British, 16th Century
Young Man in Armour

11. British, 16th Century
Bearded Man in Armour

12. Buglioni
Madonna and Child

13. Chantrey
Sir Joseph Banks

14. French, Early 15th Century
St. Barbara

15. German, 16th Century
St. John

16. German, 16th Century
Mary

17. German, 17th Century
Pieta

18. German, 15th Century
Mary, St. John and St. Mary Magdalene

19. Houdon
Voltaire

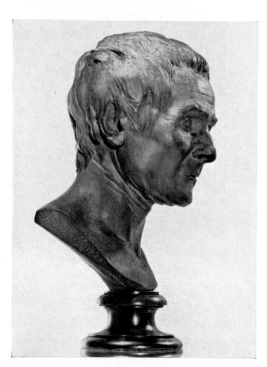

20. Houdon
Jean Jacques Rousseau

21. Italian Flemish, 16th Century
Dancing Children

23. Rysbrack
Sir Peter Paul Rubens

22. Pigalle
Georges Gougenot

24. Scheemakers
A Member of the Shirley Family

25. Scheemakers
A Member of the Shirley Family

273

26. Scheemakers
A Member of the Shirley Family

27. Spanish, 14th Century
St. Catherine c. 1350

28. Spanish, 16th Century
Virgin Enthroned with the Infant Christ

29. School of Michael Zuern
Madonna and Child

30. Chantrey
George Canning

31. Flemish, Antwerp, 16th Century
Retable of the Passion

32. Italian, Venetian, 16th Century
Anthony and Cleopatra